The Longest Climb

ABOUT THE AUTHOR

Dominic Faulkner was born in the UK but spent his early years in Nigeria and India. He spent some years with the Army and his first Everest climbing experience was as a member of the Millenium SAS team – but on that expedition he was injured and failed to summit.

In 2005 he led the EVEREST*MAX* team from the shores of the Dead Sea – the lowest point on earth – to the summit of Everest. They were the first team to make this journey and in so doing attracted worldwide publicity.

The
Longest Climb

The Last Great Overland Quest

Dominic Faulkner

Introduction by Sir Ranulph Fiennes

Published by Virgin Books 2010

2 4 6 8 10 9 7 5 3 1

Copyright © Dominic Faulkner 2009
Introduction copyright © Sir Ranulph Fiennes 2009
Maps copyright © Jeff Edwards 2009

Dominic Faulkner has asserted his right under the Copyright, Designs
and Patents Act 1988 to be identified as the author of this work

First published in Great Britain in 2009 by
Virgin Books
Random House, 20 Vauxhall Bridge Road,
London SW1V 2SA

www.virginbooks.com
www.rbooks.co.uk

Addresses for companies within The Random House Group Limited can be found at:
www.randomhouse.co.uk/offices.htm

The Random House Group Limited Reg. No. 954009

A CIP catalogue record for this book
is available from the British Library

ISBN 9780753515617

The Random House Group Limited supports The Forest Stewardship Council (FSC),
the leading international forest certification organisation. All our titles that are printed
on Greenpeace-approved FSC-certified paper carry the FSC logo.
Our paper procurement policy can be found at www.rbooks.co.uk/environment

Typeset by TW Typesetting, Plymouth, Devon
Printed and bound in Great Britain by CPI Bookmarque Ltd, Croydon CR0 4TD

I dedicate this adventure to the memory of my father,
Robert Charles Faulkner (1930–1974), and I dedicate this book
to my mother in appreciation for her support and patience in
all my endeavours.

Contents

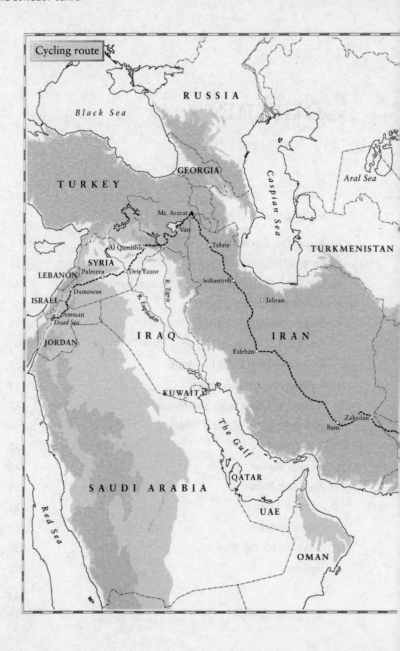

Cycling route

Black Sea

RUSSIA

GEORGIA

Aral Sea

TURKEY

Caspian Sea

Mt. Ararat

Van

TURKMENISTAN

Tabriz

Al Qamishli

Palmyra

Deir Ezzor

Soltaniyeh

SYRIA

LEBANON

R. Tigris

Tehran

Damascus

R. Euphrates

ISRAEL

Amman

Dead Sea

IRAQ

IRAN

JORDAN

Esfehan

KUWAIT

The Gulf

Zahedan

Bam

SAUDI ARABIA

QATAR

Red Sea

UAE

OMAN

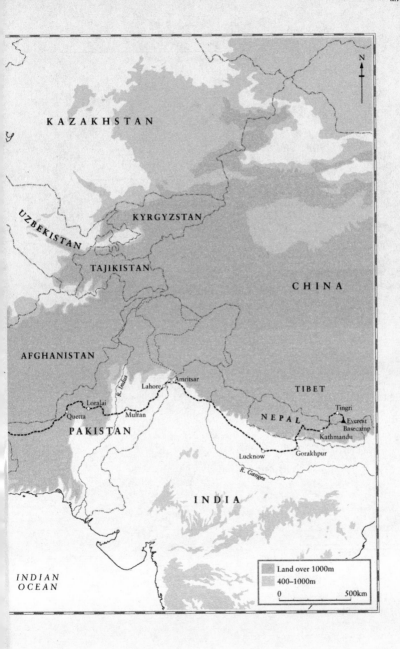

Route to the summit of Everest

Introduction

By Sir Ranulph Fiennes

I first became aware of Dominic Faulkner's attempt to summit Everest after the SAS expedition to the mountain in 2000. My involvement began after hearing of his plans to return to the mountain, and in so doing complete the ultimate ascent; I was of course delighted when he asked me to be the official patron of the expedition. Dom's commitment to his EVERESTMAX team, as well as the sheer scale of the endeavour, particularly impressed me. The combination of the formidable cycling with the summit ascent struck me as a peculiarly powerful mix, and I was keen to hear more of their plans. But I was acutely aware that these sorts of ventures are particularly prone to failure.

Selecting the perfect expeditionary team is, in my opinion, nearly impossible. No matter how rigorously one approaches the process, there is no foolproof formula and the longer the undertaking itself, the more likely each person's frailties are to be exposed by the sheer amount of time spent together. The EVERESTMAX expedition would demand months in close company on the cycling part of the trip, and would mean forming a new team to meet the very different challenge of attempting to summit Everest. Challenge enough, in my view, but this situation was further complicated by trying to then combine those two groups of people, with their different mindsets and abilities, to form one overarching group that would complete both stages of the endeavour. Bringing together these two somewhat disjointed groups, to make up a team that would achieve an extraordinary first, was certainly a feat in itself.

Dom's determination not to be thwarted on this EVEREST-MAX expedition is truly inspiring. The ability to overcome one's own limitations without putting the rest of a team in danger demands a very particular ego, and it is a reflection of Dom's own maturity and moderation that his team were, in the main, happy to be guided by a leader who to all intents and purposes looked like he would be leading his team from behind, unable to summit himself.

EVERESTMAX was a hugely successful charitable expedition, raising over £50,000 for charities including Merlin, Practical Action and SOS Children's Villages. I can think of no better reason to undertake such a challenge. That it ended successfully on the summit is the icing on the cake. If you have never climbed Everest you will be hard-pressed to find a better guide to that unique experience than Dom's account of it in *The Longest Climb*.

Chapter 1

An Elusive Summit

Everyone can recall a childhood summer, the first coming of age and the transplanting of images that will last a lifetime. Mine was in 1974, when the red-bricked house on the hill became my new home and the centre of my existence. The view across the vale was a perpetual sweep of green and yellow, the patchwork ocean of fields melting far beyond into the horizon of the Mendip Hills. In the middle distance stood Glastonbury, a lone beacon afloat in a sea of colour. It was an enticing landscape, begging to be explored, and I longed to step into its midst. But my boundary was the hedge that bordered the garden and any adventure had to be found in its confines. At least there was plenty to explore, secret hideouts, overgrown passages and, best of all, trees to climb. The tallest of these was a beech, tucked away and out of sight from the house. For weeks it seemed insurmountable, and I can still recall the anticipation, the creeping fear of that first ascent as the ground grew ever distant. I wasn't supposed to be climbing trees, but for a small boy that could only add to the sense of adventure.

Until that long summer I had been raised in Nigeria, and latterly in India, but at the age of six had come to live with my grandparents in their large and rambling Somerset home. Life had been blissful in Africa and coming to live in England for the first time was an enormous culture shock. I had grown used to cursory attendance at school, while Da'Maria our faithful gardener would wait for me on the steps outside before escorting me home along the dusty flower-lined lanes. Some adventure always ensued, catching lizards, building dens or swimming. Sometimes we went with my friend Haji to the stagnant pond in a vain attempt to catch fish. They were supposed to swim through the necks of old beer bottles. Of course it never worked but it hardly mattered. We felt like explorers dicing with death as the invisible crocodiles encircled.

Moving first to India had been upheaval enough. My father, a research scientist, was charged with setting up a new facility in the southern city of Coimbatore. Mine was the only white face among hundreds at the local school. In starched white shirts we paraded in lines before marching into class for lessons in Hindi. Away from my friends, I accepted the new regime with reluctance, but it wasn't to be for long. Our lives were upturned when my father fell ill with cancer and was rushed back to England for treatment. We followed soon after and while my mother stayed in London to be at his side I moved to Somerset.

Despite the circumstances, that summer left me with fond memories. My grandparents were affectionate and spent a huge amount of time with me. Their wonderful house was full of surprises, and even indoors there was plenty of adventure to be had. Most sinister was the drawing room, reserved only for special occasions, where the ghostly shapes of furniture draped in dustsheets terrified me. I would peek inside but then run away down the long corridor, sliding as far as I dared on the polished wooden floor, and scooting past the terrifying African mask that hung on the wall.

My grandfather's study was at the front of the house, stacked high with books and in one corner a small television for watching the cricket. Sometimes he would let me climb into the shiny leather of his reclining armchair while he worked at his desk.

Television was an entirely novel experience. I watched mostly from behind the safety of the sofa, the 'Daleks' succeeding in giving me my first nightmares. Across the hall lay the kitchen, where my grandmother always seemed to be baking, and beyond was the adjoining workshop in which my grandfather did his carpentry. They had bought the house for that very reason, so that together they could indulge in their different hobbies. Smells are so evocative that even today I can recall jumping from room to room, caught between the sweet scent of the kitchen and the raw freshness of sawdust.

After lunch they would retire for a siesta, or 'forty winks' as it was called. Initially those long afternoons seemed interminable. I had little choice but to make the most of being alone and soon began to explore. My favourite place of all was the upstairs corridor that ran to the back of the house. Here was a huge south-facing window with a wide sill where you could perch with a book in the sun. On the wall opposite hung an enormous map of the world, littered with different coloured pins. It was an endless source of fascination. Red marked where my grandfather had been; blue for my grandmother, and green for places they had travelled together. Both were born and raised overseas before they met, and for the duration of their marriage they lived and worked all over the world so it was little surprise that every continent was covered, and, it seemed, most countries. I would choose a pin and then implore my grandmother to tell me more. As a natural storyteller she would never disappoint, although occasionally she would have me fetch the diary she had kept every day of her adult life, 'just to check a few details'. On most occasions, though, her memory was clear, and she would have me crying with laughter. The youngest of six children, she had been raised in the island paradise of Montserrat, and my favourite stories were of how she and her mischievous brothers ran wild as children.

On some evenings my grandfather would take me to the railway line at the bottom of the hill where we placed copper coins on the track and waited for the next train to thunder past. It would take

3

an age to find the flattened discs, but I treasured them for years afterwards as peculiar trophies. Not so popular were the Sundays when we had to go to church. It was an unwelcome intrusion and although it was supposed to be important, grandfather always stayed at home. He told me proudly that he was a heathen, and for years afterwards I thought that must be some elitist religious sect.

On the first floor was a bedroom with a large bay window and a beautiful view across the countryside. It had been prepared for my father's convalescence but was never needed. My cosy world was shattered one morning when the phone rang on the small table in the study. I was playing on the floor but stopped to watch my grandfather listen intently. Beams of spring sunshine poured through the glass doors and caught the dust suspended in the air. Time stood still, as though the moment was somehow destined, and had to be recorded indelibly in my mind. All the while he stood straight and unblinking, concentration etched on his stern face. When he replaced the phone he glanced down at me briefly, sadly, but said nothing. I knew the very worst had happened. Confused and forlorn, I tried to grasp the fact that I would never see my father again.

I don't think anyone ever actually told me that he had died. One of the cruellest things about death is that practicality has to take over. By its very nature there are a million things to address. My memory is of everyone rushing about, while I remained a spectator to the whole event. We drove up to Surrey that afternoon, past the ghostly outline of Stonehenge, and joined my mother and elder brother at our small flat. It felt strangely empty and I was no longer sure what to call home. It seemed like an age since I had seen my mother. In a huge display of strength, she smiled warmly at me when she entered the room, before hugging me. I was too young to have any comprehension of what she had been through. Later that evening, while everyone talked, I watched the news on television, failing to understand why my father wasn't mentioned. How could it be that our lives had collapsed and no one seemed to know? The world was just so much bigger than I realised; it was a cruel awakening. Two weeks later, a formal letter from the Foreign Office arrived to say my father was to be awarded an OBE in the Queen's Birthday Honours. An agricultural scientist, his work in the developing world was duly being recognised. They were not to know he had died, of course, but for my mother it must have been yet another painful blow.

One of my father's passions was climbing and as a member of the Cambridge Mountaineering Club during the 1950s, his interest took him to the Alps and beyond. Many years later I was to climb in the remote Ruwenzori range in central Africa. These soaring peaks are like nowhere else on earth, are rarely visited, and have snow-clad summits that emerge mysteriously from the tropical jungle. There, in the middle of nowhere and on a seemingly innocuous misty ridge, I reached for the sketchy guidebook, only to see the very route was first climbed by my father. It was a faint and almost haunting link to the past and a man that I never really knew.

Cheltenham had been my father's home town and it seemed as good a place as any to settle. For my mother it was the first time she had lived properly in England and so must have been a huge change. My older brother was away at school and I too began boarding a couple of years later. I loathed it to start with, unable to escape the feeling of total abandonment. The regime was intrusive and rules governed every aspect of life. Everything was new, the uniform, the rugby, the lessons, and even the language. Words like 'quiz', 'ego', 'prep' and 'tuck' alienated me still more. Furthermore, the shock of my father's death was just beginning to hit me. Of course there was no one to turn to in those days. I would not see my mother for the entire term and aside from a weekly letter home there was little contact with the outside world. The first few weeks were dreadful and I cried myself to sleep most nights, determined that no one would see my desperation. At the edge of the grounds was a large copse, known by all as the 'spinney'. Teachers never ventured there and we were fiercely territorial. I found my refuge in a secluded corner and made a simple den, where on Sundays I could pretend I was still in Africa and nothing had changed.

On my tenth birthday, and eight weeks into term, my grandparents came to visit. I was thrilled to see them and we sat outside school in the car eating birthday cake. They said I should take the rest and share it, but I hadn't the courage to tell them I had made few friends. My present from them was a watch – my first – and I wore it with enormous pride. It was easily the best thing I had ever been given, but that night in the dormitory, more homesick than ever, I had to endure the taunts of the others as they goaded me.

'What did you get from your grandparents, Faulkner – just a watch? I get loads more than that from my parents ...'

'Yeah but he hasn't got a dad, has he? What a shame ... shame,' said Bateman as he grabbed my wrist to see the watch.

Months, or perhaps even years, of pent-up frustration came to the surface in a second. I was strong for my age but had never displayed it in anger. I pushed him away and he responded with a harder shove, laughing at me. That was it – I threw him to the floor with a crash and pinned him down by kneeling on his chest. I hit him several times until his nose was pouring with blood and it ran across his face in a sticky red mess. He conceded, and begged me to stop before I hit him once more for good measure. Afterwards I was ashamed, but also more at ease with myself, and despite my fears the incident never went further. In the dog-eat-dog world of boarding school I had earned some respect. Now I walked a little taller and boys who had never spoken to me wanted to befriend me. In time, Bateman and I became inseparable, and together we built the most elaborate den the spinney had ever seen.

On the day I left boarding school I received the news that my grandfather had also died. The house in Somerset was never the same again and my grandmother soon moved to be closer to us. My mother was about to remarry and together we began a new family life in Cheltenham. Initially I resented yet another move, but at least it transpired to be the last. The next few years were spent at the same school and the disruption was finally over. As an all-rounder I excelled at nothing in particular, except perhaps swimming. My father had taught me in Nigeria when I was very small and I had little difficulty in winning most of my races. Throughout my teenage years the pool was always a refuge, perhaps my connection to the only thing my father and I had done together. Even years after his death I would sometimes glance up at the poolside to see if he was watching.

Ten years older than myself, and a worthy father figure, my brother was the first to really take me climbing. I was very much in awe of him: he taught me all I needed to get started and bought me my first harness. Then together with my school friend Jay we launched ourselves at the crags above Cheltenham and the nearby Wye Valley. After small beginnings we challenged ourselves on the steepest and most demanding routes we could find. To us it was just one huge playground, but we took many knocks in the process, sometimes cycling the fifty-mile round trip to Symonds Yat before making it home utterly exhausted.

The prison-like regime of boarding school had given me a fierce independence and an urge to explore. I set myself ever more bizarre missions away from home. To start with I would head for the woods around Cheltenham in a bid to see how little I could survive with. Devoid of kit, I slept in a shelter made of an old fertiliser bag and drank from streams, often returning sheepishly after a night or two, chilled to the bone and with blistered feet. They were very amateurish efforts at exploration, but also some of my most treasured ones. Armed with a new bicycle, I found that horizons opened up further and the entire Cotswolds fell within reach. My initial goal was to visit all four corners of the Ordnance Survey map and I spent hours poring over the minutest detail of the route. It was always a thrill to see the features on a map come alive into actual landscape. I made it eventually, but it was much harder than I expected, a painful lesson that the best-laid plans sometimes go awry. I was making many mistakes, but unknowingly gathering experience that later would stand me in good stead.

With the heavy winters of the early 1980s, my excursions became even more intrepid. The local hill acquired an arctic mantle and for the first time I could make snow holes in the deep drifts. This was hard-core camping with little room for error, but still enormous fun. I felt like a true pioneer testing the unknown. The age of exploration may have passed, but I followed a simple premise. If it was new to me, then it was unexplored.

A gap year followed while I saved my pennies to go to Kenya with Jay and a couple of friends. We made an abortive attempt on the north face of Mount Kenya, by far our most demanding challenge to date. The exposure was frightening and we clung tightly to the face, as every few minutes loose rocks rained down like missiles from above. With minimal equipment and no helmets we were lucky to survive at all. It was also my first experience of feeling dreadful at altitude and we retreated after ten days, weak, hungry and terribly sunburned. Stung by our failure and with dented pride, we were also much the wiser. I used the remaining time to climb Kilimanjaro and begin a lifelong love affair with yet another part of the world.

It was an uneasy transition to university in London after a summer in Africa. The nights were sheer torment and back came the worst memories of boarding school ten years earlier. Never a good sleeper, I would stare for hours out of my window in the halls of residence before I took to walking the streets at night. They offered a strange comfort, some respite from the isolation, from the pressure of having to conform. I sat in Hyde Park one October night, as the great storm raged around me and huge branches crashed to the ground. Despite the hordes of people I felt lonelier than ever. How could that be in a city of millions? More and more I looked to the sky where every minute a jet carved a trail across the blue expanse. I saw them as a ticket to freedom, to undiscovered adventures. I simply had to escape.

In the summer of 1988 I joined a few friends in a hopelessly ambitious project to cycle across the Himalayas. Beginning in Pakistan, we cycled along the Karakoram Highway to remote Nanga Parbat, the ninth highest mountain on earth. As if that wasn't hard enough, we began the punishing task of carrying the bicycles up the Baltoro Glacier to K2. Despite the hardships, I had to pinch myself every day to believe I was in these surroundings, seeing mountains that I had only ever dreamed of visiting. Our descent turned to quite a struggle after we ran out of food and one of the team was badly injured.[1] With the new university term beckoning I should have headed back but was reluctant to admit defeat. It was another month before I finally reached Everest and was forced to call it a day. I could quite happily have continued indefinitely, but dropping out of university was not a realistic option. Already penniless, I survived most days by scrounging plates of dhal bhat with the local porters. I had lost a quarter of my body weight by this time and had few reserves to continue anyway.

My arrival at Everest base camp was perfectly timed. It was already late September and although there were few climbers I bumped into Lydia Bradley who offered me some lunch. Lydia was a member of a small New Zealand team, and we had met her at K2 three months earlier. She was quite a character and complete with blonde dreadlocks she had an imposing presence.[2] Later I climbed Kalar Pattar, the rocky summit above base camp which offers the best view of the mountain, and spent a long afternoon gazing up at the sharp ridges and fluted faces. It was surreal picking out features I had only read about in books. Our journey had traversed a huge cross-section of the Himalayas and I was overwhelmed by everything we had seen. Still only twenty years old, I knew I would return to this part of the world time and time again.

Living for the vacations was one thing but I wasn't coping with term-time quite so easily. I found my university years dogged by a conflict between academic progress – or rather lack of it – and travelling. I knew I was privileged to have gained a place at Imperial College but that served only to add to the weight of expectation. To me it was nothing more than a faceless concrete shell and I couldn't wait to escape. My degree course in Geology was demanding and I never really applied myself fully. Most of my lectures were spent plotting epic cycle routes and dreaming of distant mountains. For a while, climbing took a back seat as I became obsessed with skydiving. It offered the perfect weekend antidote and a chance to escape the confines of the city. An expensive sport, it was really beyond the means of my student lifestyle but that did little to stop me.

By the time I finally gained my degree I was at a complete loss. I had already dismissed geology as a career after a few months working for an oil company in London. A deskbound future held no appeal whatsoever. At least there was another option. At university I had been a member of the OTC (Officer Training Corps), cynically to earn some extra cash. In return for a weekend commitment I had set aside enough money to finance all of my far-flung trips. Being a part of the military had also given me access to subsidised parachute jumps, but while a full-time career in the forces beckoned, it was not a particularly attractive option. I had already had my fair share of authority figures, and the last thing I needed was yet more shouting. But, short on ideas, I applied to be an officer in the Marines anyway, assured that at least I could indulge in my hobbies. It was a straightforward application, but as it happened I failed the test for colour blindness, and then spent the summer fruitlessly waiting to appeal. Initially I felt let down by the system but perhaps it was for the best. The thought of signing my life away for several years had filled me with horror. Spotting my dilemma, the commanding officer at the OTC called me in. He came straight to the point and suggested I apply for selection to join 21 SAS regiment. He was more than happy to put my name forward.

'Look, it'll be just up your street. Who dares wins and all that crap. Lots of running around the mountains, or rather over the top of them! Just you against the clock, what could be simpler? Oh, and by the way, you can parachute to your heart's content with all the other like-minded nutters!'

Unbeknown to me, the direction of my life was about to change dramatically.

I knew next to nothing about the SAS, other than the kudos associated with the name. Then one Sunday morning I lined up with over a hundred other recruits at Chelsea Barracks. The first hurdle was a timed ten-mile run, which I barely passed. I was no runner, and worryingly this was called 'pre-selection', just to see off the so-called time-wasters. I failed the first medical, of course, again for colour blindness. This time the medic winked at me and handed me the failure notice.

'Might as well file that under B on your way out.'

'I'm sorry?'

'Under B. There's one in the corridor!'

During the next six months of 'selection' the numbers were whittled down. It was a punishing regime, but I found a perverse comfort in it as well. Most of the tests were long, timed marches in the hills. Fitness, map-reading and simply staying awake were the key requirements. There was no 'bullshit', no shouting and little aggression. If you were too slow, you were simply told without ceremony, to 'get on the wagon'. I have no idea what kept me going, as many of those that failed were fitter and stronger than me. There were times, alone at night in the wintry Brecon Beacons, when I simply knew I wouldn't make it, but there was no choice other than to dig deep and find undiscovered levels of stamina. The weather was dreadful and I have been colder there than anywhere else. It was a damp, penetrating cold that could take hours to recover from. Too proud to admit failure, I often resolved to carry on until I simply collapsed and the matter was settled. Of course it never happened, and from somewhere I found a previously undiscovered strength. All those adventures testing myself as a teenager had finally come in useful.

The SAS opened up a hidden world of opportunity. My love of parachuting continued unabated and I managed to leap out of every conceivable form of aircraft, from balloons to helicopters. I trained extensively in demolitions and weapons; often barely believing it was all for real. To me, it was a glorified club and a well-paid one at that. It was a great excuse to play, but of course there was a more serious side. At heart I was not a natural soldier and never felt entirely at ease among my peers. They shared a love of soldiering and hardship that astounded me. Never since have I seen a collection of such driven but modest individuals. It was an odd but very inspiring place to be.

Unlike any other regiment in the Army, the SAS is founded on quite liberal principles. Even today the use of first names among ranks is still encouraged. This suited most of us just fine as we shared a deep mistrust of the so-called 'green machine'; that is to say, normal soldiers, and even more so, their commanders. Of course, any fighting unit has to have structure, and that hierarchy was still present, albeit more subtly. Being recently 'badged' meant a formal introduction to the squadron, which had the potential to be a humiliating experience. A week earlier, grasping the hard-earned sand-coloured SAS beret in your hand, you felt invincible, the proudest man alive. Now, in front of sixty others staring you down, it was like being a five-year-old again on the first day of school. Only the brave and quick-witted could hold their own in such a forum. Most of us knew better and stayed quiet.

One Bear Grylls, fresh-faced and with a plummy Etonian accent, was introduced a couple of years after I joined. The scene was set for a showdown with the boss. The tension was killing us.

'What kind of ridiculous name is Bear, then? Stand up so we can see you!'

'It's my nickname, sir. My sister gave it to me.'

'Don't call me sir, and don't cause me any trouble! I've got my eye on you.'

This is part of what made the SAS special – it was a great leveller; you were all accepted as part of something special. If you had passed selection then that was all that mattered. And of course the regiment attracted alternative characters.

As new members we sat at the back of the drill hall, roughly moving forward a row a year. At the front, by nature of their seniority, sat the 'old and bold'. Their reputation was questioned at your peril and newcomers soon learned where they stood in the grand scheme of things. The more experienced had acquired, or perhaps just perfected, the casual disregard of the 'thousand-mile' stare; an intimidating ability to look at you without focusing. That said, the weekly 'prayers' meeting where grievances were aired often descended into hilarity. I made many staunch friends over those years, but only after time. It was an environment where you all learned to keep your distance and remain self-contained. Those I had initially resented often turned out to be the most loyal in times of crisis. Some were very complicated characters, and all I could decide was that first impressions counted for little.

It was never going to be a permanent career but I resolved to make the most of the opportunity. Later this came in the chance to train as a medic and I moved into civilian hospitals and on to ambulances to gain experience. It was a thrilling time and I briefly considered going back to university to retrain as a doctor. I had never realised that such an adrenalin rush was possible in a routine job. It hadn't even occurred to me at school that I should pursue this as a career. I was doing something useful for once and with regret realised that I had missed my true vocation. Most of our training was, by its very nature, destructive, but now for the first time I was helping others. Much of my time went in suturing wounds, dealing with trauma and helping in theatre. It could be tough emotionally, and that was often far harder than dealing with the blood and gore.

In hospital my partner and I were often called upon to help eject troublesome patients. One such character obliged willingly only to head for the lift a minute later behind our backs. He got out at the top floor, broke a window with a chair, and jumped ten storeys to his death. I heard the dull thump and screams outside. When I got to him he was gulping at the air desperately trying to breathe through his blood-soaked throat. His legs had disintegrated from the impact on the hard concrete. He lay unblinking at the sky above him as his fist clutched emptily, pathetically. It was the first time I had seen someone die so needlessly.

Just a few months later it was almost my turn. Our regiment was being deployed to Poland for 'cross-training' and a large joint exercise. These were often political events where we flew the flag and worked alongside the local soldiers. We were to arrive in style, by making a low-level parachute jump into a small airfield before a host of dignitaries. The massive Hercules was bucking wildly on the approach and I had to steady myself against the fuselage. I was last through the door and exited badly as the plane banked steeply at the end of its short run. Within seconds events went horribly wrong. My parachute had twisted so tightly the canopy was barely half-open. I raced towards the ground at an alarming rate, hurtling past the parachutes of my colleagues. That fateful slow motion began in my mind, every action recorded like a still frame, despite the rush of adrenalin. I made a conscious effort to resist the nauseating fear that was sweeping through me. Below I saw people racing, running panic-stricken across the drop zone. 'Someone else is injured,' I realised. 'No . . . shit! They're coming for me. They think I'm going in . . .!' Fear was replaced by stubborn determination and training took over. 'This simply can't go wrong . . . it can't.'

Too low to open a reserve, I had little choice but to brace myself for the impact. 'I can do this . . . brace yourself . . . chin on chest, knees together, legs bent.' Crash! When the impact came it was with a sickening thud that jarred my body to the core. It felt as though my internal organs had exploded into my chest cavity.

The entire episode was over in only twenty seconds from plane to ground. I lay there for a few minutes, struggling to absorb what had happened, unable even to acknowledge those leaning over me. Eventually I was helped to my feet, bruised and battered, but with no serious injury. It was a wake-up call and the near escape left me in no doubt that enough was enough. It was the first mishap in hundreds of jumps, but I didn't want to push my luck any further. I was out of hospital the next day but could barely move and ached in every joint. It was definitely time to quit while I was ahead.

21 SAS
'Everest 2000'
Climbers needed.
Selection in Skye at Easter.

My heart raced when I saw it. Short and to the point, those few words were to alter the direction of my life yet again. It was an opportunity I could not afford to miss. Climbing Everest was an expensive undertaking and here it was being offered on a plate. Further investigation revealed that not only would we be paid, but also extensive training would be available during the months prior to the expedition. This was a chance not only to get back to the Himalayas, but to climb the mountain I had seen twelve years earlier.

It was an exhilarating time. We made several trips to the Alps and even to Nepal the October before the main expedition. Mounting a team from a small regiment such as ours was an ambitious undertaking, hardly surprising as our entire strength numbered no more than 150. Nevertheless, the SAS had a strong association with Everest and the pressure was on to succeed.[3] The night before our final departure a macabre sweepstake took place in the squadron bar as to how many toes and fingers each climber would return with.

Between us we had a lot of climbing experience but nothing at the extreme altitude that Everest demands. We were ambitious but also extremely naive about the challenges the mountain would present. We had at least all worked together before and gelling as a group was hardly a problem. We hoped summit success would very much stem from our ability to be an effective team. While this was all very well in theory, rivalry between us was inevitable. The SAS thrived on the competitive instinct after all, or else would never have attracted the people it needed. The result, though, was a pace that led to my undoing. Even on our arrival at base camp, we had noticed the Russians stealing the best rocks from our designated area. Not to be outdone, we plotted a midnight raid when we should have been resting and acclimatising. But now in our element, with barely a sound, we moved several tonnes of boulders back into our camp. By morning we had constructed fortress-like walls around our tents and were not challenged by the Russians again.

Never quick to acclimatise, I should have had the strength of character to bide my time and rest. Instead, I fell dreadfully ill with pulmonary oedema and was evacuated down the mountain after just three days. Our emergency plan swung into action and a Chinese driver was found to take me to the Nepalese border by jeep. Undaunted I got off an hour later in the Rongbuk Valley and a thousand metres below base camp, dismissing the confused driver with a generous tip. I crawled into the nearest building I could find, a disused school open to the elements. The drop in altitude was enough, and after two days lying amid the rubble I felt much stronger and started the long hike back up to base camp, bivvying on the hillside each evening. It was infinitely preferable to our rushed ascent of the previous week and it reminded me in no small way of the expeditions I had made as a youngster. On the last night I kipped just below the Rongbuk Monastery at a height of nearly 5,000 metres. It was bitterly cold but the compensation was a sky littered with a billion stars. Lying awake I wondered seriously if this mountain was for me. In my rucksack was a detailed map of Everest and its surrounds. It was of little use on the mountain itself but we were encircled by remote peaks and valleys begging to be explored. I had pored over that map in the weeks and months before the expedition. It was such a temptation just to wander off and ignore the honey-pot that was Everest, drawing all of us blindly towards its summit.

The others were surprised to see me so soon, but equally relieved that I had recovered. Although thankful to be back with the team, the pressure was, if anything, more intense. The others had already been to Advanced Base Camp (ABC) and returned to rest. Anxious to re-establish myself, I joined them on their next trip up, an utterly exhausting six-hour walk across glacial moraine. Once at ABC we learned that no team that season had yet made the North Col, and the chance to be first fed our competitive instinct. It would, of course, also mean the best and safest tent spots. It was another chance to show the Russians who was boss, and so the next morning four of us set off. I felt good initially, but the ascent was far too premature. Every few steps we were left gasping and doubled up, each movement unbelievably hard as our lungs strained at the effort. We were all extremely fit but that was no substitute for lack of oxygen. Again, bravado had left us carrying much of the load, while more experienced Himalayan climbers know that the Sherpas are far better at doing the hard graft. We made the Col after a punishing five hours and staggered back to ABC, only to collapse in a heap. Despite our exhaustion we were pleased with our efforts, proving to ourselves that we could climb on the mountain quickly and as a team. The others were impressed that I had kept up after my illness, but there was a heavy price to pay when I woke the following morning.

For a long time I had revelled in that blissful state of exhausted half-sleep, getting my bearings and recalling the events of the previous day. Everything's a gradual process at altitude – you have to identify each aching part of your body and will it into action. Eventually I unzipped my sleeping bag a fraction, releasing a cloud of steam into the tent. With my eyes and lips glued shut I had to gently force my eyelids back before trying to focus on the yellow material above me.

Something wasn't right. Blurred smudges confused my vision, and it was impossible to focus. I tried to persuade myself that it was the wind shaking the tent, but the icy stillness around me said otherwise. In desperation I forced my right arm out of the bag and reached for my book, flipped it open and tried to read. The words were obscured and through my right eye alone the page was totally unreadable. It was as though someone had smeared Vaseline over my eyes. I clutched at explanations, but instinctively knew what had happened. My retina had haemorrhaged and the blood inside my eye was disrupting my vision. Other high-altitude climbers had suffered from it in the past and now it was my turn.

The events of that morning put paid to my newfound optimism. Everything was a blur as I pulled on my down suit and boots to walk across the moraine and into the dining tent. I had little appetite but instead sipped on a huge mug of sweet tea. There was a gentle game of brinkmanship developing, a habit we had developed over the last few months of training, with one of the team suggesting we go back up to the North Col that day. We all knew we were too exhausted, but the trick was not to be first to admit defeat and therefore be labelled as the quitter.

When asked for my thoughts, I was forced to confess that all was not well. It was a difficult admission, knowing that any injury would jeopardise not only my own summit chances, but also those of the whole team. Nevertheless, it was time to be realistic and head down to base camp. Every step of the fourteen-mile descent over rough glacial terrain was demoralising. I couldn't ignore the fact that it was an inglorious and premature retreat. My head was spinning with the possible implications, not only for my chances on the expedition, but for my eyesight as well.

Our team doctor descended back to base camp a few days later. Although an experienced surgeon he quickly stressed that eyes were not his area. Despite this he had an ophthalmoscope with him, and through it he painstakingly sketched the view of my retina. The result after an hour was an impressive piece of artwork, liberally strewn with patches of red crayon. Anyone could see that it spelled the worst. There was a further delay while he emailed a colleague back home to seek advice. The reply, when it came, wasn't good. On no account should I ascend higher and I would do well to seek specialist advice as soon as possible. It was a bitter blow and signalled the end of my expedition. Only three weeks after arriving I descended across the plateau and back to Kathmandu. Passing the Rongbuk Monastery, I stole a last glance over my shoulder at the majestic north face. From this side the enormity and grandeur of the mountain could be fully appreciated. That day the summit was clear and a long plume was being swept off the top by the jet stream winds. It was an evocative sight and I can't deny that I felt a pang of jealousy for those who still had a chance for the top.

My stony-faced Chinese driver and I sat in silence during a bumpy, frustrating journey. This time there was no jumping off early. As we descended on to the Tibetan plateau we swept through the local villages, horn blaring, without stopping, just as we had done in reverse a month earlier. Local children paused to stare but made no attempt to wave or acknowledge us. They had seen plenty of rich Western climbers pass along this road, spending thousands of dollars in a rush to fulfil their ambition. A mountain like Everest deserves reverence and being whisked back and forth seemed an injustice. In George Mallory's day, the climbers had taken the train as far as Darjeeling in India before walking across the Tibetan plateau. I longed to make a similar journey and relive that style of expedition. Only in the previous year had his body been found on the upper slopes of the mountain. It was a stark reminder of how much the mountain had changed in the seventy-five years since his disappearance. In all likelihood my condition was at least in part the result of ascending too quickly. A gradual approach to the mountain would be much kinder, to both mind and body.

The feeling of failure is a miserable condition. I rented a small room in Kathmandu and spent hours staring at the walls feeling sorry for myself. Eventually I dragged myself to the Canadian clinic by the embassy to seek treatment. By putting things off I hoped to have at least delayed the bad news. They were unable to treat me but said I was in luck as a world expert on retinal haemorrhages ran an eye clinic in Kathmandu. He had seen many such injuries over the years and would probably be able to help me.

When I arrived at the doctor's large home I was greeted warmly and ushered straight to the front of the queue. I felt very humbled and more than a little embarrassed. In the waiting room were severe cataract cases and small children with seemingly very little sight. I now felt ashamed for thinking that my world had fallen apart, while around me were far more pressing cases. I still had perfectly reasonable sight and the quality of my life at least would barely be affected. So what if I couldn't climb Everest? While the prognosis was mixed, it was a relief to know the outcome. He had seen many such cases before, he reported, although mine was unusually severe. The haemorrhages were on and very near the macula, the most sensitive part of the retina. It was likely that my sight would be affected but to what degree it was hard to tell. However, he was certain that I would see a marked improvement over the coming months. He advised me not to fly for a month or so if I could avoid it, and on no account to head back up the mountain.

I spent the next few days wandering the streets of Kathmandu, desperately trying to work the frustration out of my system. In my urgency to climb the mountain I had always seen failure alongside frostbite or broken limbs, but now I didn't even feel ill. Still the advice was sound, the blurred vision in my eye wasn't going away and returning to the mountain was no longer an option. Even if I could surmount the hurdle of red tape and visa problems, I would be much too far behind the others. After all, trying to catch up had been my undoing after the first week. The advice not to fly was a complication but also a blessing in disguise. Heading home would only have compounded the sense of failure. There was also the issue that I was still on duty and being paid by the Army. If I had been able to travel home I could in theory be reassigned straight away, although in my condition that was unlikely. My ticket was still booked with the team and the return flight was another month away. I simply had to pick myself up and make the most of an opportunity.

It was twelve years since I had been to the Annapurna region, during our epic crossing of the Himalayas by bike in 1988. On that occasion we had only partially completed the Annapurna circuit and I had always meant to return. It was a three-week hike, which would fit in perfectly; all being well I would be back in Kathmandu to meet the others on their descent. I could at least fly home with the team and salvage a little pride.

My heart wasn't in it at first. After so many months preparing for a bigger challenge this would always feel like second-best. I took a bus to Besisahar and stayed in a miserable hotel, feeling unable to mix with the other travellers. The initial few days' trekking I spent entirely on my own, until by chance I fell in with those on a similar schedule. Over the following days, I joined a multinational group from Holland and France. The scenery was simply magnificent and I have never enjoyed better company. My new friends were intelligent, well travelled and unbelievably relaxed. It even gave me the chance to practise my French, and was the perfect antidote to the competitive military environment I had been immersed in.

Just as I began to feel at ease with myself, we returned to the lakeside town of Pokhara. The experience of trekking with my new friends had given me some much-needed perspective. They had little in the way of ambition and had brought me firmly down to earth, even if it was short-lived. Our Everest team had a website and I logged on, desperate to read the latest update. Splashed across the homepage was the news that two of them had reached the summit. My head reeled, shocked at the impact of the news. While I had come to terms with my own failure, I was totally unprepared for the success of others. I am ashamed now to admit that I was jealous. I knew I had been every bit the climber they

21

were and felt success had been snatched away from me. Selfishly, it would have been so much easier to handle if no one had made it, but that's hardly a worthy sentiment.

Everest had left a big hole in my life and I needed a challenge, one that would consume me completely, both mentally and physically. Something where I could pore over maps hour after hour as I had done so many times before. I wrestled with a few ideas, but nothing seemed to grab me. In the end, there was no denying that Everest was unfinished business. Returning was simply inevitable. Exactly how was another matter.

Chapter 2

On the Shoulders of Giants

'We knocked the bastard off!' Sir Edmund Hillary's words to his colleagues on descending to the South Col seem devoid of any sentiment. It surprises many that the first man on the summit of Everest didn't seem particularly in awe of his achievement. Perhaps it was his Kiwi pragmatism that prevented him from getting too emotive? That casual disregard may have been intentional at the time, but Everest remains a mountaineering ideal for many. Even for Hillary it was to have a huge effect on the course of his life. It may have lost some of its mystique since the early days, but it is still the mountain that many aspire to.

George Mallory, of course, has much to answer for. He was a fitting ambassador for the mountain – young, gifted and brimming with ambition. Ultimately his obsession with Everest led to three expeditions there in just four years, and despite the lack of summit success, the efforts of those early pioneers caught the public imagination. Mallory's death in 1924, along with that of Sandy Irvine, for ever sealed Everest in the public's psyche and marked the mountain's place indelibly in the history of exploration.

Whether their efforts were in vain or not has been much debated by both mountaineers and commentators. Just as with Scott of the Antarctic, the English have a particular appetite for a hapless hero suffering a glorious and poetic death. However, neither came home, and certainly on Everest any mountaineer will tell you that getting down is the hard bit.

The British refused to admit defeat and during the 1930s further expeditions were mounted, none of which succeeded. After the war, Tibet became off-limits to Western teams, just as Nepal began to open its borders. Climbing from the south had never been an option in Mallory's time and now there was the promise of a new and more accessible route to the top. The Swiss came close to summit success in 1952, but it was John Hunt's team that finally succeeded with Hillary and Tenzing Norgay the following year. Never mind that neither was British; the news broke on Coronation Day and it was seized upon with relish in the bleak post-war years.

In the eyes of mountaineers it was perhaps inevitable that Everest would be conquered sooner or later. Scientists, however, were not so sure. The atmosphere at the height of the summit is perilously thin and many considered it impossible that life could be supported at such elevations. Their assumption was in fact well founded and based on a logical calculation. Atmospheric pressure has long been known to decline with increasing altitude. This is due to the decreasing density of the air as you move higher. At sea level we are in effect sitting at the bottom of an ocean of air. Early efforts at calibrating altimeters for aviation assumed a standard decrease in pressure with height. Accordingly, the summit of Everest was estimated to have an atmospheric pressure of about 236 torr.[4] Only in 1981 was the true pressure at the summit first recorded. It is in fact closer to 253 torr, a small difference perhaps, but with significant implications. The error stems from the fact that the atmosphere is noticeably thicker nearer the equator than at the poles. In fact, were Everest situated further north, an oxygen-free ascent would be impossible.

As it is, 253 torr is still barely sufficient to support human life, as oxygen forms only a fraction of this total pressure. Furthermore, the lungs are saturated with water vapour to a higher proportion than at sea level. All this conspires to put the mountaineer right on the edge of what is humanly possible. It is for this reason that some mountaineers climbing oxygen-free have been caught out by even minor fluctuations in the weather. The onset of a depression will lower the pressure still further and perhaps lethally. For myself, and other mountaineers, this physiology has an almost perverse attraction. Where else can you step so close to the margins of human endurance?

The science was not fully tested until 1978 when Reinhold Messner and Peter Habler reached the summit oxygen-free. Messner recounted later that he felt like 'nothing more than a single gasping lung'. Their achievement stunned the worlds of both mountaineering and science, and although some have followed, it is still a rare breed that makes it to the top unassisted by extra oxygen. For most people, it is certainly beyond their physiological limits and no amount of training will remedy that.

For many, the success of Messner and Habler was a closing chapter in the mountain's history. That's not to say there weren't other credible achievements and fine ascents, but the talk was now of records being broken rather than tackling the unknown. My first visit to the mountain in 1988 was a case in point. Not only was Lydia Bradley about to become the first woman to summit without oxygen, but base camp was still buzzing with the achievement of Jean-Marc Boivin.[5] A multi-talented climber and extreme skier, he had made the summit the previous morning on 26 September. Unfurling his homemade parapente, he had then flown from the top in a flight lasting just twelve minutes. The Himalayas had now become the new Alps. The games that climbers had developed for years, in resorts such as Chamonix, had now arrived on a bigger stage. To a young man such as myself it was a thrilling spectacle, but equally it left me feeling a bit despondent. What was there left to do that hadn't been done? I wandered back down the Khumbu glacier afterwards, determined to try and find my own first.

During the years since, records have continued to tumble with ever-increasing obscurity: the youngest to climb, the oldest, and then even the first blind person. New routes were still being forged, of course, and in ever-smaller teams; ascents were being made in different seasons; and then even the number of individual summits began to be counted amongst the Sherpas.

Accounts of these early expeditions struck a very personal chord. While I considered myself a climber, my first love was for travelling and it was the approach to the mountain that most intrigued me. On numerous previous expeditions, I had always been the slowest to acclimatise and as a result had fallen ill. I longed to approach the mountain at my own pace and, if possible, enjoy the revelation of actually feeling well on a mountain. In Mallory's time, the climbers had to endure a six-week trek from Darjeeling, but the walk was spectacularly beautiful, and en route the team acclimatised gently and improved their fitness. Any journey in itself would be an added bonus, amid incredible scenery and cultures. Here I knew was the challenge that I needed, the fusion of an epic overland journey with the ascent itself.

Yet I thought someone must have at least attempted the ultimate ascent. It was a simple challenge in principle, travelling from the Earth's lowest point to the highest in a single journey. I searched the internet in vain, trying to find some account of an attempt. Surely it was too big a goal to have been overlooked? Much to my amazement, not only did the challenge remain, but, to the best of my knowledge, no one had even attempted it. My initial excitement was short-lived, and after reaching for my trusty atlas my heart sank. It was easy to see why no one had ever undertaken the journey. The 8,000-kilometre route from the Dead Sea to Everest is a dangerous one, if only politically. That is before you begin over 9,000 metres of climbing: the greatest ascent possible.

Despite this, I spent hours plotting and scheming my way across the page. How many routes were there and how long would they take? When would one have to start to arrive for the best season on Everest? What would be the best mode of travel – on foot, by motor vehicle, or by bicycle? The first would take too long, the second would be less of a challenge. It simply had to be the bike.

The route to the north and through the old Soviet republics looked intriguing. But I knew the winters there would be unforgiving. In order to arrive on the mountain for the spring season, any expedition would have to travel overland during the winter months. Another route lay to the south, perhaps through Saudi Arabia and across Iran. The latter was the only country that could not be avoided, whatever the route. This went some way to explaining why the challenge had never been attempted. Since the revolution in the late 1970s, it had been very much off-limits to Western travellers, in part due to the bitter war that had raged between Iran and Iraq for eight long years. Now restrictions had eased and Westerners were beginning to travel more freely. A friend of mine had recently journeyed by bus through the country and reported a warm welcome wherever he went.

I wrestled with these ideas for months and, plagued by self-doubt, dismissed any serious notion of an expedition. After all, if it could be done surely someone else would have done it? On the other hand, the world was changing, and I knew if I didn't seize the chance, someone else certainly would. I might then spend the rest of my life kicking myself over the missed opportunity. With the idea refusing to settle, I drew up a tentative proposal, as much for my benefit as anyone else's. I needed something tangible, something to help unravel my own thoughts. I half expected to draft it, and then, embarrassed, throw it in the bin before anyone saw it. Instead, I plucked up the courage and sent it to a few friends, sat back, and waited.

'Blimey, Dom, have you seen these countries? If you need a name just call it "The Axis of Evil Expedition!"'

'Why don't you do it the other way round? If you started at Everest it would be downhill all the way and you could finish with a swim!'

It was a mixed response. Although I wasn't totally discouraged, there were two major problems. Most of my friends were now either settled with families or entrenched in careers. The expedition would last six months and taking that sort of time off wasn't easy. In addition, not everyone wanted to cycle and climb. The mountain appealed to most, but the overland journey to very few. I had always assumed that some might be able to join the expedition halfway through. It was easy to arrange but would do nothing towards meeting the original objective. Someone had to go from the lowest to the highest.

The first of those to commit was Sebastian Bullock, a teaching colleague of mine, and coincidentally a former member of my regiment. Our paths hadn't really crossed in the Army, but we shared a common experience and had since become firm friends. Seb was a very strong endurance athlete who liked nothing more than testing himself in the hills with long runs. He was quiet and self-contained but also displayed a steely determination. As an experienced climber he was itching to have a go at Everest, but his work commitments and two small boys meant that he was very unlikely to get time off for the entire trip. At least I had one team member on board, even if it wasn't for the whole expedition.

Others came and went, as it became increasingly clear that for most the trip was just too long. Some also raised perfectly valid questions about the finances, something I had yet to address, but on a personal level felt relaxed about. The overland trip would not be particularly expensive, and the mountain costs could be kept to a minimum if I organised our own logistics. But for those with busy lives, families and jobs, the uncertainty was a step too far. They were reluctant to commit without guarantees, something I could blatantly not offer. I needed some free agents who were prepared to take a leap of faith, share some ownership of the project, and actually make it happen.

From the outset, I was anxious to give the expedition a name. An identity would help marketing efforts, both for finance and recruits, as well as providing a point of focus. We had discussed this at the first meeting but most of the suggestions seemed too long. Of course it would also help if the name we chose was available as a website. After much deliberation, the simple title of 'EVERESTMAX' emerged after we decided it best summarised our efforts. The 'Max' of course would be shorthand for 'the longest climb on earth'.

Next to commit was Seb's brother-in-law, André Zlattinger, who worked for Sotheby's in London. André had long held an ambition to climb Everest. Not only was his enthusiasm infectious, but his endless list of contacts would also prove useful. But even a year before departure I was left with very little 'team' to speak of. Not only that but I had set a date the following April to officially launch the expedition. I had asked Bear Grylls, from my old regiment, to come and give a talk. Having departed the SAS he had since gone on to climb Everest, and in so doing became the youngest Briton to make the summit. I hoped that same evening to launch our own plans and perhaps even get a few sponsors, but now it all started to seem very premature. I briefly considered cancelling the event; after all, it would be a bit embarrassing with a team of just three. It would also mean we were beyond the point of no return as the expedition would be in the public domain. Postponing until I had a stronger team would have been a cautious move.

Instead, I threw caution to the wind and pressed on regardless. I was anxious not to lose momentum and things looked up immediately with the recruitment of Nic Clarke. He came with the personal recommendation of an old army friend, although he had no connection with the military himself. I warmed to Nic instantly. He was very quiet and sincere but struck me as completely genuine. Everything about him was precise and considered and I had little doubt he would prove valuable to any team. It was obvious he was a very self-disciplined individual and one that needed to be occupied. He routinely competed in triathlons and marathons and had just returned from climbing in the Himalayas. Not only did Nic have the right balance of experience, but he had clearly considered the commitment very carefully before putting himself forward. He was – by his own admission – up for a 'serious adventure' and had already made enquiries about giving up work. Here at last was someone with exactly the necessary credentials.

The other welcome addition was Jamie, the son of Chris Rouan, a teaching colleague in Cheltenham. Jamie had an easy-going nature and was great company, the sort of person that would slip effortlessly into any team. Despite being only twenty-two, he was already an experienced climber and seasoned traveller. He was about to graduate, but luckily for me had no idea what to do next. Departure that winter would be ideal timing, giving him a few months to earn some welcome cash.

Finding Jamie and Nic at last bolstered my efforts. Both were committed and reliable from the start and that alone counted for a lot after months of uncertainty. Soon there were others expressing an interest as well. Typical of these were Vicki and John Parfitt, a local couple I had met through work. Not only were they passionate travellers, but Vicki was also a keen cyclist and climber. She was taken straight away with the project and began to make moves to secure six months away from work. John's job with the RAF meant that he was unlikely to join us, but he was keen to help with the organisation in any way he could.

We now had the semblance of a team, with four of us up for the whole journey. Along with Seb and André who were joining us for the climb that made for a total of six. We were still a long way short of the number I had envisaged but it was a start. I had hoped, perhaps naively, that we might find eight for the entire journey, to be strengthened by a further four for the mountain. At least with a small team in place we began to pick up momentum, with several people looking in turn for others.

Dickie Walters was another character introduced to me. He had spent a few years in the Navy and still worked for them on an ad hoc basis. Dickie was a jovial character, round-faced and constantly chatting, with an endless stream of stories. I imagined him as a pub landlord or a friendly local butcher. He was well travelled and had experience organising a whole host of activities. His latest job was running the press side for the Navy's forthcoming Trafalgar celebrations and it was clear he would be able to bring some much-needed marketing expertise to our efforts. Dickie, by his own admission, enjoyed a few beers and was desperately out of shape. He quickly counted himself out of any cycling effort, but suggested helping in a support capacity such as driving a vehicle. This, I realised, was going to prove essential. While I wanted to cycle the overland journey, ideally unsupported, that was ambitious. We would have a mountain of equipment with us, including spare bicycles and even a generator to power laptops and so forth. As this was all too heavy for the bikes, a vehicle of some description would be necessary to carry the extra equipment. I guessed that finding someone to drive was going to be tricky, so I seized upon Dickie's offer readily. We now had a support team, even if it numbered just one.

Bear spoke superbly at our launch evening and we even had a few sponsors in place on the night. John Parfitt, Vicki's husband, had wasted no time in writing endless letters to companies seeking support. Mostly the response was negative but small successes served to spur us on. The biggest surprise came from Whyte Bicycles, who in principle agreed to provide custom-made Marin bikes for the entire journey. It was a huge boost and meant that for the cycling team at least a significant part of the cost would be saved. With over 300 guests at the launch night, we also gained valuable publicity for new team members.

Friends in the audience came back to me a week later and recommended a local girl called Sarah Lyle. Sarah had just graduated in Geology from Cambridge having secured a first-class degree. Her plans to work in Africa for a year had recently fallen through and she found herself in desperate need of a project. She was enthusiastic but cautious on the phone and we agreed to meet at her home near Cheltenham. By the time I had finished explaining the expedition to her, she could barely contain her excitement. On paper, she seemed a strange choice, as she had next to no climbing experience. Despite that, she was very well travelled and into a variety of sports, including rugby and rowing. Her determination was obvious and with still over six months to departure, she resolved to spend the summer climbing.

I had little doubt that Sarah would rise to the task, but our team for the entire journey was looking increasingly weak. In terms of climbing, I feared we would be very inexperienced for the demands of high altitude. My previous trip to Everest had been with a team of ten, some very experienced. Even then, only two had made the top. On paper at least, the odds seemed very much against us.

With new momentum, the plan was to train in the Alps during the summer of 2005. We were still relative strangers and although I was apprehensive whether we would all get on, I needn't have worried. There was a casual confidence among the others that caught me unawares. It was immediately obvious that I was among people used to aiming high and giving every project their all. In truth this was almost nothing to do with me, as in effect the expedition had become self-selecting. I had little choice but to accept whoever could come along. All I had done was to emphasise to every individual the magnitude of what we were attempting. Those that now remained were naturally motivated for such a challenge, or they simply wouldn't have been there in the first place. We might be inexperienced but, at long last, we had the makings of a team.

The following week we climbed Mont Blanc with surprising ease. For me it was the third time on top and I knew it could be tough. We had made a similar ascent with the Everest 2000 team as part of our preparations, and for my own peace of mind, I needed to make a comparison between that team and this. It was perhaps useful that the conditions were far from ideal. The temperature was bitterly cold and the wind gusted strong enough to check our progress. Still, Sarah handled the ascent comfortably and proved to be as strong as any of us. We returned to the campsite after an eighteen-hour day and dropped with exhaustion, but Sarah was still bouncing with energy.

'Is anyone up for a quick mountain bike ride?' We stared back in horror. She was undoubtedly a force to be reckoned with. The others were equally impressive. Jamie and Nic had already forged a strong partnership and were working well together. André suffered with the cold but it was evident that he had few problems with his fitness. It was clear that our team was talented and very strong and I for one felt hugely relieved.

On returning from Mont Blanc, I had barely stepped through the front door before the phone rang. The woman at the other end babbled away excitedly, almost uncontrollably, in a cockney accent, before introducing herself as Pauline Sanderson.

'Right, look, here's how it is – about this trip of yours . . .'

'Do you have any experience?' I replied.

'Oh yeah, buckets of it. I used to live in Nepal. I've been climbing and cycling for years!'

Pauline worked at Glenmore Lodge, a climbing centre in Scotland, alongside her husband Phil, who was an instructor. I had sent a number of flyers a few weeks earlier to some of the climbing schools hoping to attract a few more recruits and my efforts had clearly paid off. Pauline's enthusiasm was unbounded and furthermore she was up for the whole expedition. Phil would not be interested in the cycling, she explained, but she was hoping to persuade him to join us on the mountain if there was space. She was so desperate to be involved we agreed to meet as soon as we could to talk things over.

Sadly the news wasn't quite so good with John's wife Vicki. She too had climbed Mont Blanc in the summer but, unable to join us on our training, had done it prior to our arrival. During the descent she had aggravated an old knee injury, which now required an operation. It was looking increasingly unlikely that she would be able to join us. It was a disappointing setback. John and Vicki had been major supporters of the project since its inception. To their credit, they resolved to stay fully involved and they remained tireless in their efforts.

In October, Sarah and I flew up to Inverness to meet Pauline and her husband Phil. We survived Pauline's suspicious cooking, stayed over, and enjoyed a great evening. Phil was naturally sceptical about the expedition, but that was to be expected. He had friends who had climbed on Everest and knew just how demanding it was. We talked into the early hours about every aspect of the logistics, from what food we would take to how much oxygen we would need. He was clearly a cautious individual and at times it felt like a cross-examination. That was no bad thing and it was better for any potential problems to emerge early on. He was reluctant to make a decision that night, but I hoped he would be able to join us on the mountain. His expertise would add some credibility to the climbing team.

Pauline herself was quite clearly a natural traveller and I could see she would be a huge asset. She had that positive 'can do' attitude present in people who thrive on life. She was a very different character to Sarah, if only because of their ages. Pauline was forty-one and so there was nearly twenty years between them. Sarah was more academic where Pauline was more pragmatic. Nevertheless they seemed to get on well, which was lucky, as without Vicki they would be the only girls on the main team. We now numbered six for the whole expedition, plus Dickie, and then hopefully with Phil on board, another four climbers to join us.

There was also good news from Dickie, who had met and secured the services of Rowena Wright to help with the support driving. Ro was a talented marine artist, based in the Isle of Wight. Another avid traveller, she was keen to drive with Dickie, and maybe do some painting en route. With these late additions, our team was all but complete. Five of us would be aiming to tackle the whole journey by cycling to the mountain and our numbers would be at least doubled for our arrival on the mountain.

Things took another leap forward when we had a farewell dinner in late October. It was the bicentennial Trafalgar celebration and a suitably patriotic night for the occasion. An 'auction of promises' enabled us to raise valuable funds and the publicity helped enormously. With only six weeks to go, the momentum carried us through and André organised a similar evening of fundraising a fortnight later at Sotheby's. That too spread the net further and we started to recruit our first 'official supporters'. We had put a modest dent in the overall expenditure but were still falling short of what we hoped to raise. In truth, the cost of the trip was not enormous as the very nature of the overland journey meant that daily spending would be kept to a minimum.

The final fortnight wasn't without setbacks. The bicycles arrived as promised, but were much delayed, and I got to ride mine only once before departure. Our Iranian visas proved elusive and we were twice forced to delay our flights to Amman in Jordan. It was a tense waiting game, and, with everything in place, there was nothing else to do. We simply had to be in Kathmandu by the end of March, so frustratingly the clock was already ticking. With such a small and inexperienced team, getting just one of the cyclists to the top was very ambitious. That, of course, assumed that we all made it to the mountain. Between the Dead Sea and Everest lay 5,000 miles of untold adventure.

Chapter 3

The Road to Damascus – Jordan and Syria

The lights of Amman sprawled for miles below as we circled into the city. The task ahead was almost upon us, and felt more daunting than ever. There had been a knot in my stomach for hours, tight with anticipation. Arriving in a foreign city at night was intimidating enough, but our one-way flight seemed to compound the sensation of heading into the unknown. If all went to plan we wouldn't be returning this way, but flying home from Nepal. Still, none of us had even booked a return flight – it would have seemed premature and overly confident. Perhaps we were just hedging our bets a little? After all we were still relative strangers and Pauline had met the others for the first time at the airport. While we had tried to plan for every eventuality en route, we simply might not get on with each other. It was quite possible that we might all fall out over the next few days, and have to return home humiliated. I tried my hardest not to even entertain the thought.

Until our departure the expedition had existed only on paper. Ideas were bandied about freely and we could have backed out at any time. Finally, setting off had added some much-needed realism. But it still seemed bizarre to me that we could skip over one continent so effortlessly, while the next would be full of adventures. I had never quite come to terms with the magic of air travel and how deceptively small it makes the world. It is only when you cycle across a continent, or sail an ocean, that you appreciate the magnitude of long distance. I had spent most of the flight switching my gaze between the map on the screen and the window. We were chasing the sunset effortlessly but the map reminded me that we would need to cycle a quarter of the way around the globe. With only three months to complete a huge distance the pressure was on, and I had to wonder if we were asking too much of ourselves. Aside from the demands of cycling there were just so many unknowns. This was no longer a game and for the first time I felt the heavy weight of responsibility. The team believed in my idea and I was desperate not to let them down.

Our first stroke of luck had been at Heathrow. Armed with bicycles and huge amounts of kit, we had been fully prepared to pay for extra freight. In fact I had even budgeted several hundred pounds of our precious budget just in case. Much of our climbing equipment was already being freighted ahead, but we were anxious to keep hold of the crucial items, especially the bikes. In the event the queue was so long, and the girl at the counter so fraught, that she simply waved us on at no extra cost.

Pauline was naturally vivacious and wasted no time in getting to know everyone, walking up and down the plane chatting to us all in turn. Dickie and Ro seemed engrossed in conversation, which was just as well. They would be in each other's pockets over the coming months far more than the rest of us. Nic and Jamie had also hit it off, as I knew they would, having climbed well together during our summer trip to the Alps. The fact that Sarah seemed to get on with the other two girls was a blessing.

They were all quite different to each other and there was quite a spread of ages.

After landing, we were met by a couple of drivers from our hotel, the Al-Saraya, the most intriguing I could find on the web. The owner was known simply as Fayez, and had a reputation as a rather colourful character. By the time we arrived downtown at the Reception it was gone two in the morning and we were shattered. That didn't put off the suave-looking Fayez, who, despite the hour, was immaculately dressed in a shiny blue suit and red silk tie. With a nonchalant click of his fingers he ordered our luggage to be taken straight upstairs, while we joined him for coffee in his palatial office. We sat back on the faded leather chairs and did our best to stay awake. He was utterly charming as he explained he would be of whatever assistance he could with what he called 'the big bicycle ride'. However, he clearly hadn't grasped the magnitude of what we were attempting.

'And where will you be cycling to?' he queried.

'To Tibet and Mount Everest,' Sarah replied on our behalf. There was a pause while he frowned slightly.

'But this is on the far side of the world!' He gestured casually out of the window as if to indicate the precise direction of Everest. 'Please – you must be mistaken. It will be very far for you, I think.'

'About 8,000 kilometres. It'll only take us three months,' said Pauline.

'Only you crazy English would think of such a mad journey!' he tutted while shaking his head. 'What will you do when you get there?'

'We will climb to the top!' I said a little too confidently for my own liking, '. . . we will try to climb to the top.'

A lawyer by day, Fayez ran the hotel in the evenings. Ensconced in his office he spent the entire time entertaining guests, while the staff hovered loyally, hanging on his every word and command. His consumption of strong coffee and cigarettes was mind-boggling. Fayez clearly revelled in the cult status his hotel had acquired and many journalists had used it over the years as a stopping-off point en route to Iraq. A few years previously, many of those attempting to form a 'human shield' against the American-led invasion had landed up here. Their efforts to stop the second Gulf War were of course in vain, but at the Al-Saraya many of the protesters gave ongoing press conferences and interviews, much to the delight of Fayez. His walls were covered in memorabilia and pictures of him with former guests and travellers who had passed this way.

We had many discussions with Fayez over the following days. He was certainly well travelled and, at least on the surface, apolitical, fascinated by other people's views and experiences. A mine of information, he helped us enormously in finding where to secure various items. Our shopping list was exhaustive, from pots and pans, to tarpaulins, fuel, food, and of course a vehicle in which to carry it all. The last was proving the trickiest to resolve. If we had been staying in Jordan, or even returning that way, the process would have been straightforward. The problem lay in the fact that we would be effectively exporting the vehicle out of the country, which presented us with an administrative nightmare. An alternative was simply to hire a different vehicle in every country, but it was likely to prove more expensive in the long run, as well as make us less independent. I had researched the problem extensively back at home but, despite my best efforts, I had failed to secure any kind of vehicle in Amman before leaving.

With the help of Fayez we made contact with Hassan, the Jordanian president of the RAC. His desk and office were indeed presidential and he lectured us from a good five metres away. He spoke slowly and with enormous gravity about our 'dangerous undertaking', occasionally leaning low across the desk in a hushed whisper for extra effect. After dire warnings about crazy Iranian drivers, robbers and bandits, he briefed us on the legalities of buying a vehicle and taking it out of Jordan. He also arranged a visit to the so-called 'Zarqa duty-free zone' from where we could buy and officially export a vehicle, in this case to Nepal. After purchase, the vehicle would have to leave Jordan within a mandatory twenty-four hours. The fact that we would not actually reach Nepal for another three months seemed fairly academic and of little interest to Hassan. The key issue was that we had to be out of the country in the stipulated time. It all seemed very fanciful and I left feeling a little dubious. I gladly passed on the small print to Dickie, who was emerging quickly as the team optimist. So much so that I sometimes felt like shaking him through frustration.

'Oh, don't worry, Dom, I'm sure it will all turn out fine. We'll just go with the flow on this one. You've got to trust these people.'

'Great, Dickie, but what if it doesn't work out? We'll be completely stuck.'

'Oh, don't worry, we'll cross that bridge later . . . It will sort itself out . . .'

Nothing seemed to dampen his spirits, but I had spent so long planning the venture I didn't want to leave anything to chance. Ro had already teased me that my glass was always half-empty, and we were still only two days into the trip. But my attitude was that if things turned out better than expected then there was no harm done. Dickie's carefree attitude also extended to the finances and he had little hesitation in throwing money at a problem, a habit we couldn't sustain. I had asked him to keep track of everything we spent but was starting to regret the decision. His wallet was already a pile of crumpled receipts and mixed currencies. On our third day I accompanied him back to the airport in Amman to collect our freight. What we had hoped would be straightforward became a marathon of endless offices, strange officials, cups of black tea, and pile upon pile of documents. We raced from room to room at the heels of our earnest translator. Every paper needed a stamp and every stamp required a fee.

The final customs fees were so exorbitant that we had no choice but to refuse to pay. The only way our items could be released was by paying a modest amount for official seals. We were then warned that breaking these seals in Jordan would result in a stiff penalty or even imprisonment. While this was a temporary solution, it meant that we would be in the odd position of having all our kit, but not being able to use it until we entered Syria and the seals could be broken. Their customs in turn might levy further charges if they spotted the imported equipment. It was all very confusing and the final straw came when we tried to exit the warehouse, complete with sealed crates. Only yards away from freedom, the same suspect security guard in a grubby T-shirt, who had charged us to get in, was now trying to charge us to get out. As he tucked our last wad of notes into his belt I badgered him for a receipt as Dickie pulled me into the taxi. The quicker we were on the bikes and away from Jordan the better for all of us.

To save time in Amman we split up as many of the tasks as we could. Nic and Jamie toured the city looking for a suitable cooker to last the journey. A tougher mission was finding a gas cylinder to supply it, until we realised that the depot lay just two doors away from the hotel. Nic, in particular, showed a dogged determination in anything he was asked to do. He liked nothing more than to be occupied and the trickier the task the better. Jamie was the true team player, happy to tag along with anyone and do anything asked of him. While Pauline and Ro also scoured the shops for cooking equipment, Sarah and I remained in the hotel. I was determined to sort out the finances and I had asked her to work on the website. Her job was without doubt the most stressful. Although the website was up and running, we had always updated it from home and through a decent internet connection. Any changes on the journey would have to be made through our small satellite link, which we had received only a week earlier and was yet untested. This proved to be a technical hurdle, which would have defeated all but the most determined. Fortunately Sarah was not easily put off. For most of the first three days in Amman she sat over the computer, sometimes in tears of frustration. I tried to be supportive but also knew that we simply had to get it working. After numerous phone calls and test-runs it finally came together. We wrote our first blog and transmitted it from the roof of the hotel, then five minutes later we logged on through the hotel internet terminal and cheered our success.

After a couple of visits to Zarqa, Dickie and Ro promised me they had secured a vehicle. It was a blue diesel van, perfect for our needs, and with two compartments in the rear it could easily seat five. As this was surplus to requirements the idea was to rip out the back seat and install a temporary kitchen and larder for the journey. However, the van would not be ready for another two days and we were falling dangerously behind schedule. Anxious to make a start we decided to head south and down to the Dead Sea the following day by taxi. The sixty-kilometre journey from Amman was supposed to take about only an hour and then our first day's cycling would be straight uphill and back to the hotel. From there, assuming the van was ready, we could press on to the Syrian border the next day. In total we would be cycling for just two days in Jordan.

With departure now imminent we tracked down the only pizza restaurant in the city and enjoyed a good meal. We felt a bit guilty about not eating local cuisine but this was no time to be choosy – every calorie would count in the morning. The restaurant was full of middle-aged ladies wearing revealing and untraditional outfits. Their faces were plastered with make-up and they were positively laden with cheap jewellery. They smiled constantly in our direction, much to the disgust of the girls but to the delight of Dickie. By the time we realised it was a brothel we were halfway through our pizzas and it was too late to leave. We returned to the hotel and under duress I let the others shave my head. Nic and Jamie had cut their hair that morning and they were adamant that we should all look equally stupid.

Nerves were tight on the chill morning of 21 December 2005. Before dawn we piled into the same jeeps that had picked us up from the airport and headed out through the silent grey suburbs of the city. Mile upon mile of faceless concrete buildings extended into the surrounding desert. At least the sun was fully up by the time we reached open country and the temperature climbed still further as we descended. It was disconcerting to be heading downhill out of a city, especially as we would have to reascend every inch the hard way. Amman lay at an altitude of 800 metres and we were descending that and another full 400 below sea level. The day ahead, although short on distance, promised to be one of the biggest climbs of the trip. I was starting to feel nervous, knowing my serious concerns about lack of fitness were about to be realised. My planned and comprehensive training programme had collapsed into a few desperate rides around the Cotswolds during the last fortnight. The day ahead promised to be a rude awakening.

Sarah echoed my thoughts, although she had little to be worried about. 'I don't like the look of this hill. I thought the first day might be a nice gentle start. This is going to be a nightmare!'

Nic was less concerned and was clearly relishing the climb ahead while Jamie looked equally relaxed. I knew he and Sarah had done a hundred-mile ride together only a week earlier. Pauline was unusually quiet and, I sensed, very nervous. As the oldest member of the team she had her concerns about keeping up. We all knew the day ahead would be one of reckoning and would in many respects also define how we would cycle over the coming months.

We seemed to be dropping endlessly, as the modern dual carriageway wound down and around curve after curve in the road. Our altimeters indicated the moment we dropped below sea level, but still there was no sign of our destination. I had always imagined this to be a desolate wasteland but here were hotels, offices and gaudy conference centres, despite the sub-zero elevation. When we finally caught sight of the Dead Sea it revealed itself as more of a blue haze nestling deep within the surrounding landscape. For a while we drove along the shoreline searching for a beach that Fayez had mentioned. There were numerous small resorts and hotels offering restaurants and private beach access but there were no tourists to be seen anywhere. I couldn't decide if it was tacky or just plain weird, but it was unlike anywhere else I had been. What should have been a beautiful landscape, if only for its desolation, was scarred by over-development. I was only glad we weren't here to stay. Love it or hate it, this was the very lowest point on earth.

We pulled up and unloaded the bikes, before paying a steep entrance fee to get to the water's edge, a good hundred metres away across a sandy beach. At least the view now was impressive, looking west across the Dead Sea itself to the buff-coloured mountains of the West Bank and Israel. The so-called sea is poorly named, as it is in fact a lake fed only by the river Jordan from the north. The water drains into the enclosed basin and with no outlet to the ocean it can only seep away or evaporate, accounting for the very high salt content. The last few decades have seen a rapid decline in the water level as the river Jordan is being ruthlessly tapped. Israel, Jordan and Syria are all accountable for its demise, and of course the ensuing tension that lack of water causes. The resort where we now stood was constructed originally on the water's edge. Now it looked faintly ridiculous, as the line of plastic table umbrellas was forced to extend ever further as the water receded.

In an effort to restore the lake, moves are afoot to link the Dead Sea to the open ocean. Water would bizarrely flow out of the ocean downhill, and thereby replenish the dying lake. En route the water would be desalinated for drinking, with the salty excess deposited into the lake, closely matching its present composition. The so-called Red–Dead Canal would have enormous benefits, but politically it is still some way from being realised.

The high salt content makes for an unusual attraction and we weren't going to miss out. We plunged in and the extra density of the water made us float with incredible buoyancy. In a bid to outdo each other we tried to dive below the surface and start our journey even lower. It was next to impossible, and we emerged spluttering and laughing after every effort, the salt stinging our eyes and throats. We messed around for half an hour, putting off the inevitable, before posing for pictures with Dickie and Ro who were heading back by taxi. After they departed we were very much on our own, with just the bikes for company and a solitary man raking the beach fifty metres away. He was oblivious to the moment as we lined up our back wheels in the water. What had now been years in the planning was about to become a reality. On the count of three, we pressed hard and tried to cycle up the sandy beach. Our efforts ended in farce as we all tumbled off in the wet sand and rolled around with laughter. The man even stopped his work, looking up to see what all the fuss was about. It was a very long way from Everest as we reluctantly wheeled the bikes back up to the road before heading on our way.

No sooner had we begun to cycle than the stresses of the last few weeks just vanished. Despite my role as leader, events were now very much in the hands of the whole team. We sped along the smoothly concreted road, blue sky above and even a light tailwind gently pushing us on our way. It was a perfect day, and released from the burdens of organisation we were all relishing the fresh air and warm sun. We were none too keen to reascend the busy dual carriageway, but luckily after just half an hour we reached a T-junction where a back road wound its way steeply up into the hills. It would be longer and more undulating than the direct route but was a lot more tempting. In another hour we had already reached sea level and a third of our total ascent for the day. I stopped briefly to take a photo while the others carried on, struggling to believe that here on a steep mountainside we were at zero-elevation. I sat back on the bike stretching, before my phone rang and shattered the peace.

'Hello?'

'Dom. It's Kenny here. Sorry not to get back to you about that trip you were planning. I'm still keen to join you if it's on. When are you heading off?'

I struggled to contain my laughter. Kenny hadn't been in touch for months. 'About an hour ago, mate. Oh, and we've reached sea level already. You're a little late!'

We both chuckled. 'Oh, no worries . . . Well, you'd better have a good trip then . . .!'

The scenery was bleak but there was a mystical quality in the landscape, a biblical and earthly feel that had probably changed little in centuries. This area had after all been at the centre of civilisation for millennia, and now, amid the turmoil of Middle Eastern politics, the region was still making history. I slowed on a bend in the road and watched a young boy amble past with a shepherd's crook. He was barefoot and wore a simple brown shift, his head bowed to the ground. The small herd of goats ran ahead, bells tinkling around their necks as they nibbled the meagre vegetation. It could have been a scene straight from the Old Testament. He looked up before waving hesitatingly at me, then ambled off into the scrubby wasteland below the stark outline of the mountains.

The first village didn't offer much in the way of a welcome. A group of half a dozen young boys stood idly at the side of the road and gut instinct told me something was amiss. We stared each other down as we rode past in convoy, only to be met with a hail of stones from behind.

'They bloody hit me!' Sarah didn't hold back, just as another one glanced off Pauline's foot. I wheeled the bike around and yelled at them as they scarpered into a narrow alley between two buildings. Thankfully there was no serious injury but the situation was repeated twice in the next few hours. They were mostly children and probably no more than twelve years old. There was little we could do, but we resolved to cycle closely together for the rest of the day. Spreading out just gave them time to prepare and arm themselves fully. It was unsettling and made for a less than ideal first day – all the more so as there was no apparent reason for their animosity towards us.

It was a demanding first day and not just because of the stone-throwing. The hills were relentless and made worse by frequent small descents that only added to the overall climb. The downhill offered a welcome respite with a refreshing breeze, but then two minutes later we were sweating our way up the next incline. By early afternoon we finally crested a high plateau and the gradient eased for good. We had reached Mount Nebo, reputedly the spot where Moses gazed over the 'Promised Land'. It was certainly a staggering view. Below, the Dead Sea was barely visible through a haze of low cloud, but far beyond the mountains of the West Bank were clear. To the north, but indiscernible, lay the Sea of Galilee through which the river Jordan flowed. We were now over 800 metres above sea level, and well over a thousand higher than we had started that morning. In fact our altimeters recorded that our total ascent was nearer 2,000 metres thanks to all the up and down. Much to my relief, I was feeling fine, although my lower back was already aching from the climb. I was glad not to be the only one and Nic led us in stretching exercises while everyone mocked my inflexibility.

An hour later we passed through the pleasant town of Madaba and found ourselves again on a dual carriageway. A fat police motorcyclist appeared from nowhere with his siren wailing and lights flashing. At first we thought we were being stopped but he beckoned us onwards, even stopping the traffic to allow us to pass safely. We waved back at him, his generosity making up for our earlier welcome. It was another tiresome thirty kilometres to Amman and by the time we reached the suburbs dusk was falling. We had underestimated the sheer size of the city and wound our way awkwardly through the gridlocked rush hour looking for familiar landmarks. Tired and hungry, it was gone seven by the time we arrived at the hotel. Fayez had promised to take us to dinner and was waiting on the steps to greet us. His usual grin was broader than ever and I swear he expected us to quit there and then.

'How was your day? Did you have a pleasant bicycle?'

'Yes. Thank you, Fayez.'

'Not too many hills for you, I hope?'

'Not at all.' I lied. 'All very easy, except for the children throwing stones.'

47

He dismissed this with a nonchalant wave of his hand. 'Ahh, they are just children. That is their way of saying hello.'

Dickie and Ro had picked up our new vehicle and had only just returned themselves, thinking it wise to get a full service while the facilities were available. A new roofrack and ladder were another useful addition and it looked ready to go. We all stood around in admiration. Much to the disgust of us boys, the girls insisted on naming it. This had been the subject of some discussion over the last few days but the final choice was 'Martha' after the Nepalese name for Everest, 'Sagarmatha'. Nic especially was aghast at such sentimentality and swore to call it the 'van' for the duration of the expedition.

Fayez was very quiet over dinner and, I think, genuinely concerned for our welfare. It was now clear to him that we were indeed off to Syria, and – to his horror – Iran. Of the former his praise was gushing and we were assured of a good welcome. Iran on the other hand was a dangerous place, he warned, especially for us English. Nevertheless his generosity was unending. We settled the pitifully small hotel bill later that night and at less than a hundred dollars between us for five nights it was probably half of what it should have been. Despite our tiredness and the promise of an early start, we enjoyed another late night in his company, sweet black coffee a recipe for very little sleep.

With a border to cross, we were again up and away early. Syria lay just eighty kilometres to the north. This time we climbed gently out of the city and on to a featureless desert of dull brown scrub. It took a while for the stiffness of the previous day to ease, but I could already feel my fitness returning. At least it was flat and we sped along for an hour before being battered by a strong headwind. The rain then appeared and followed in bouts of intense showers. I pulled alongside Pauline who was less than impressed.

'You come all this way to a desert and it's just like a bad day in Scotland!' She was gritting her teeth while hunched over her handlebars, but still in good humour. Pauline's style was distinctive and she held her bike like she was wrestling a bull by the horns. A couple of hours later we arrived at the sprawling border complex of Jabal, complete with restaurants and even a duty-free shop. Much to our amusement the seedy official took an instant fancy to Jamie, ignoring his passport and looking up and down his Lycra-clad legs. 'Jamie? Yes, nice name . . . very nice . . . nice, Jamie. You will return to Jordan?'

Dickie and Ro had already been there for two hours, but there were still more forms to complete. Our Jordanian friends had advised us that there would be no fees to pay on leaving Jordan and entering Syria. This was clearly not the case and Dickie had already spent $200 to secure the necessary documents. I shouldn't have been surprised but it was enough to leave me anxious for the rest of the day. Every penny counted on the trip and our daily budget extended to just a hundred dollars a day for the team. With a hundred-day journey ahead, that meant a total expenditure of just $10,000.

Over a coffee we got chatting to Alison, an English lady who lived and worked in Jordan as an archaeologist. She often visited Syria and was fulsome in her praise for the country and its people. Intrigued by our journey, she armed us with plentiful advice. One of our concerns was a repetition of the stone-throwing we had endured the previous day. Alison did her best to reassure us, and was adamant that we would receive a warm welcome and experience few difficulties.

It was three o'clock before Dickie and Ro, together with Martha, finally cleared customs. Despite being some $300 lighter, the customs had failed to search Martha. Our cargo was purposely buried beneath a casual-looking mountain of clothes and bike spares. That meant that we were at liberty to remove the customs tags that sealed our bags and would pay no extra duties. We decided it might be best to wait for a more subtle location, and after inspecting the map decided to make for Derra. The small town lay a little off our route, some twenty kilometres away, but with any luck we might be able to find a cheap hotel. Derra in turn would put us within reasonable distance of Damascus the following day. Our original aim had been to reach the capital in time for Christmas itself and as the next day was Christmas Eve we were still on track. We turned off the main road and cycled five abreast, reliving the day and congratulating ourselves on making our second country already. Conditions were much improved and despite the delay the border had gone pretty smoothly.

Derra began as one long street that ran for mile after mile – grubby shops and run-down businesses on either side. Most operated out of simple concrete sheds, hastily erected and poorly maintained. Others were boarded up and some even lay in ruins. Litter lay everywhere, strewn liberally by the sharp gusts of wind that swept in from the desert. Paper, tattered plastic sheets and broken glass lined both sides of the road. We fell silent as a group, all of us reluctant to be first to express our disappointment. The only signs of life were the mangy dogs that picked through the debris. It stank of neglect and I started to have second thoughts about finding somewhere to stay. The other option was to backtrack and stay at the expensive hotel back at the border, but with little warning we arrived at a small grassy central square complete with a bustling market. It was a big improvement but still very dilapidated. A few locals and teenagers stopped to gawp, but no one approached us. We munched on a few bananas bought at the nearest stall and waited. Dickie and Ro were ahead of us, and hopefully investigating somewhere to stay but it was another thirty minutes before we spied Martha coming round the corner. They pulled alongside, and as Ro wound down the window I saw they had picked up a passenger, sitting between her and Dickie.

'There's good news and there's bad news.'

'So long as there's somewhere to stay?'

'Well, there's a very nice little hotel here. Unfortunately it's full . . .'

'You must be joking. In this place!'

'Well, you're not going believe this, but there's a tour group of thirty German cyclists staying.' We had to meet Germans here of all places, I thought.

'Mahmoud here is the owner's son,' continued Ro. 'He feels bad about having no space so he's trying to help us find somewhere.'

What followed was a fruitless half-hour cycling around town, trailing Martha, all to no avail. Eventually we ended back at the hotel where Mahmoud said we could at least eat in the restaurant. It was good news as we were pretty sure that once we were established they would be unlikely to chuck us out. If we could just get a floor to sleep on we would be quite happy.

We watched with interest as our passports were photocopied and a runner quickly dispatched to take the papers to the police station. The owner seemed ill at ease with an unscheduled group pulling into town and earnest discussion began in the back office. Despite the Germans, tourists were a rarity in these parts, and at best our hosts seemed very nervous. Our plan did at least work and after dinner no one seemed too bothered about us moving. Just as we prepared to bed down on the floor, Mahmoud appeared to tell us a room was available after all. He looked uncertain as to whether it was for the girls or us boys but he needn't have worried. We grabbed our kit and all traipsed up together. It turned out to be more of a suite and with four beds it was better than we expected.

Right up until our departure the next morning the Germans stoically avoided us. It seemed rather comical considering we had something in common and were so far away from home. A quick breakfast from a bakery saw us on our way and with a tailwind we sped along for a couple of hours before the wind and rain set in. Lunch was delicious, a spread of fresh bread, cheese and olives. We stood shivering and jogging on the spot in a bid to keep warm, but at least we were out of the weather. The respite was short-lived. Within minutes of setting off we were soaked to the skin and were again shivering violently. It wasn't just the rain, it was bitterly cold and the damp penetrated our light cycling tops easily. The weather relented for a bit, but by the outskirts of Damascus the torrents returned. Out of desperation we stopped under a canopy outside an official-looking building and it didn't take long for the owner to come storming out. He was fierce-looking, well built and sported a big black beard.

'Where from?' he snapped. 'Where you go?' By now we were growing used to the usual greeting but this was considerably less friendly.

'We're from England,' I replied. 'We are going to Damascus. Very bad weather, yes?'

'England!' He turned his head and spat on the ground. 'USA! George Bush!' He pulled his finger across his throat to indicate what he would like done with the latter.

I thought it best to make a move and we started to get back on the bikes.

'Wait. Wait please,' he softened his tone and broke into a broad smile for the first time. Now that we had dealt with the politics, he turned to bark an order through the open doorway. Right on cue a boy appeared, carrying a tray of steaming tea glasses. Our now genial host gestured to us. 'Please. Please drink tea. You are my friends. You are very welcome in my beautiful country. You like Syria . . . yes?'

Our encounter, we were soon to learn, was a typically Arab one. Politics was always at the forefront of daily life and conversation, but once dispensed with, it was not permitted to cloud a traditional welcome. The episode was repeated again when we stopped at a small market and were besieged by locals asking the same questions.

'What is your name? Where from? Where are you going?' Whether friendliness or mere curiosity, it was a relief to know that we could travel freely. Syria's reputation abroad was not always favourable, but our welcome was undiluted.

The long road into Damascus was interminable. Biblical associations were quickly dismissed as we entered an industrial suburbia heaving with traffic. Anonymous factories and ware-houses stretched away into the distance, clouded in an unhealthy haze. Each side of the road was bordered by a strip perhaps twenty metres wide. Here, every conceivable activity took place. Markets selling fresh food vied with bicycle repair shops and tyre depots. Abandoned cars and buses were being stripped for parts and heavy black oil soaked into the stained earth around neat piles of stacked oranges and vegetables. Basic carts were the transport for many, their entire livelihood pushed before them in a constant quest for business, selling cigarettes, batteries and cartons of juice. The noise of traffic was exaggerated by the bedlam of hammering, revving buses, welding and shouting, so to hear each other was next to impossible. The more established businesses worked out of premises away from the highway, but the vast majority of activity simply took place at the roadside. Anxious to reach the centre we pressed on as quickly as possible. It was certainly no place to have a puncture.

'Stop!' yelled Pauline. It was her second of the day. Anxious not to be separated, we set about fixing it as fast as we could. We needn't have lifted a finger. The inner tube was snapped from our grasp and run into a nearby repair shop where a huge patch was applied. A minute later and it was being subjected to an industrial tyre inflater. It was the developing world's equivalent of a Formula One pit-stop. I wondered what attention we would have received if the girls hadn't been with us. We had already noticed that women in Syria were rarely seen, with all of the businesses around us run exclusively by men. In fact, we had to look hard to see a woman at all, except perhaps in the food markets or on buses. Pauline, we now realised, was an expert in these situations, putting others at ease and breaking down barriers. She soon had the entire workforce at her disposal.

'Oh, you're a gem, you are . . . what a star. Look at this tyre everyone!' she shouted, holding it aloft. We were now surrounded by dozens of bystanders. 'If you need something fixed, Moham-med here is your man!' The crowd laughed and applauded while our mechanic looked very chuffed with the free publicity.

We were now dripping wet and the road had flooded inches deep in grimy brown water. We negotiated the traffic as best we could. Lorries, buses and taxis swerved wildly, blasting their horns as they dodged the donkey-pulled carts, stranded in the rising floodwater. One nonchalant driver even had an open fire roaring behind him on his flat-bed trailer. Then, with little warning, we came upon the city centre and an immediate sense of calm ensued. The modern buildings were taller, the roads better and even the drainage had improved. It could have been a city almost anywhere, and was a world away from the chaotic outskirts. Many of the road signs were in Arabic and English so we had little difficulty in finding our route. We had long since lost Dickie and Ro but made our way to a previously arranged hotel. It was Christmas Eve and we had decided to treat ourselves.

The owner almost had second thoughts as we trailed muddy boots and wheels across the marbled lobby, but like many foreign hotels the upstairs didn't quite match the façade. Even after ten minutes the taps offered barely tepid water and the radiators were stone cold. Our kit was soaking wet and cloaked in grime and oil, so I simply chucked it all in the shower tray in an effort to remove the worst. The best plan seemed to be to head out. Alison, the lady we had met at the border, insisted that if short of time we must at least visit the souk, and luckily it was only five minutes' walk away. Dressed in an odd array of dry clothing, we wandered through the brick arches and vaulted ceilings of Al-Hamidye. Lying at the heart of the city it had done well to survive the encroachment of modern buildings and traffic-thronged streets. Although bustling with people, it was a respite from the outside world, a complete contrast to the Westernisation all around us.

The souk was impressive if only for its sheer size and thousands of stalls. At least half were bright dress and material shops and many of the others were selling cheap tat. Every shop owner beckoned us in. 'Hello, my friends. Where are you from? Very cheap price . . . yes, very cheap. Your wife is very beautiful, yes. Please, please. Looking is free.' Staring vacantly ahead and walking on was the best policy. Merely breaking your stride or glancing in their direction was sufficient to trigger the second phase of marketing. An order would be shouted into the shop, no doubt the Arab equivalent of 'On your feet – we've hooked one here!' A junior assistant would promptly appear with samples of the said merchandise, usually squares of material or dates on a tasting tray. Entering a carpet shop would result in an endless stream of rugs being unrolled in front of you that you knew would take an hour to put away again. Within a minute tea would be produced and a chair offered to make you comfortable – all designed to maximise the guilt, ensnare you and grab your custom.

Despite the welcome, above us was a more sinister reminder of the politics underlying modern Syria. Strung across the main entrance to the souk was a vast red banner bearing a stark warning:

From Syria the country of peace and loving to the aggresive Israel and its Allied America ... We refuse your democracy after what we have seen in Iraq and Palestine and how your democracy builds on people's bodies where you bombed innocent civilians ....

Bashar Al-Assad

We debated over dinner what we should do the following day. I had always thought Christmas Day should be celebrated in style, at least with a day off, but we barely deserved it after just three days' cycling. Our delayed departure meant that we really needed to push on and the others felt the same. My sister-in-law had recently emailed, saying that she had read about a new five-star hotel in Damascus, so I suggested a compromise. After a short lie-in, we could enjoy a slap-up Christmas brunch in the morning and then hit the road, albeit with a late start.

Despite having washed our clothes, we felt instantly grubby on entering the sparkling Four Seasons hotel, with its marbled floors and immaculate dining room. The service was exquisite and much to our delight they offered the most enormous buffet spread for a mere ten dollars each. Jamie and Sarah led the way as we stocked up on crêpes, poached eggs, pastries and freshly squeezed juice. It was easily our best meal so far and, unbeknown to us, the best we would enjoy for many months.

Chapter 4

Across the Desert – Syria

Despite the better weather, leaving Damascus on Christmas afternoon was chaotic. We needed to head east out of the city, but every road led us in a gentle curve away from our intended direction.

'Is this the way to Palmyra?'

'Yes, yes,' came the reply, with furious nodding. I would then do a test by pointing in the other direction. 'Palmyra – is it this way?'

'Yes, Palmyra,' came the identical reply. Nic was more persistent and step-by-step we made our way to the margins of the city through the heavy flow of traffic. Cars beeped at us continually and with every stop we were besieged by curious onlookers. It was as though the entire population were in attendance, shopping in the numerous markets that lined the city streets. Everywhere was a juxtaposition of new and old. Modern office blocks crowded ancient mosques, and even churches, interspersed with heaving roundabouts and frenzied junctions. It would have been pleasant without the constant traffic and stench of diesel. We found ourselves on an ugly freeway for a few miles before turning off on to the quieter roads of the suburbs. Gone were the crowds of people and we found ourselves in a residential area. A grubby and modest signpost finally marked the turn towards Palmyra, our next destination over 600 kilometres away.

The road took us through a lorry park, the road stained heavy with black oil and littered with glass. Sarah picked up her third puncture in as many days but we made the most of the winter sunshine while we fixed it. A pleasant poplar-lined avenue then led us to the very edge of the city where we crested a sharp incline. The view was so magnificent that we were left speechless. Never had I seen a city finish so abruptly. Before us lay the vast expanse of the Syrian desert, the road running straight as a die across the scrubby plain and bounded to the north by a steep rocky escarpment. To the south, the distant horizon simply merged into what was now a heavy and threatening sky. It was a timely reminder that it was already four o'clock and we needed to press on.

We shot off down the hill, gaining the momentum we needed to find a steady rhythm on the flat. Thankfully there was a narrow but well-maintained hard shoulder, which offered some respite and a margin of safety from the trucks that thundered past every few minutes. We made good time but I was becoming concerned that we had seen no sign of Dickie and Ro. We had left Damascus ahead of them, since they had a couple of things to buy, but they certainly should have caught us up by now. As the daylight faded, the temperature began to drop steadily – something we were ill equipped to deal with. What had been a pleasant tailwind in the afternoon was now bone-chilling when we stopped for a couple of minutes. We had hoped to be able to camp, but having never pitched the tent before we didn't fancy doing it in the dark for the first time. Instead we began to scout each side of the road, looking for any sign of habitation or shelter. If Martha, together with Dickie and Ro, didn't find us soon we were going to be in trouble.

The sun dropped below the horizon and within the space of a few minutes we felt the penetrating cold. We had foolishly relied on the vehicle for all our warm clothing and food, leaving us far too vulnerable. In the gathering gloom we rounded a gentle bend in the road and, down to our right, I could see a small cluster of concrete buildings. There was no light, or other sign of life, and it looked as though they might be deserted.

'What do you reckon?' I said to Jamie and Nic, who pulled up alongside.

'I'm not sure we've got a lot of choice. We should at least go and take a look,' said Jamie.

'The girls aren't far behind,' said Nic. 'I'm happy to wait here so they don't miss us.'

Jamie and I made our way down the rough track, our teeth already chattering. We walked briskly for five minutes until we drew close to the first building, and then proceeded more cautiously. It was actually a concrete complex of half a dozen rooms, and appeared completely abandoned. Broken glass had been swept into the corners and the remains of open fires were scattered on the concrete floor. The walls were open above chest height and the wind whistled eerily through the gaps and swept through the building. By ducking down we noticed you could escape the worst of the chill and be relatively sheltered. Although there was no sign of life, not a single light to be seen in the blackness, I still felt nervous. After all, this wasn't a country where we could easily explain ourselves. On the other hand, it was only for a night and now that it was dark we were unlikely to be disturbed. Jamie and I agreed that if we were on our way first thing in the morning we would probably be fine.

We jogged back up to the road until we could make out Nic's profile through the gloom, just a few metres away. All of a sudden came the familiar and metallic double click of a weapon being cocked. It froze us in our tracks and we stood stock-still. I hadn't heard the sound in years but the effect on me was electrifying. I feared we might be fired upon in the dark but we had no choice except to stand our ground. Nic and Jamie were impressively calm and we all strained our eyes to make sense of the shadows. I could hear the muttering of nervous whispers and then three figures slowly emerged from the darkness. They were soldiers dressed in simple green fatigues and armed with sub-machine guns, faces almost obscured by woollen scarves tightly wrapped around their heads. They seemed young, very cold and just as nervous as we were. They raised their weapons and gestured along the road. We feigned confusion and I tried to greet them in Arabic.

'Sala'am.' I moved tentatively forward to shake hands but they stepped back sharply and continued to wave along the road, trying to urge us on our way. I pointed in the opposite direction and down to the buildings where we planned to stay, but this only aggravated them further and they peered into the darkness, now aware that there might be more of us. Instead of departing we embarked on some furious sign language to allay their fears. We showed them the bicycles and mimed that we had been cycling along the road. Now we were tired and wanted to sleep. Tomorrow, I tapped my watch, we would be on our way again, gesturing north along the road.

They seemed a little placated, but further attempts at conversation proved futile as they spoke no English and our Arabic was pitiful. We tried to beckon them down to the building. Perhaps if we could offer them a hot drink maybe they could see we meant no harm, but they refused. It was just as well, I remembered, without Martha we had no food or drinks to share anyway. We must have been an unusual sight, foreigners with short haircuts riding bicycles across the desert on a dark night.

Still they refused to leave us and instead turned to mutter quietly to each other. They were clearly deciding what to do next and the tension was unbearable. I was sure they meant us no harm, but if they chose to arrest us or escort us somewhere else it would at best be a major inconvenience. The stand-off lasted another couple of minutes before they simply turned and melted away into the night. We stood silently until we heard a vehicle start up in the distance and presumed they were leaving the area.

Our encounter had been a strange one; miles from the nearest town it was an odd place to bump into soldiers. The girls soon arrived but it was another half an hour before we saw lights in the opposite direction and eventually Dickie and Ro pulled up alongside. By now we were jogging furiously on the spot in a bid to keep warm.

'What happened Dickie?' I said a little curtly. He looked taken aback.

'Not much – sorry we're a little late. Just had the shopping to do – took a lot longer than we thought really . . . then had a cup of tea . . . managed to get plenty of food, though!'

Before the soldiers had arrived I was getting increasingly annoyed. Now I was just relieved to have us together again and in one piece. It wasn't long before we were all ensconced in the concrete building and Ro wasted no time in getting a meal started. We had a lot to unpack but I was anxious that we should keep the lights down as low as possible. Any activity would be visible from miles away and although I hoped the soldiers had left the area they could easily return. We had enjoyed enough excitement for one night and desperately needed some rest. Dickie had secured some duty-free champagne from the border a couple of days earlier and we toasted each other over a pasta supper. Amid the excitement we had almost forgotten it was Christmas night and the mood relaxed over pasta and the dubious-tasting bottle.

Despite our fears, the night passed uneventfully and we woke to a frosty but beautifully sunny morning. Now the road seemed just a stone's throw away and the buildings looked much less daunting than they had in the pitch-black of night. The wind had also dropped away completely, making for ideal cycling conditions. We were soon under way and made quick progress along the desert highway, the sky an enormous cobalt blue dome against the dull desert scrub. Everything but the sky was a study in brown – the ochre soil, the twisted rocks, and the buff-coloured sandstone cliffs to our left. Through it all, like a steel-grey ribbon, carved the road, with the only vivid colour anywhere being the bright yellow line down its centre.

For the first time on the trip we began to settle into our own pace. Nic and Jamie forged ahead while I stayed in the middle, with Pauline and Sarah never far behind. We experimented with the idea of doing legs of about twenty-five kilometres, which equated to about an hour's cycling. The theory was that whoever was in front would stop after that distance from the last break to allow everyone to close up. That way, if there were any problems, no one would be left too far behind. If there were any junctions, or a possible discrepancy over the route, then the leader would call an early halt. It seemed to work well and despite spreading out we all arrived within a few minutes of each other at the first stop.

Our flexible approach certainly had its merits. Since arriving in Amman we had been in each other's pockets day and night. I was thrilled at how well we were all getting on but there was no need to feel obliged to each other. We had a long trip ahead of us, and for now I was enjoying the solitude, feeling truly relaxed for the first time in weeks. The only sound, barring the odd lorry, was the purr of a new bike and the gentle hum of the tyres over the road. My fitness was returning and the miles were already coming more easily. Cycling like this was complete freedom and a perfect mode of transport for the landscape. To drive would be an injustice to a country like this, its landscape and its people. We could stop whenever we liked, and if we ever grew bored we would soon be twenty miles down the road. I settled back and admired the view of endlessly shifting desert hues.

We were not long into our second leg when Dickie and Ro caught us up in Martha. They had clearly detected our annoyance the previous evening and were anxious to make amends. We decided to 'leap-frog' each other and so they pushed ahead to the fifty-kilometre mark, where we would have some brunch. The idea was that we could then get back on the road while they packed up, before passing us again and looking for somewhere to stop that evening. On paper at least it seemed to be the most efficient system and by the time we arrived Ro had worked wonders. The kettle was on and laid out next to Martha were the results of yesterday's extended shopping trip: dates, fresh tomatoes, dried apricots, together with pitta breads and cheese. We were constantly hungry and burning up every calorie we could consume. Jamie, in particular, was already very lean and had little to lose. He had serious concerns that a 5,000-mile bike trip might leave him skeletal before he even arrived at the mountain, but for now we were just plain hungry, and demolished all we could.

The distance flew by after lunch and we soon reached our intended minimum of one hundred kilometres, before keeping an eye out for somewhere to camp. We could have cycled further, but after the excitement of the previous night, were determined to find a place where we could feel secure. By five o'clock the late-afternoon sun was striking the high rocky ridge to our left. It was a captivating sight watching the cliff luminesce in reds and oranges, and all the while trying to keep the bike on the narrow hard shoulder.

Dickie and Ro had found a bumpy dirt track leading off the main road that could just be negotiated by Martha, and had parked several hundred metres away on the open plain. It was certainly not out of sight but there was little we could do surrounded by a featureless expanse. We hoped that just being well off the main road would be enough to deter all but the most curious. Our tent could easily accommodate all seven of us with plenty of space for cooking and equipment inside. We soon had the cooker on the go and even fired up the generator to get everything recharged. It was all very luxurious and more than any of us were used to on the average expedition, but it had always been my intention that we should make ourselves as comfortable as possible. Five thousand miles would be demanding enough, so a few luxuries were a sound investment. After all, we still had the small issue of climbing Everest afterwards.

The cold night passed slowly before I woke to a heavy frost and the comforting sound of the gas burner. Nic was up first again, although not quite as readily as the previous day, and Jamie and Pauline were also stirring. It was quickly becoming apparent who the early risers were. From Dickie there was little sign of life except for the gentle snoring that had kept me awake. Stiff from the previous day, I had to press my limbs into action just to get out of bed. After a speedy breakfast we packed away the tent, before a couple of young Syrian girls approached across the empty desert. They were tending a small herd of goats and were dressed traditionally with coloured silk scarves wrapped around their heads and long dangling earrings. We beckoned to them before they overcame their shyness and came closer. They smiled warmly with our gift of empty water bottles and took as many as they could carry.

I cycled at the front with Nic for an hour and we powered our way up the first hill, the incline making a pleasant change from the flat. We passed through a complex of ugly quarry workings bordering each side of the road, the first civilisation we had seen since leaving Damascus. On the second leg I pressed ahead of the others until we reached a prominent junction marked only by a disused petrol station now abandoned to the elements. It must have once been a major truck stop, but now there was no activity. To my right the road continued into Iraq and a small pick-up headed that way loaded with dozens of red plastic barrels. They were stacked so high they dwarfed the actual car beneath. The others soon arrived and we opted instead to turn left. The road would take us into the north-east desert, and hopefully that night to Palmyra, our next major stop.

We called a lunch halt at the curious Bagdad café, presumably named after the film of the same name, which is set in the heart of the American Mojave desert. It was actually more of a curio shop than a café and stood in splendid isolation, adjacent to the road, but miles from the nearest settlement. It had to be the most bizarre place possible to open a business, but we weren't about to complain. Surrounded by fossils, minerals, blankets and random bits of pottery, we sat down to enjoy a cold drink and some respite from the open road. The owner insisted on treating us to a traditional, but very painful, Syrian tune on his homemade violin. It consisted of an empty tin of cooking oil to which he had attached a single wire. The resulting screech was nearly enough to get me back on the road, but he summoned up a passable tune. He persuaded us to have a go and Sarah, a talented cellist, responded impressively with a variety of carols, much to the owner's chagrin.

Outside and around the back of the café stood a traditional 'beehive house'. It was deserted and we took the opportunity to sneak inside. The design is thought to have changed little in thousands of years and probably evolved in response to the harsh conditions of the desert. A simple conical structure, it was constructed from thick clay walls to keep out the heat of the midday sun, while the round shape offered stability against the frequent earthquakes that have blighted the region. In 1089, a devastating quake had destroyed neighbouring Palmyra completely, after which plundering of its antiquities sent it permanently into oblivion. Next to the house was a Bedouin tent, more mobile and easily moved, if only on a seasonal basis. The thick woollen walls must have provided protection against the heat and cold in equal measure. We browsed the owner's collection of brass pots and hubba smoking pipes under a sign that read 'Arab antiques'. Pressed to make a purchase, we apologetically pointed towards the bikes and made our escape.

Palmyra came into view at least half an hour before we arrived, a vivid sweep of green oasis at the base of a rocky bluff. In my research on cycling routes nearly two years previously the name of Palmyra had always cropped up. Many cities lay claim to being on the 'silk road', probably in a bid for some historical kudos, but here there could be no dispute. Location had virtually guaranteed prosperity and for centuries it formed a crucial link between Mediterranean ports to the west and Asia to the east. Traders and nomads had little option but to stop their camel trains here for water, and the inhabitants grew wealthy on taxes imposed on the passing traffic. For two centuries it had marked the eastern edge of the newly expanded Roman Empire, managing to cling to some hard-fought independence.[6]

We were starving by the time we had located Dickie and Ro and made straight for the local pancake house, demolishing some enormous helpings before finding a simple guesthouse with a view across the city. The modern town consisted of little more than a few streets, but in every direction lay the backdrop of ancient ruins. Tall Corinthian pillars and broken arches stood like sentinels against the jagged skyline. Later we sauntered along the main street, or colonnade, remarkably preserved and blissfully free of people. Only the ubiquitous camel-drivers were touting for business, but were still relaxed and friendly when we declined. Instead we wandered freely and took photos as the sun warmed the stone. It was a relief to drop the hectic pace for a few hours and behave like tourists. The setting was magnificent, the desert backdrop only adding to the grandeur and sense of isolation. It was difficult to unravel the full magnitude of what had taken place here. The streets would once have been alive with commerce, thronged with travellers from across Asia, all drawn to this lonely spot. One can understand large cities being influential by their mere presence, but Palmyra's impact on the traveller lies in its location. It was extraordinary to think that entire armies had fought bitterly for this patch of desert – its place in history so disproportionate to its modest size.

We resisted the urge to eat more pancakes for dinner and instead made for the traditional option across the street. It was a bad decision and we struggled through stale bread and a dubious goat stew that was dense with gristle. While we waited for a coffee, I headed for the computer in the corner. John Parfitt, our contact back home, had forwarded an email from a man in Germany who was relaying us some 'bad news'. He purported to be the support team for an Austrian mountaineer named Gerry Winkler. They had been following our website and our stated aim to be the first to travel from the lowest point to the highest. With 'some regret' he informed us that Herr Winkler was also aiming to do the same and what's more was some two months ahead of us. Having crossed Iran, he was now entering Pakistan and was already over halfway through his cycling journey.

I was gob-smacked. The others crowded around the computer as I relayed the staggering news. We logged on to Winkler's website and translated what little we could from the German. It was obvious from the maps, though, that his route was exactly the same as ours. Jamie was the first to react and didn't hide his irritation.

'He's copied the whole bloody idea,' he blurted in disgust. 'Look at the map! His route's exactly the same. He even came through Palmyra.'

Nic's response was measured. 'Look, I've got a mate back home who's a fluent German speaker. I'll get him to have a good read of it all and get back to us. Then at least we'll know the full story.'

I had no idea if Gerry had copied us, but having spent weeks researching the journey I knew there was only one realistic route – apart from cycling through Iraq, which was hardly a sensible option.

'It's possible he's never heard of us,' I countered. 'Why would his support team get in touch with us now? Surely if he was ahead they'd just keep it quiet?'

Although I was defending Gerry, I wasn't entirely convinced by my argument. Our website and route detail had been out on the web for almost a year, ripe for any ambitious adventurer to chance upon. I had no choice but to accept this as a risk, as we needed to raise the profile of the trip early on. Our own expedition had taken at least a year to organise, so I was confident that anyone starting from scratch would be unable to steal a march on us. But Gerry seemed to be keeping it simple, and without support team or vehicle his journey would have been much easier to put together, albeit harder to complete. Presumably this was why he had set off so early. He would need to be on the mountain at the same time as us, thereby taking a whole extra two months to cycle the same route. Whatever his motivation, and wherever he got the idea, there was nothing we could do. I consoled myself with the knowledge that the odds were very much against him. Our chances had to be slim and we were a team of five. He was on his own.

There was another reason why I felt relaxed about the competition. I was simply enjoying the journey too much to be bothered by someone else. My original motivation had been to achieve a first, but now the trip was under way I was determined to make the most of the experience. The day in Palmyra particularly had brought this home, and talk of records seemed a bit trivial. The others had mixed feelings and I had to admire the pride that they already had in our expedition. Jamie remained convinced that Gerry had stolen the idea and gave him short shrift. Pauline was also very competitive and I sensed in her some disappointment. Nevertheless, we composed him a goodwill message, which we posted on his website, playfully suggesting that we would wait for him on the summit.

'Bring it on,' said Pauline defiantly. 'Let's show him what we're made of!'

There was a sinister side to Palmyra, which thankfully remained hidden from our view. Recent events were if anything more macabre than the ancient battles that had raged in these parts. I knew from my research before the expedition that Palmyra was also famous for its high-security prison. It has a grim reputation and gruesome reports appear on websites championing human rights. Hundreds, if not thousands, of political prisoners had been executed within its walls, many of whom were connected to the outlawed Muslim Brotherhood. They launched several successful bomb attacks against the secular government and in 1980 even an attempt on President Assad's life. He personally kicked away one of two hand grenades that had been launched at him, while a bodyguard sacrificed himself by diving on a second. The President's revenge was swift and brutal. His brother led a massacre of Islamist prisoners within Palmyra jail and hundreds were summarily executed. The stories told by those who survived the prison are horrific. Even today it remains home to many political prisoners and torture and mistreatment are rife.

Our stop in Palmyra was all too short and I couldn't help but be jealous of Gerry Winkler as he had had the time and flexibility to spend a couple of days in interesting places. It was tough heading back into the desert, but we soon settled into our routine of twenty-five-kilometre legs. We hoped for lunch at the end of the second stretch, but still there was no sign of Martha. With no visible evidence of habitation we followed a road indicated on the map that led us to a village north of the highway. Half an hour later we arrived in the near-deserted central street. A couple of men eyed us suspiciously while we walked along looking for any food for sale. A fridge in the corner of an empty room was a promising sign, but instead the reluctant owner produced some luke-warm Cokes from the crate in the corner. We sat on his small terrace, surrounded on all sides by a steel metal grille. A few passers-by stopped and idly stared as though we were animals trapped in a cage. We seemed to be the objects of curiosity like never before, but it was little surprise. Syria has few visitors and certainly none would ever stop in a village like this. The locals had almost certainly never seen a Westerner before, let alone a cyclist.

The numbers swelled rapidly until there were at least fifty gazing through the bars, and we started to feel uncomfortable. No sooner had we decided to make a move than the owner produced some limp-looking salad and we felt obliged to stay. Before we could take a mouthful a crowd of children, numbering almost a hundred, emerged from the next street and ran en masse to get a closer look at all the commotion. The children were far more excitable than the disapproving and twitchy adults who merely kept their distance. They began to prod and poke at the bikes. The shop owner grew increasingly agitated and started shouting at them, before attempting to beat them back with a tea towel. He was promptly ignored of course and the hysteria continued to build. We left a few notes on the table and decided to make a dash for it through the scrum.

A night in a perfect spot, completely hidden from view, was a recipe for a good night's sleep. Sarah introduced us to her favourite breakfast of flatbread smothered with chocolate and bananas before we were back on the road. Our destination for the day was Deir Ezzor where we would cross the Euphrates, our first geographical milestone. If our journey proved successful, we would cross another three major rivers: the Tigris, Indus and the Ganges. Progress was quick and with a steady tailwind we flew through the first fifty kilometres and were back on the bikes after a quick lunch. Only ten kilometres along the road I pulled up behind Jamie and Nic who had stopped in a small layby. Set back from the road was a traditional Bedouin tent and a car. A striking-looking girl stood a few yards away, silently staring back at us, and trying to smile seductively. She wore a long traditional dress, low-cut and sleeveless, more like a ball gown. It was odd attire for the desert and her thick plastered make-up was more comical than attractive. I was a bit slow on the uptake until a man scurried from the tent, still rearranging his clothes, jumped into his car and disappeared. Jamie asked her if he could get a picture, at which point another scrawny-looking man came running out of the tent to shoo us away. Pauline and Sarah arrived right on cue and watched with total bemusement as we were chased down the road.

We could detect the presence of the Euphrates long before we reached it. Houses on each side of the road increased in number and for the first time in days we saw evidence of agriculture and irrigated farmland. Dickie and Ro had already driven ahead and found a hotel for the night. They returned to meet us on the edge of town.

'All sorted for tonight,' said Dickie proudly, as we pulled alongside. 'But you'd better follow us through – you're not going to believe how crazy this town is.'

The crowded marketplace was too hectic for anyone to pay us much attention. Shops on either side spilled on to the street, selling every possible product, while traders shouted their custom from behind wooden carts, struggling to be heard over the tooting horns. We wound our way between neatly stacked vegetables, hawkers, beggars and, of course, the relentless traffic. Cycling was a delicate balance of trying not to collide with something, while also taking in the sights and sounds. With the exception of the cars, the scene could have been straight out of medieval England, and after the austerity of the desert the colour, smell and noise were unbelievably intense. Even the goats and chickens wandered freely between the legs of oblivious shoppers. For a traveller in ancient times, reaching the Euphrates after weeks of journeying, the sight of all this abundance must have been overwhelming. We made our way to the far side of town and close to the river found a modern three-storey hotel complete with en suite rooms and even radiators. The latter were a real bonus and meant we could wash our clothes and get them dry by the following morning. At $50 for seven of us, it was expensive but just within budget, and we had after all saved money by camping in the desert during the last week.

After the usual round of chores, we headed off to a restaurant recommended by the surly owner of the hotel. We found it down the street and entered an enormous open room with high ceiling fans and art deco fittings, more like a 1920s music hall for afternoon tea dances. It was busy with seemingly affluent local Syrian families and workers, presumably from the nearby oilfields. There was the distinct whiff of money that we had not detected elsewhere in Syria, and for the first time we saw fat children. A similar sign of affluence were the Western-style burgers and pizzas that the restaurant served. Unable to make up her mind, Sarah had both. The size of her appetite and the rate at which she demolished her food amused us boys and appalled Pauline who ate very lightly. Dickie was long overdue for a haircut so after dinner we spent a hilarious half-hour watching him frantically trying to restrain the barber. All to no avail as he emerged looking entirely different but, we all agreed, a lot tidier.

'Guys – you'd better come and have a look at this,' shouted Jamie as he knocked on our door the following morning. Dickie and I were sharing a room while across the corridor he and Nic overlooked the front of the hotel. They had been keeping half an eye on Martha, which was parked opposite Reception on the busy street. We had unloaded all of the valuable items but there was still a lot of equipment inside that we couldn't afford to lose. I feared the worst but the van wasn't the issue. Parked perhaps ten metres behind Martha was a plain white saloon car, inside which were two burly-looking men. One stared fixedly ahead while the other was reading a newspaper. It looked innocent enough but Jamie wasn't convinced.

'Look – I went down to the van half an hour ago and they were there then. They could be police, but why would they be following us?'

It was like a scene from a spy novel and I was convinced that Jamie was being paranoid. But they were still there when we loaded Martha an hour later. I glanced in their direction and they instantly retreated behind their newspapers. The incident was all but forgotten as we set off across the Euphrates and paused for a quick photo call on the bridge, the wide sparkling river a welcome sight after endless dry desert. On the far side the farmland and greenery continued for some miles, irrigated by canals extending from the river. We stopped to fill our bottles where a water channel ran close to the road and it wasn't long before Dickie and Ro caught us up. Sure enough the white car was still there, trailing Martha at some distance. It stopped about fifty metres away, sufficiently near enough to make it obvious that we were being followed. Pauline suggested a simple solution while we took a drink.

'Look, it can't do any harm. Why don't we just go and ask them what they're up to? I'd rather know now than out in the middle of the desert! What if they're going to rob us?'

It was a fair point, so Dickie and I plucked up our courage and walked towards the car. The two men cautiously stepped out as we approached. I could see they had the air of police or security about them, albeit plain-clothed. Maybe it was the black leather jackets or their swarthy appearance, but they definitely fitted a certain stereotype. We greeted them but maintained our distance a little.

'Sala'am'. They responded curtly but politely, bowing their heads slightly as they spoke.

'Do you speak English?' I asked hopefully. They both shook their heads and raised their palms to us defensively. We had to establish what their motive was, so I pointed at them and then the car.

'Police?'

To this they nodded, a little too readily I thought, and their tension eased. I wondered if this meant they weren't really police but were happy for us to think so. They looked more like members of a dubious security service. I pointed in the direction of Al Qamishli, the border town with Turkey, still two or three days' ride away.

'Al Qamishli? You follow us?'

They nodded furiously. 'No problem. No problem,' they countered, their palms raised again for reassurance.

They were keen to put us at our ease, but I felt very uncomfortable. Having an escort in itself was not a problem, but we had hoped to camp in the desert again that night before pushing on. It was hard enough explaining to someone who spoke English the purpose of our journey, but this was nigh on impossible. At least the bicycles helped confirm our status as overland travellers and being a mixed group meant that we didn't present much of a threat. Still, the police were sure to take a dim view of us just turning off the road to camp and I was worried about all our equipment. Any search of Martha would quickly reveal laptops, video cameras and the satellite link. Despite being for an entirely innocent purpose, their use would be hard to justify to foreign police. The company who had supplied us with our communications kit had explained firmly to us that we were on dangerous ground using it in countries like Syria and Iran. The sale of it to these nations was prohibited under an embargo, and therefore the use of it by Westerners would certainly merit attention from the authorities. Any police who suspected what we were using would be justified in confiscating the kit and we could find ourselves in a heap of trouble.

As things stood, we could hardly ask them to leave, and simple friendliness was definitely the best policy. We were soon back on the bikes and heading back into the featureless desert as our distance from the river increased. The police seemed more relaxed now and stayed closer behind us, even getting out to stretch their legs and have a smoke when we stopped an hour later. Following bikes in a car can be painfully slow, so we hoped boredom would soon get the better of them. But there was no such luck and it looked increasingly like they were with us for the duration.

Unlike the desert highway, there were far more settlements and we wound our way through small dusty villages that recurred every few miles along the road. We stopped for a break adjacent to a water tower, and were watched by some aggressive-looking teenage boys who kept their distance. As we departed, a couple of stones were thrown half-heartedly in our direction. I looked back at the police, hoping to salvage some benefit in having them near, but they simply pretended not to notice. It was the first time this had happened since the Dead Sea but I was sure it could be attributed more to boredom than politics.

It was late afternoon before we approached Hassake, the last major town before Al Qamishli and the border. A second police car now joined our little convoy, further restricting our movements. We had hoped to lose the one car each time we separated from Martha but the new escort beckoned Dickie and Ro ahead and into the city. We did our best to confuse the other car by heading around the city on an ugly bypass. It was too soon for us to stop cycling and the last thing we wanted was to negotiate the streets of Hassake. We could see it was a miserable and godforsaken place. On each side of the main road lay a dirty strip of land, where stray dogs picked their way through knee-high piles of litter. Small clapboard shops were protected by heavy metal shutters, while strung between them dangled bare electricity wires. Behind this façade we could see the tin roofs and plywood walls of very basic slum housing. Again, the traffic bedlam was horrendous, with a constant blaring of horns and clouds of diesel fumes that had me longing for the open desert. We attracted shouts and gestures from everyone we passed; mostly friendly, I think, but it was hard to tell. We couldn't escape soon enough and ten minutes later the town finished abruptly and we were back into open country.

We now faced a stand-off with the local police who were still on our tail. They must have expected us to follow Martha and stop in Hassake, but here we were disappearing off into the desert again. It was already gone four o'clock, the light was quickly fading and we would need to find somewhere to camp. There was still the odd house every few hundred yards, which meant our presence would be all too obvious, but about twenty kilometres out of town we crested a small rise and ahead of us seemed to be just empty road. A dirt track led off to the left, meaning that Martha could follow easily enough. We all stopped and Nic and I took the chance to recce for a possible site. The ground was stony but drivable and about 600 metres from the road there was a slight bowl in the terrain. It was very exposed ground, but far enough from the road to put off all but the most determined onlookers.

We returned to the others only to find the police very agitated. They couldn't possibly understand why we would want to stop here in the gathering dark and cold. Sign language was proving futile and then right on cue Dickie and Ro arrived. They had been directed to the main police station in town and quizzed about our activities before being offered tea. The whole episode had taken two hours, although we suspected this was partly Dickie's fault; he loved nothing more than a cup of tea and a good chat. Ro at least had a great solution to our language barrier with the policemen. She promptly grabbed her sketchpad and within three minutes had rustled up a beautifully drawn tent, surrounded by a van and cyclists. There was some hesitation while they whispered to each other, probably wondering where the tent was. Much pointing at the back of Martha ensued before the penny finally dropped. They seemed quite understanding and I really hoped they would now leave us to our own devices. Unfortunately the two police pick-ups still followed us across the stony plain. It was now getting cold so we elected to pitch the tent as quickly as possible and sort ourselves out. Perhaps if we looked efficient and organised they might be tempted to leave us, if only for the night. The police kept their distance, but showed no inclination to move. I finally went over to investigate further.

'You will sleep here?' I asked, pointing at them and laying my head to one side and on to my hands, in the universal sleep symbol. He nodded defiantly and pointed back to Hassake and then the ground. 'Six . . . police here', he confirmed by holding up six digits and tapping his chest. I had only counted four police and said so. Again he pointed to Hassake. 'Two men more. Three cars.'

I was amazed. Not only were they planning to stay, but they were now calling for reinforcements. He proceeded to point out where the three cars would be placed around us. I thought it a bit of overkill, but now was not the moment to argue about use of police time.

'Is it dangerous here?' I ventured. I gestured slitting my throat and pointed to the surrounding desert.

'Yes, yes. Danger, much danger,' he replied gravely.

'It will be very cold,' I pointed out and shivered with my arms wrapped around me.

He just laughed at this point and shook his head. 'No problem. No problem'.

I began to feel a bit sorry for them. They had no personal issue or grievance with us but this must have seemed a lousy posting. I could only hope they were getting some decent overtime. Their boss, whoever he was, had obviously tasked them with watching these mad cyclists, no matter what they got up to. I wondered if it had something to do with our visit to Palmyra. Because of the prison it was a highly sensitive area and any visitors would normally be under the auspices of an official group. I was nervous about us uploading to our website that evening, but once night fell, we easily slid the small plastic dish under the bottom flap of the tent. The policemen were oblivious, happy in their vehicles with the engines running all night in a bid to keep warm.

We were up early. We were keen to get under way and as close to the border with Turkey as we could, so we took our grateful guards tea, thinking we might as well keep them on side. Together with Jamie, I managed to tuck into the slipstream of a tractor for about fifteen kilometres. We weren't too sure here of the cycling ethics, but it took the edge off the headwind and we nicknamed the process 'tractor surfing'. Its benefits were more psychological than anything else, but at least it broke the monotony. We made quick time during the morning, and by early afternoon had covered well over a hundred kilometres. The escort was still with us and we were all reluctant to spend another night in the desert in the same circumstances. Later, as darkness fell, Nic inspected the map.

'Guys, we're only fifty-six kilometres from Al Qamishli and the border. What do you reckon?'

Our moderate days were barely stretching Nic, and I could see he was in the mood for a big push. There were also likely to be hotels and that was a big incentive. It was New Year's Eve and I too was in the mood for something a bit different.

'Tell me you're having a bloody laugh!' Pauline wasn't impressed and I could see that she was already shattered.

'What about a decent bed for the night though? A few beers even?'

There was a pause while she reconsidered. 'Oh, go on then – we might as well get on with it,' she said with a resigned sigh.

By the time we set off it was fully dark and we cycled in close convoy. We had only two bike lights between us, so instead used our head torches, which barely sufficed. Dickie and Ro in Martha drove close behind us, which provided some extra light against the pitch black of the desert.

The police were still with us, but clearly deduced that we were going for the border and I sensed their interest in us rapidly waning. The feeling was entirely mutual. We were ready for a new country and hopefully a little less scrutiny. Now they chose to drive ahead several hundred metres at a time and then wait for us to pass. We made a steady pace and after an hour and a half stopped for another brew while Dickie and Ro went on again to find somewhere to stay. After they left, the dark and silence were all-enveloping. There was no ambient light so we took it in turns to cycle at the front where it was trickiest. Only by following the thin white line edging the hard shoulder could we identify the road at all. We all felt drained but fought off the exhaustion with constant bites of food from the pockets on our shirts.

Another hour brought us to within ten kilometres of Al Qamishli, where a beaming Dickie and Ro greeted us. They had clearly made a discovery. We followed them for another twenty minutes to a plain but modern-looking hotel on the outskirts of the town, where we were instantly surrounded by helpers. They took the bikes inside and offered us tea, even carrying our bags upstairs. Pauline was so excited at the prospect of a real bed after a hundred-mile cycle that she jumped up and down on it like a six-year-old before collapsing in a heap. We enjoyed a late meal and were just in time to toast the New Year with non-alcoholic beer. It was a relief to be free of police scrutiny. They had melted away without a word.

Ultimately Syria would leave me with mixed memories. The kindness and welcome of the people was traditionally Arabic, but beneath the surface was a sinister undercurrent. Our stop in Palmyra had left me confused, even haunted, not from what we had seen, but from what was hidden from us. Despite our mode of travel, here was proof that our journey gave us only a tiny insight into the lives of Syrians. I came away with a sense of loss, a failure to understand the politics of a repressed people and a nation that had lost its way.

Chapter 5

Winter Shadows – Turkey

New Year's Day was always destined to be a late start. My head was still ringing to the sound of Pauline's mouth organ, which appeared on the stroke of midnight, her rendition of 'Auld Lang Syne' leaving the hotel staff lost for words. Too shattered after our ride of nearly 170 kilometres and a full twelve hours in the saddle, we had also neglected most of our routine chores.

After a hurried bid to catch up, it was nearly eleven o'clock before we were under way and entering Al Qamishli, the border town through which we would cross into Turkey. There was a friendly and bustling feel in the narrow streets as we squeezed through in single file. It was obvious where we were heading, and unprompted, helpful shouts directed us to a side alley, at the end of which was the border bounded by high wire gates. Dickie and Ro had driven ahead to begin the paperwork and we could see Martha parked nearby. The customs officials were in cheerful mood and offered us sweet black tea while we waited in the office. As always, the problem was destined to be with Martha rather than us cyclists. Apparently, on entering Syria Dickie had declared by which border crossing we would be departing. He had done this correctly, but the form said otherwise, stating Bab Al-Hawa, rather than Al Qamishli, where we were now. There was a sudden commotion and much rustling as we unfolded our maps. We knew it wasn't close when the customs men began arguing, unable to locate it themselves. It turned out to be over 500 kilometres west of Al Qamishli, meaning that Dickie and Ro would have to drive a round trip of at least 1,000 kilometres, just to reach the other side of the gate barely ten metres away. It was a ludicrous scenario and we spent a fruitless couple of hours trying to persuade the officials to take pity on our situation. While they were sympathetic there was no backing down.

I felt for Dickie and Ro, but to their credit they proved unflappable. The situation would have infuriated me but they quietly resigned themselves to driving through the night and hopefully reaching the border the following morning. All being well they would get through easily and could potentially rejoin us the following evening. We hastily grabbed a few things, including our sleeping bags and a change of clothes so that we could be independent for a couple of days. Our own crossing of the border was seamless and we received a warm welcome and a steaming cup of coffee as we stepped into Turkey.

I had been to Turkey as a tourist before, but never to this far south-eastern corner. Few travellers venture here due to the tense security situation between the government and the Kurdish people. Numbering some fifteen million in Turkey as a whole, they represent about 80 per cent of the local population. The Kurdistan Workers' Party, the PKK, is recognised by many nations as a terrorist organisation. Their campaign against the central government in Turkey has been brutal, and for fifteen years between 1984 and 1999 there was open warfare between the two sides. The government responded mercilessly by wiping out almost 3,000 Kurdish villages in this area of the country, deporting many of the population to central towns where security was easier to administer. The aftermath of this recent history was all too evident as we cycled the short distance into Nusaybin, on the Turkish side of the border. The dirt road was lined with tall watch-towers, sentries and numerous armoured vehicles. We passed through a final gate manned by a few bored recruits, and suddenly we were in the town. I had barely walked a few yards before an old man in a long trench coat, clutching a stick, shuffled up to me. He raised his head with some effort and smiled warmly. 'Welcome to Kurdistan,' he whispered.

First impressions of Nusaybin were favourable and we strolled along the main street feeling more relaxed than we had in days. It was great to be away from the scrutiny of the police and the escort that had dogged our every move in Syria. Much to our relief we found a cash machine on the first street corner. Having seen only one in Syria, and that in Damascus, meant that we had been eating into our dollar reserves far too quickly. It was already three o'clock and without the tent we were too late to cycle further that day. We checked into a dingy hotel on the main street before wandering the town in search of food.

The town wasn't as prosperous as we had first assumed. Most of the shop fronts were actually banks or hardware stores. There were plenty of coffee shops, but little to actually eat. Eventually we found a small restaurant, which at least displayed a poster of a pizza in the window. It took an hour before anything resembling the picture appeared, but it was good and helped to nourish us a bit. We chased it down with a cake each for dessert and retired back to the hotel. We were all thinking the same but Jamie was the first to announce his dissatisfaction. 'I'm not sure about anyone else, but I'm still hungry – could anyone eat that again?' We trooped back to the restaurant, barely an hour after leaving, and ordered exactly the same meal from the bemused waiter.

The following morning dawned grey and overcast. There was a definite chill in the air and we knew it would get colder still. The flat plain of the desert was behind us and now we would be heading into the hills. We needed to cycle north-east through some steep terrain until we met the enormity of Lake Van, still some 300 kilometres away. From there we would skirt the eastern shore of the lake for three days before breaking off east towards the border with Iran, at the town of Dogubayazit. If things went well, the journey would only take a week, but much would depend on the weather, and of course how Ro and Dickie fared at the border.

Our peace and quiet at breakfast the following morning was shattered by hordes of school children arriving to buy their lunch. They pointed and sniggered at our Lycra kit, while we laughed at their attempts to look cool with ties undone and shirts hanging out; some things are the same the world over.

The road out of the town soon led us into a narrow and winding gorge. It was blissfully free of traffic but the road surface was much rougher than we were used to in Syria. For the first time in two weeks we were also climbing – a steady gradient that followed a small river switching back and forth between towering ridges. There were very few homes and no settlements, but lots of small cafés and sheds boarded up for the winter season. In summer it would be an idyllic spot to sit by the river, but now the ground was covered in a heavy frost that even the weak sun couldn't melt. Our pace was leisurely and not just because of the hill. The efforts of the last few days had left us feeling washed out. We took the chance to cycle beside each other, chatting away as the valley carried us ever upward. In places the switchbacks were perched high above steep drops and we saw the wreckage of a lorry that had plummeted several hundred metres off the road.

We had naively been expecting Dickie and Ro to join us in the small town of Midyat that evening, but we received a text to say that they were only just through the border, having negotiated with customs all day. Furthermore they had parted with an enormous $1,500 deposit, as a returnable bond for the vehicle. This was to be expected but it left me again worrying about the finances, although – in theory at least – it would be reimbursed on leaving Turkey. As we returned to our hostel we noticed dozens of armoured vehicles coming and going from the local barracks. The soldiers clearly enjoyed making their presence felt.

We weren't sorry to leave Midyat the following morning. The route out of town was straight and featureless but soon we turned off on to a narrower mountain road completely free of traffic. All being well it would take us the remaining seventy kilometres to Batman, the largest town in the area. We climbed our way up through smooth, green rounded hills and repeated switchbacks. Nic was loving every minute and yelled back over his shoulder with a big grin on his face. 'It's beautiful – we could be cycling in Provence!'

I had to agree but in the distance we could see a line of ominous-looking snow-capped mountains to which we were drawing ever closer. An hour later and we reached our high point at a windy pass and stopped to soak up the precious rays of the sun. It felt gloriously warm with the clouds now far below, but bouts of chilly mist soon blew up again from the valley. Sarah had picked up a slow puncture and, glad for the stop, we adjusted our bikes and checked our brakes while she fixed it. The map indicated that from here it was downhill for a full twenty-five kilometres into the next valley, so we planned on gaining some serious speed. At the bottom we would cross the Tigris, the second of the major rivers we would encounter en route.

The others jumped on their bikes and disappeared straight into the clouds while I sorted myself out. Just as I was about to set off I noticed that I too had a flat tyre. I unshouldered my rucksack in order to fix it, annoyed with myself for wasting the ten-minute stop. Then I remembered with horror that I had just lent my pump to Sarah, who was now on her way down the hill. Without a moment to lose I dropped everything and sprinted. They were only a minute ahead, but by the time I reached the first corner it was already too late. At such a speed they were well out of earshot and I couldn't even see them through the mist. Dejected, I made my way back to the bike. I reached for my phone knowing that Nic always kept his close, but of course there was no signal. We were as remote as we had been on the whole trip. There was no traffic whatsoever on the road, so there was precious little chance of getting a lift. Then I reminded myself that wasn't an option anyway; we were aiming to cycle every inch of the way, after all. Short of bright ideas, I decided I might as well start walking. If the road was downhill as the map indicated, the others would be at the Tigris in little more than half an hour, and walking the twenty-five kilometres I estimated would take me at least five hours. That meant they would surely realise something was up and head back to find me. I imagined them all pulling straws to see who was going to cycle back uphill for two hours. Even then would they bring a pump? At least it's not raining I thought as I hobbled along miserably in my cycle shoes.

The scenery had now changed from sunny Provence to Snowdonia on a wet blustery day. I kept sliding on the steep, slippery road, muttering under my breath and cursing my stupidity. It would have made for a fantastic descent, in fact the only big downhill we had encountered so far. After an hour of walking I spied the first building ahead. The road had briefly levelled out and in the distance was what appeared to be a petrol station. To save time I started to jog, wheeling the bike alongside, and in just fifteen minutes arrived at the dilapidated structure, unable to believe my luck. I could fix the puncture easily enough with my patches, and if only they had an air supply I could be on my way.

I was quickly disappointed. The forecourt was all but deserted and there was certainly no air supply available. A fat dishevelled man appeared and ambled over from behind the office, pulling up his trousers as he approached. I pointed out the flat tyre and lifted my hands up in a desperate 'what do you do?' gesture. He crouched down and poked the wheel a few times, tutting away to himself and shaking his head. It was utterly useless and I was simply wasting time. I certainly didn't need a second opinion on whether it was flat or not. He rose to his feet and pointed into the distance, then back at the bike. I had no idea what on earth he was talking about and could see nothing ahead. There was little choice but to start walking again.

The road was still heading downhill, but more gently now, and over a wide open plain. The weather was good but the wind was picking up and I was getting hungry. The other issue was water as I had barely half a litre left. Ahead in the distance emerged a small lonely wooden shack, set back from the road with what appeared to be a motorbike outside. A few minutes later I was at the open door and shouting inside.

'Merhaba,' or hello, was one of the few Turkish words I knew. A wiry middle-aged man emerged promptly from the back. At least he seemed a bit more energetic than my previous encounter. He chewed on a toothpick as he wiped his hands on a greasy rag, which he then returned to his back pocket, while behind him I spied lots of old motorcycle wheels and tyres on racks. It looked promising. I pointed to my flat tyre, and tried to explain that I just needed air. 'Pssshhh' was the best I could muster for a translation as I pointed at the valve. He beckoned for me to hand over the wheel so I unclipped it from the frame and obliged. Never have I seen a puncture fixed so quickly. He pulled off the tyre in a single yank and soon had an oversized motorcycle patch over the small hole. I took the chance to inspect the inside of the tyre and found the offending article, a tiny shard of glass. He had an industrial compressor and within five seconds it was fully inflated and ready to go. My whole visit from start to finish had taken less than three minutes. He grunted a few times, before ambling into the back of the shed, disappearing as quickly as he had arrived. Unable to believe my luck, but with no idea how much I should pay him, I left some notes on his bench equivalent to a couple of pounds. It was probably far more than the going rate but I was over the moon at the prospect of being back on the road.

I had come so close to being denied the rest of the downhill that it seemed all the sweeter. The road descended in wide, gently sweeping turns, so it was possible to build up quite a speed. In less than half an hour I pulled into the village of Hasankeyf, spotting the other bikes outside a small bakery. It was a relief to see them and it felt like a reunion with long-lost friends. Needless to say, they had barely noticed my absence, and had spent an amusing hour in the local school, Jamie opting to play football in the playground while Sarah delivered a quick English lesson. Nic and Pauline perhaps had the toughest chore, enduring tea with the headmaster. The bakery we now sat in was a welcome shelter from the bitter wind outside. A young man was sliding flat dough on a wooden paddle into a vast bread oven. The heat radiated across the room tingling one side of our faces. Within a minute it was cooked and he delivered it hot and crispy straight to our table. It melted in the mouth instantly, and was one of the most delicious things I had ever tasted. He laughed, unable to believe the rate at which we demolished it before signalling again and again for more.

With our stomachs stretched full, we freewheeled the last few hundred metres down to the Tigris. There is now a modern road bridge across the river, but from its edge we could see the ancient crossing for which the village is famous. This had been a Roman town before the Arabs conquered it in the year 640, but there is thought to have been a settlement in Hasankeyf for at least 10,000 years. They built the high bridge resting on enormous stone piers and in so doing provided a vital and strategic river crossing. As long ago as the eleventh century the bridge needed restoring. These days only two of the stone piers remain, but it must have been a formidable structure in ancient times.

The future of Hasankeyf and the bridge look fairly bleak. Recently the Turkish have begun construction of the Illisu dam further downstream, part of the enormous South-East Anatolia Project (GAP): a complex series of twenty-one dams throughout the south-east of the country. Tens of thousands of people will have to be displaced, and many villages, including the one where we stood, will be underwater. Tragically, many archaeological treasures will also be lost. The surrounding gorges are littered with ancient cave dwellings and the remnants of early inhabitants. The area between the Tigris and the Euphrates is thought by many to be the cradle of modern civilisation. The local people have enlisted international help to try and halt construction, but opposition is painfully weak. After the rural clearances of Kurdish villages, the population is thinly spread and it would appear that the fate of Hasankeyf is already sealed.

We left the village and cycled parallel to the river, savouring the magnificent view along the valley. On each side were the remains of abandoned homes, many burned to a shell, although it was unclear just how old they were. The sun came out as we began a long but gentle climb out of the valley on the still-deserted road. Only ten kilometres outside Batman we rounded a bend in the road to be greeted by the sight of Martha, complete of course with Dickie and Ro. It felt as though we hadn't seen them in weeks; in reality it had been just three days. They had endured an incredible level of bureaucracy and looked exhausted after their epic drive.

'It's been a very, very long trip,' said Dickie. He looked utterly finished and I couldn't help feeling that for once we cyclists had enjoyed the better option.

Frustratingly there was nowhere to camp and so we headed into the curiously named city of Batman. This turned out to be short for Bati Raman mountains, and was the provincial capital. I also knew it to be at the forefront of the Kurdish resistance movement. But at first sight the city didn't seem to have much to offer and we booked into an anonymous concrete hotel. The lobby at least was smart and we secured two enormous rooms between us for less than twenty dollars. Just as we were leaving the Reception area we noticed a door marked 'Hamam'. Unable to believe our luck, we booked ourselves in before heading upstairs. I was too slow and suddenly seemed to be at the back of the queue. Pauline, never one to miss an opportunity, was already heading down the stairs as I was still heading up. 'You snooze, you lose!' she taunted me.

Jamie and Nic were back in the room an hour later, looking suitably refreshed and almost unrecognisable they were scrubbed so clean. Each session was supposed to take about half an hour, so I headed down to take my turn after Sarah. I was handed a token towel and directed to the steam room before taking a shower. Unfortunately for me, the man in charge clearly got

87

carried away with Sarah. By the time they had finished, I had been in and out of the shower three times and couldn't have been much cleaner anyway. She emerged looking very pleased with herself and so relaxed I thought she was about to keel over. 'That was just . . . just amazing,' she muttered as she headed upstairs.

I was desperate to see what all the fuss was about. In the washing room was a large marble plinth in the centre, around which were seating areas and more marble sinks. The masseur directed me to lie on the table before my tired limbs were extended in turn and ruthlessly scrubbed. I decided I would happily cycle any distance if this were on offer at the end of every day. The brief head massage also felt fantastic and left me with a floating hypnotic feeling. Unfortunately, me being seventh in line meant that he was getting bored and my time was up after barely fifteen minutes. I left praying that it wouldn't be the last hamam we encountered in Turkey.

After the delights of the massages we were a little too relaxed the following morning. Although I now had my puncture fixed, there was yet another problem with my back wheel. Both Nic and I had suffered from broken spokes. We had plenty of spares but foolishly had not brought the correct tool to remove the rear block of cogs. Without it, we couldn't replace the offending spoke and on the rough roads the bikes were taking some punishment. My wheel was now wobbling slightly as a result and I really needed it fixed before it became any worse. The young lad behind the desk in the hotel thought he knew a man who could help, and after leading me through endless back streets he deposited me at a small mechanic's shop, similar to the one I had encountered the previous day. It was well equipped but everything was covered with a thick layer of black grease, with a naked bulb the only source of light.

If you could have had a Dickensian bike shop, this would surely have been it. There was nothing new for sale. Racks of spare and recycled parts lined every available space on the walls and ceiling, and along one side, an enormous tool bench supported heavy metal crates full of spanners. I was becoming fairly adept at sign language and had brought a new spoke with me, a prop to indicate exactly what needed replacing. While he examined the wheel he barked orders at his two young assistants, who flew into action and began rifling through the metal boxes for the correct tool. There was a lot of coming and going before, much to my relief, the spanner was found. He soon replaced the spoke and then, as an added bonus, began straightening the wheel, placing it in a vertical wheel brace and checking it was 'true'. Mostly he did it by feel, his head cocked to one side checking the alignment, while he carried on a conversation with another customer. Tiny adjustments of the spoke were followed by a rapid spin of a couple of inches, before repeating the process. He must have done it thousands of times and his two young apprentices looked on admiringly. The wheel emerged as good as new, perfectly straight, and all for less than a pound.

We headed out of Batman in a thick Gotham City-style mist. The first twenty-five kilometres were grim, along a busy main road and without the benefit of good visibility. After renewing their haircuts Nic and Jamie were even faster than usual, spurred on by delusions of Lance Armstrong, while Sarah took a bit of a tumble an hour later after a brief disagreement with a tractor. Angry with herself, she dealt with it by speeding off during the second leg while we all trailed in her wake.

At midday, the traffic eased when we turned off the main highway, and right on cue the sun broke through the mist to reveal a stunning landscape of rolling green hills. We stopped in a hillside village for lunch and Pauline and Sarah headed off to a nearby house, where they negotiated the purchase of eggs, bread and strong homemade goat's cheese. Dickie and Ro had some shopping to do in Batman but they shouldn't have been too far behind. The last three days on our own had been remarkably stress-free, despite having to carry rucksacks full of our gear. Now we were back in the situation of not knowing what to take each morning or how long we would be on our own. We could always carry more equipment and be more independent but that defeated the object of having a support team. Again I was jealous of Austrian Gerry Winkler's freedom, but having our huge amounts of equipment carried was a massive bonus, and was making the cycling much more pleasurable.

The scenery after lunch became more dramatic by the mile and was uncannily similar to the 'badlands' of the American Mid-west. Large rolling sand dunes cut by small gorges ran all the way down to the roadside. In the distance, the snow-covered peaks we had first seen a couple of days earlier drew ever closer. As always, the last hour before sunset was the most vivid and the mountains in the distance positively glowed. With the plummeting tempera-ture, mist collected in the valleys and hollows on each side. The road itself was slightly higher than the surrounding terrain and the effect was unearthly, as though we were cycling above the clouds on some aerial viaduct. We were determined to camp for the first time in days and began to look for likely spots through the gathering gloom. Foolishly, we passed several possibilities, always on the lookout for something better. As darkness fell, we entered a narrow steep-sided gorge, which funnelled the wind ferociously into our faces. The intermittent gusts almost brought us to a standstill and we battled for over half an hour to fight our way through to where the valley widened. We were shattered, but just before eight o'clock came Dickie's welcome shout down to one side of the road.

They had driven Martha across a small stone bridge where there was a neat field perfect for the tent. It was already dark but we entered into our practised routine, and got the tent up quickly and the kettle on. Only an hour later, and just as we were settled in, we heard the unfamiliar noise of a vehicle. We had seen no traffic all day so it was something of a surprise. It pulled over the bridge, the lights glaring through the tent fabric and we heard shouts outside. I was writing my diary on the laptop but quickly hid it in my sleeping bag before we emerged to see who it was. At least four or five soldiers were paying us a visit but they didn't seem too threatening. I just prayed they weren't going to make us move on in the dark. As before, the old 'offer of tea' trick worked wonders and broke the ice successfully. After much laughing and gesturing at our bikes, they clearly decided we were mad but harmless and disappeared into the night.

We didn't sleep well in the bitter cold, especially Nic who had lost his sleeping mat and was suffering in the conditions. I woke to what I thought at first was a heavy frost on the tent, and emerged to see the gorge for the first time in daylight. There was actually a light covering of snow and the nearby river was choked with blocks of ice from upstream. The valley floor was still in shade and frozen in an icy stillness. I turned around and emptied my bladder against a rock, producing a cloud of steam into the air. Above our camp was a steep slope which culminated in a rocky outcrop barely fifty metres away. I couldn't believe my eyes. The summit was fortified with sandbags and poking over the top was a huge machine gun and the heads of three soldiers. They smiled and waved at me while I zipped myself up and returned the gesture. No wonder we had been paid a visit the night before. Further inspection revealed at least two other machine-gun nests within shouting distance, and a barracks around the corner. Having passed half a dozen remote campsites we seemed to have picked the most unsuitable place imaginable.

We set off uphill through the gorge and again found ourselves battling a fierce headwind. It was now a dirt road and as the gusts whipped the dust into our faces our pace reduced to a crawl. Pauline had woken with an upset stomach and had eaten no breakfast. She was a strong character but by the first stop she was some way behind and I could tell she was struggling. As we climbed higher, the snow lay heavier on the verges, but at least the roads were clear and the wind thankfully eased. Snow ploughs passed us frequently, heading up towards Bitlis, apparently one of Turkey's main ski resorts. We planned to take lunch there and I arrived in the village a few minutes after Nic to find him visibly shaken. He had slipped on black ice coming into the main street and fallen into the path of an oncoming lorry. Dickie, driving behind, was just in time to see him roll out of the way with a second to spare. Thankfully they waited to warn the rest of us and we quickly dismounted and skated down the main street together.

On the other side of Bitlis the road wound ever higher into the mountains and a thick mist descended. We desperately needed to reach the town of Tatvan on the shores of Lake Van itself, but this was still a good thirty kilometres further. With my energy fading in the bitter cold, a snow plough passed me at a perfect speed. I accelerated hard and tucked in neatly behind, inches from the massive wheels draped in thick metal chains. The shelter from the cold wind was immediate and the heat from the engine was funnelled back towards me. It might have been a tropical sea breeze and I enjoyed an idyllic ten kilometres before the driver turned off with a cheery wave.

Concerned about the visibility, we decided to regroup for the last section into Tatvan. A car pulled up ahead of us and the driver frantically waved us to a stop from the open window. Out climbed a well-dressed young man who introduced himself as Nazim, in surprisingly good English. He owned a restaurant in town and insisted that we must come and eat on our arrival. We normally did our best to avoid over-committing ourselves, but on this occasion there was no escape as he was waiting for us again when we arrived. Tatvan was a hive of activity, the main street lined with small boutiques, mobile phone shops and cafés. The population seemed younger than in other towns and Nazim himself turned out to be a bit of an entrepreneur. His restaurant consisted of a coffee and cake shop downstairs with a second enormous café upstairs. It all had a very modern feel and he was clearly trying to establish a Western-style outlet to attract young professionals. He soon had a waiter scurrying over to serve us. Having had our fill of traditional food at lunch, and craving quick calories, we asked if he had pizzas.

'Pizza no problem,' he said nonchalantly, waving his hand. 'What you like? Margherita, Hawaian, Vegetarian?' Despite having ordered one of everything, we shouldn't have been surprised when they all arrived looking identical. We were too hungry to care, though, and it tasted pretty good. Nazim insisted on staying with us and he slumped casually in his chair, one leg hooked over the armrest, soaking up the greetings and praise from passing customers. He was justly proud of his business, but I sensed he was desperate for our seal of approval.

'Nazim – how long have you had your restaurant?' I asked between mouthfuls.

'This place here?' he replied flippantly. 'Just few months. But this is nothing – I have many businesses. My family is from Istanbul. You must come and visit when you arrive.'

'We're cycling the other way, towards Iran,' said Jamie.

'Iran! You are crazy!' Nazim sat up sharply as he spoke, before receding back into his chair. 'This will be big problem for you. They are very dangerous people. They will not like good people like you. Why you go this way?'

'We're cycling to Everest. To climb the highest mountain in the world.' Sarah repeated the well-worn routine, but geography was not Nazim's strong point as we soon realised.

'Istanbul I think is a better way for you. Only one week from here. You can stay with my family. We are very rich.'

Sarah's eyes lit up at the last comment and she pestered him as to why he wasn't married. She and Pauline loved to quiz the locals and get to the root of their personal lives. Nazim, in turn, thrived on the attention, revelling in his status as everyone's friend. Every couple of minutes his phone would go off and without apology he would stop mid-sentence and babble away, issuing instructions. After one such conversation he hung up and turned to us.

'That was my farm,' he said in an uncharacteristic hushed whisper, leaning in close towards us.

'What sort of farm is it?' I replied, feigning interest. His eyes darted left and right to make sure no one was listening.

'It is a pig farm! It is in the mountains.' It took a few seconds for the penny to drop. 'A pig farm in a Muslim country. Is that good business? Who can you sell pork to?' I was curious now.

'Many people want pork,' he replied. 'But it is very dangerous. If they catch me, I could be killed.'

I wasn't sure if he was joking or not, but it seemed an odd way of earning a living. Nazim was a helpful source of information but was very sceptical about our chances of reaching the larger town of Van the next day. We would have to climb to almost 2,000 metres, the highest point yet on the trip and there was every likelihood that the road would be blocked with snow. We had already negotiated some severe conditions and that was at a much lower altitude.

The scene was set for one of the most difficult days of the trip, with Van over 140 kilometres away. The previously unseen lake came into view straight away, a bold jade green, alluring against the backdrop of snowy hills. It was by far the largest lake in Turkey, nearly 100 miles wide and in places 500 feet deep. On the horizon we could see the remnants of the ancient volcanoes marking the remote western shores.

For the first two hours we hugged the shoreline, passing high above the water on rocky headlands where the road had been blasted into the cliff side. At times the road ran flat along the lakeside, where tall feathery reeds strained in the wind. The margins of the lake were heavily iced and the surface sparkled in the sunlight as we rode past. The wind lifted the thin dusting of snow, sending it spiralling away in every direction. It was a bleak and austere landscape but hauntingly beautiful. The sight of the lake was so captivating it was hard to turn your eyes away. Sadly, the road turned inland for a while and so began a long climb. By the time we stopped for lunch, Sarah and Pauline had fallen some way behind. They were both suffering from the cold so the lunch stop was doubly welcome. We ate as much as we could, fuelling ourselves against the weather, and quickly downed huge mugs of hot chocolate. Barely a week earlier we had enjoyed lunch in the desert sun and now our mugs sank deep into the snow at the side of the road.

An hour later and we found ourselves on the steepest hill of the journey so far. We could see a lorry high above us on the switchbacks long before we began the ascent. Jamie and Nic decided to stretch their legs and race to the top, outpacing us all. As usual, I was content in the middle, safe in the knowledge the girls were behind me still. The ascent was hard-going but a welcome change from the flat. I had discovered my cycling fitness and was enjoying the sensation of climbing higher with every turn in the road. At the summit pass we played snowballs but the novelty soon wore off. It began to snow heavily and we desperately needed to keep moving. With no sign of the girls, we decided to have a brew stop and make the best of it. Sarah was only a few minutes behind but by the time Pauline arrived conditions were a complete white-out. She was still suffering and for her the timing of a long cold cycle couldn't have been worse.

Painfully short of warm clothing, we pulled on all the kit we could. The descent from the pass promised to be bitter and visibility was now so poor that we couldn't speed up for fear of losing the road. Perhaps it was just as well as our hands and feet were already freezing, even in our gloves and overshoes. We stopped every five minutes, shaking our hands to keep the circulation going, but by the time the descent levelled out we were suffering badly. The bottom of the hill coincided with an army roadblock and full-scale checkpost. The soldiers were in cheery mood and beckoned us off the bikes and over to their heater, a rusty wood-burning stove by the side of the road. It had built up such a fierce heat that the chimney pipe was glowing red hot and looked close to melting. We stood as close as we dared and with my clothes drying by the second the warmth quickly returned. We thanked them and got back on the road in the encroaching gloom.

The final fifty kilometres were relentless, a neverending succession of small hills and gusts of chill wind. Jamie and Nic were both delayed by punctures but I pressed on with Sarah and Pauline, knowing they would catch us up soon enough. We were now back along the lakeside but could see nothing of the view, isolated by the darkness and the freezing rain that hammered into our faces. We stopped at a junction. It was so dark that I had to use my torch to read the sign. It was lucky I did, as to the right the road led off towards Iraq. It enforced our vulnerability still further and I only hoped that Jamie and Nic would also turn left behind us. Frustratingly, we could see the lights of Van ahead in the distance but they never seemed to draw closer. I felt surprisingly strong but could tell the girls were fading. It was gone eight o'clock by the time we finally arrived in the city, and the boys followed soon after. Pauline was later to say that it had been one of the most gruelling days of the entire trip.

Camping again was out of the question and we checked into a large rambling hotel. The owner Ahmed was thrilled to see us and wasted no time in ensuring we had somewhere to store the bikes. Having already planned to take a rest day, we intended to spend two nights here. We had now been cycling for fifteen consecutive days, and a break was long overdue. Ahmed told us that the town was buzzing with news that three people had died of bird flu that day. It was already hitting the international headlines and the staff were crowding around the small television in the lobby. We found a café near the hotel but were simply too tired to eat much. There were several options but tactfully we avoided the cheap chicken. We headed back and collapsed into bed with the welcome prospect of our first lie-in.

It was just as well that it was a rest day as we woke to find it had snowed in the night. A few inches had fallen and the streets were pleasantly quiet outside. It was a beautiful sight and it made not having to cycle even more welcome. We had a lazy breakfast in the hotel, the usual mix of bread, hard-boiled eggs, olives and sugary black tea. There was precious little sign of the girls and we decided to let them sleep. Unbeknown to us they were lying in bed and using the laptop to watch all six TV episodes of *Pride and Prejudice*, too busy swooning to be disturbed. Jamie and Nic headed off to check out a local bike shop for spare tyres while Dickie and I sat down to tackle the finances – Turkey had proved quite expensive and not being able to camp was also draining our resources.

In the afternoon we made our way to a local internet café. The atmosphere was stifling, with young Turkish men playing computer games and idly smoking themselves to death. We checked Gerry Winkler's website to see how he was progressing with his own journey. He hadn't moved much in the last week, and through a translation that Nic obtained, it transpired that he was in hospital with an abscess on his backside. Jamie could barely contain himself and felt it was nothing more than he deserved for nicking our idea in the first place. I also read up on the bird flu situation and the news was not good. There were reports that Iran was considering closing the border with Turkey as a precautionary measure. This filled me with horror as we could in theory be stranded indefinitely waiting for it to reopen.

That night it started to snow again, this time more heavily. There was no wind but silent clumps fell relentlessly as we watched from our hotel bedroom. Beautiful as it was, our prospects were not looking good for the following day and sure enough we woke to at least eight inches of snow on Martha outside. The city remained deathly still and very few people emerged. It was doubly frustrating as we had just had a day off and would rather have pressed on. We had calculated that we could only afford to rest about one day in ten and time lost now would have to be recouped elsewhere. We considered whether it might be possible to battle on and have a shorter day and although Nic and Jamie were keen, I was sceptical. We could hardly camp in these conditions and towns were now few and far between. Here at least we were secure and warm in our hotel until conditions improved.

Having bought some snow chains, Ro took Jamie and Nic in Martha to recce the route out of town. Even if we went nowhere, information on the road ahead would be useful. While they were gone I used my bike to test the conditions on the local streets. The snow ploughs were now out in force, along with an impressive army of workers, shovelling furiously to get the town moving again. Trying to cycle was tricky as the road was being cleared to allow one lane of traffic and the snow ploughs simply dumped the excess on what had been the hard shoulder. But the biggest danger – and what we all feared most – was the ice. Nic had already flown off once and was lucky to come away unscathed. We knew that one bad slip resulting in a broken wrist, or worse, would be the end of the expedition for that person. By the time I returned to the hotel I had already made up my mind. Moving today was simply not an option.

We spent an amusing afternoon being interviewed by the local TV channel. Ahmed had apparently given them a call after hearing of our expedition and was eager to act as interpreter. He later produced maps to show how hazardous the next couple of days would be, probably in a bid to make us stay. It would be two full days until we reached Dogubayazit on the Iranian border and en route we would cross another pass, only this time it was 600 metres higher than the last one. We remembered how bitterly cold we had been only a couple of days earlier, but we had little choice but to continue after two days off. Once in Iran we would start to head south and, fingers crossed, conditions would improve.

We left early the next morning and followed the lake shore again. It was an arctic-like cold but there was little wind and we soon built up some warmth with a steady pace. On the edge of the town we met a roadblock where vehicles were being disinfected by men in protective white suits, no doubt in response to the recent bird flu outbreak. They weren't quite sure what to do with bicycles and so we passed through unchecked. At least the weather was holding off, although dark clouds overhead made for a forbidding atmosphere.[7]

Nic and I led the way into Muradiye just after darkness. We had been offered floor space in a local school for the night. When Pauline arrived a few minutes later, she looked utterly drained. She grabbed a large bottle of water and retreated straight to her sleeping bag, determined to recover. By the time the police arrived to check our papers we were surrounded by a dozen curious locals in the common room area. I was never at my most sociable after a long day's cycling. It was tiresome repeating yet again the purpose of our trip when food and sleep beckoned. On this particular occasion, the formalities lasted at least two hours, much of this taken up with the police laboriously copying our passport details, including date of birth and even father's Christian name, on to a scrap of paper that would never see the light of day. By the time we were given a room to sleep in we hadn't eaten for over eight hours and there were still jobs to do.

Pauline emerged bleary-eyed the next morning after a mammoth twelve-hour sleep. I was worried for her as ahead lay a very demanding day. Although she looked a little stronger she had eaten almost nothing in the last twenty-four hours. It was minus twelve outside and as we tried to fill our bike bottles the water froze instantly. We needed all the protection we could muster, so we wrapped up in everything we had, including our neoprene overshoes. Despite the temperature, a weak sun offered some comfort as we found our way back on to the road and veered away from the lake. Ahead lay a desolate sixty kilometres to the pass we had to cross. The road was clear and a gentle wind lifted the powder snow into swirls and patterns across our path. The effect was mesmeric and it soon became hard to focus on the road surface ahead. At least the gradient was gentle but as we climbed higher we found ourselves cycling on hard compacted snow for the first time. The tyres crunched and bit the surface reassuringly, barring the odd patch of ice, and we managed to maintain a decent speed. Jamie was the first to take a tumble, emerging with a grazed and bloody knee but no serious injury.

The first job for Nic at any stop, even before eating, was to clean his bike. All of ours were new at the start, but his was still in mint showroom condition, while mine already looked a year old. He would remove the slightest speck of mud at every rest break and he repeatedly told Jamie and me, 'If you look good, you cycle good!' We had been wondering what he would do after a morning of cycling over pure virgin snow but we needn't have worried. The bikes had acquired a thin sheen of ice over the entire frame. Nic slowly extracted his bike tool and gently prised off the frozen layer. He always tried to do this subtly, while Jamie and I did our best to catch him and, where possible, record his efforts on film. For once, Dickie and Ro arrived right on cue and we cooked up a cheese pasta from the back of Martha. The combination was a winner and gave us some badly needed energy.

It was late by the time we reached the sleepy town of Dogubayazit. We checked into the only visible hotel on the main street, collapsing on to the damp musty beds. Having arrived in darkness I had no idea of our surroundings until I scraped the ice from the frosted window the following morning. I quickly got Jamie and Nic up, and together we braved the freezing air on our tiny balcony. Over twenty kilometres away to the north rose the enormous and breathtaking sight of Mount Ararat. The snowy volcanic cone rose majestically above a layer of white cloud circling the lower slopes. It looked close enough to touch, and reminded me of seeing Kilimanjaro for the first time. Lost for words, we admired the view for perhaps half an hour before the sun rose fully and the mountain was tantalisingly enveloped by cloud from the surrounding plain. It disappeared as if sinking away to the horizon, an invisible hand easing it slowly from our grasp.

The news from Dickie at the Iranian border was not good. Deciding to get a head start, they had driven on the previous evening but were still on the Turkish side and yet to even begin negotiations with Iranian customs. The problem centred over the $1,500 bond we had paid for Martha on entering Turkey. Although guaranteed to be returned, as long as we left with the vehicle, the customs were now disputing this. Any money also had to be reclaimed from the National Bank, and there was a branch in Dogubayazit. Conveniently, a public holiday had just begun and furthermore it was to last another four days. We promptly went to the bank just to double check but it was plainly shut. On the phone I got annoyed with Dickie, who seemed convinced that we could just pick it up at a later date, even in London if necessary, where the bank had a branch. We had a piece of paper saying that we had parted with $1,500, but I found it hard to believe that a bank on the other side of the world would happily hand over that sum of money. But at customs posts you are in no position to bargain. If you need to get a vehicle across, the officials can name their price.

Dickie suggested we have a rest day while he continued to sort things out. There was little point in us all going to the border only to wait around. It seemed like a sensible suggestion, but again time was slipping away. That afternoon we took a taxi about half an hour out of town and up a steep, icy, winding road. It was strange to be travelling in a car again after so many miles on the bike, but our destination was the Ishak Pasha Palace, which had been built in the 1600s by the Ottomans. As it was winter it was closed to tourists, but it was worth the drive just for the view. Poised at the head of a snow-covered valley, and above a steep hillside, the setting was magnificent. We could see for miles across the snowy and desolate plain across to Mount Ararat, whose outline was again visible through the cloud. It was a mystical landscape, vast but so vivid and close you felt entirely in its midst. In every direction the view was washed in blue and grey: the marble of the palace walls and spires, the purplish haze that hung beneath the mountain, and the rolling iron-grey clouds in the sky above. I felt sure we were gazing on the true centre of the earth, the cradle of civilisation, even the supposed resting place of Noah's Ark. It was ethereal, primeval even, and I felt as though we had stepped into a painting.

Before us lay an unknown country, three times the size of France, the enormity of Iran. Tomorrow we would set off, come what may.

Chapter 6

The Land of Kindness – Iran

The border consisted of an extensive complex of low-lying buildings, straddling a barren and snow-covered mountain pass. I couldn't have imagined a lonelier spot. We spent the last of our Turkish lira in the over-priced café and wandered through a bleak no mans land between the two nations. En route, the girls pulled out the headscarves they had brought especially. By law their hair had to be covered in Iran and now was no time to test the rules. We passed hundreds of parked lorries, presumably awaiting permission to travel onwards. Row upon row of barbed wire marked the boundary of the holding area while beyond, the hills rose steeply to where both countries had erected high watch-towers. Ahead, and for the first time, we could see the red, green and white stripes of the Iranian flag. As a group we fell silent, intimidated by the austere surroundings.

'Welcome to Iran!' The passport official spoke good English and inspected our visas carefully against his details on a computer. The buildings of passport control were surprisingly modern and well equipped, contrasting sharply with the primitive infrastructure on the Turkish side. Despite my concerns, there was no problem and to my relief we were ushered straight through without any further checks. Our timing was perfect, as Dickie and Ro, together with Martha, had just been cleared for entry. They looked exhausted and it was little surprise. It had taken them forty-four hours to travel barely 200 metres, and again they had negotiated a minefield of red tape with good humour. The Iranian bond for Martha was less than $200, which was a welcome relief. There was the nagging issue that our number plates had been confiscated, but Dickie assured me he would deal with that en route. His optimism knew no bounds.

We couldn't wait to get going and left the border thrilled at the prospect of a new country. The weather had already eased and improved further as we descended steeply from the pass, free-wheeling downhill for a good ten minutes into the border town of Bazargan. We would need to press on further, but it seemed like a good place to grab a quick lunch, and we didn't have to look far. The owner of a local café spotted us and even crossed the road to secure our business. He barked orders at a young lad to watch the bikes and ushered us into the steamy fug of a smoke-filled room. Curious glances from the clientele greeted us, some acknowledging us with a nod of the head, before settling back into their conversations. All sat cross-legged on low carpeted tables around the edge of the room, puffing away on their hookahs or water pipes. We had seen them before in Turkey, but not quite on this scale, three foot tall and incredibly ornate. The smell was heady but not unpleasant, most likely a mixture of mild tobacco and herbs. Almost all the men were bearded and middle-aged and had definitely settled in for a long afternoon. You couldn't help but wonder what they did the rest of the time. We sat ourselves at the more familiar tables and chairs in the centre of the room and were quickly served black tea, poured theatrically from a great height into tiny glasses. We had no idea what food to order and a menu was nowhere to be seen, not that we could have read it anyway. Fortunately we had Pauline, who was not shy in coming forward in these situations. She loudly hailed the manager at the back of the restaurant. 'Hello, cooey, yes . . . you! We need some help over here.' The conversation around us died abruptly and the locals looked up in total bewilderment as our host scurried over. The customers began laughing, mocking him as he came running.

'We need food. Very hungry . . . much cycling!' Pauline's accompanying sign langauge was something to behold. The manager merely shrugged and babbled back at her, leaving us even more confused and certainly no better off. Out of frustration Pauline jumped to her feet and tugged at his sleeve. She led him past the chuckles of customers and straight into the restaurant kitchen, only to emerge a couple of minutes later.

'Hey guys, come and look at this!'

We passed through the double doors to see in the far corner an enormous oven where piles of flatbread were being baked. It smelled divine. Adjacent to it stood a stainless steel hot water bath where the smiling chef was proudly holding open the lid. Inside were densely packed clay pots, all the size of large mugs, each one simmering gently with a colourful vegetable stew.

'Sabzi . . . sabzi,' he repeated pointing at the pots. It looked and smelled delicious and we indicated that we would need seven. The manager and chef were thrilled. It clearly hadn't occurred to them that we would actually like to eat, and a couple of minutes later we were tucking in, to the delight of the locals. It was a brilliant hour and we ate well, all for 10,000 rials, or about 50p each. They didn't seem the least bit bothered by female company either. Coffee shops and restaurants were by no means off-limits to women, but the girls had been understandably nervous about what sort of reception they would receive. We posed for pictures with our newfound friends before getting back on the road.

Our first full day in Iran dawned cold and wet. We would have preferred fresh snow rather than the ugly grey slush that covered the roads. It was like a bad day in Scotland, my feet were soon soaked and I quickly lost sensation in my freezing toes. We had all started the trip with neoprene overshoes, but mine had already fallen apart in Turkey and now I was paying the price. The bikes were also taking some punishment, filthy with the oily grime that sprayed up from the wet road. It was a fairly miserable day by any measure and morale was low, our optimism in a new country already checked. The poor visibility prevented us from seeing what the guidebook described as spectacular views and then Nic broke a spoke. His frustration was immediate, such was the pride he took in keeping his bike pristine, and unlike in Turkey there was little prospect of getting it fixed.

The day was spent on a succession of dual carriageways and highways and despite the conditions we made rapid progress, helped by the gentle decrease in altitude. Our main concern was finding somewhere to sleep. Hotels, although cheap, were few and far between and the language barrier had caught us all unawares. We longed for the simplicity of camping again but there were few suitable places, with many of the roads fenced off or the land in use. It seemed a long time since the carefree existence of the Syrian desert, where all we had to do was turn off the road.

Late that afternoon, we pulled up at a dirty petrol station full of trucks belching diesel fumes. The drivers were incredulous to see the bikes but beckoned us over to where the lorries were being hosed down with a pressure washer. They had the bikes sparkling within two minutes and refused to accept any payment. Not for the first time we heard the same sentence repeated again and again. 'Welcome to Iran . . . welcome to Iran.'

Dickie and Ro had paid a visit to a local Red Crescent clinic just a few hundred metres away. Not only had they offered us beds and the use of a kitchen, but even a garage to store the bikes in. When we arrived the medical staff were incredibly polite and welcoming, but only one spoke a little English. He showed us to an immaculate room containing four hospital beds while the small kitchen lay along the corridor. It was a welcome respite from the difficult conditions outside, and yet another sign of Iranian hospitality. There was no sign of any patients or treatment under way, but the staff seemed to be on continual standby. I knew they shared the same foundation and principles as the Red Cross, and we could only assume they were here to treat casualties from road accidents. From what we had seen of the local drivers there would be no shortage of patients.

In the morning we tried to give our hosts a 'donation', but they adamantly refused, despite our suggestion that the money go direct to the Red Crescent. While the cyclists had a challenging day ahead, Dickie and Ro had decided to detour in search of a new number plate for Martha. If everything went to plan we would meet up later in our first Iranian city, Tabriz, 135 kilometres to the east. Separated from any support, we lunched on pre-cooked rice eaten out of a plastic shopping bag under a tunnel in the road. I found myself longing for the empty expanse of the desert again, and the near perfect conditions we had enjoyed at the start of the trip. This was miserable cycling, the scenery was uninspiring, and still the freezing mist and cloud refused to lift.

Dickie and Ro met us on the outskirts of Tabriz, complete with a shiny new number plate for Martha and a guide by the name of Mister Hossain, who, refreshingly, spoke fluent English. He had helped secure the necessary documentation for Martha but I was a bit confused as to why he was still sitting comfortably in the front seat. Despite his assurances otherwise, I knew he would want paying at some stage, but Dickie naively thought otherwise. He did at least help guide Martha through the mayhem of traffic and identical-looking streets while we followed. We were un-prepared for the city's size and the sheer volume of traffic, which increased in intensity as we neared the centre and hit rush hour. It was now dark but the city had come alive. Not knowing what to expect, I was amazed at the apparent affluence around us and we spotted numerous Western-style stores. Shop windows dis-played stereos, computers and mobile phones, and fashion bou-tiques and restaurants were all doing good business. The streets and pavements had a cosmopolitan feel, and if it hadn't been for the weather we could have been cycling down the wide boulevards of a Spanish city on the Mediterranean.

Mr Hossain guided us to a laughably expensive hotel. He looked vexed when we rejected it, as he had probably lost his commission; instead we suggested finding one at a fifth of the price. When we did, it was right on the main street and ideal for our needs. Grandiose, with high ceilings, it had original art deco features and was incredibly cheap. Hungry and eager to explore we headed straight back out into the city. On the surface at least it had such a relaxed feel that we had to remind ourselves we were in a hardline Islamic state. I had expected to see a dour-looking population, spartan grey shops and potholed roads. Instead there was colour and vibrancy all around, and even as Westerners we attracted far less attention than we had in the countryside. The biggest surprise was to see so many women on the street. They chatted and walked together just as they might in the West, but of course the law dictated that at least their hair must be covered. Most wore the *hijab* that hid all but their faces, but younger women wore a simple headscarf, often pushed far back on their heads and in practice covering little. Very few wore the *burqa*, an all-concealing garment with a mesh grille through which to see. The men, too, seemed relaxed about their dress, if modest. Most wore long-sleeved shirts and certainly long trousers. Back at the hotel, and thinking of our own safety, we asked Mr Hossain about our cycling shorts which stopped well above the knee.

'No problem, no problem,' he said dismissively. 'There are different rules for sport and you are doing sport, so no problem. But in the city you must wear long trousers.'

This seemed fair enough to us, but of course the girls were not so fortunate. There was no special 'allowance' made for girls to do sport in Iran. Indeed, women are still prohibited from attending major sporting events in public. This meant they would have to keep cycling in their *hijabs* and long trousers and sleeves. While it was so cold this wasn't really an issue, as we were all trying to wear more clothing, not less.

Leaving Tabriz was every bit as chaotic as our arrival and in the traffic I noticed something that had escaped me the previous evening. Almost all the cars were identical and all from the same manufacturer – Iran Khodro. They were devoid of style, angular and square, in profile exactly the car that a child would draw on paper. But the biggest hazard was the hundreds of mopeds that weaved their way in and out of the traffic, making progress treacherous. There was little road sense and we found ourselves in friendly arguments on several occasions. The drivers were good-humoured, their frustration worked out by repeatedly pressing their horns.

By the time we reached the city margins the traffic had thinned and we were climbing steeply again, our first uphill for some days. Fresh snow had fallen and the surrounding hills were beautifully stark in the weak sunlight. It was still piercingly cold but at least the roads were wide and for once well gritted and completely free of ice. Jamie was unusually quiet and I could tell he was having to dig deep to keep himself going. He'd thrown up in the night and was looking distinctly under the weather. We stopped briefly and he crawled into the front of Martha for a few minutes' sleep before we had to wake him up. After just two hours we crested a pass and began a rapid but cold descent into the town of Bostanabad. Dickie and Ro had gone ahead to find somewhere to stay but yet again they had simply disappeared. We waited fruitlessly by the side of the road for half an hour, growing colder and more impatient by the minute. Nothing we could do seemed to instil any urgency in them. We retreated to a coffee shop where I could see Nic was growing increasingly tense. Waiting was not his forte, especially when it was time that could be spent doing something else. The owner kindly lit the gas fire in the corner for us and slowly we felt some warmth returning.

It was another half-hour before Nic leaped to his feet. He had spotted Martha cruising past and we all raced outside. The excitement was too much for Jamie, whose strength was exhausted. His legs buckled and he fell to the floor, his face an ashen grey. When he came to he still looked completely dazed, but recovered soon enough in the fresh air to make it to the accommodation Dickie and Ro had found nearby.

It wasn't, strictly speaking, a hotel. The building was quite clearly a restaurant, but upstairs was a series of about six rooms off a large central landing. It was dirty and plain, but we were too tired to care and were certainly not heading out again. That night it also became obvious that we were going nowhere the following day. Sarah was back and forth for hours, throwing up her kebab dinner. She seemed to have picked up the same bug as Jamie, albeit more severely. Over breakfast we had no option but to declare a day's rest, deciding it would do Jamie no harm either. He too was still low on reserves.

A rest day in itself was not a problem, but after Jamie's shaky recovery I had real doubts that Sarah would be sufficiently well the following morning. After all, Jamie had ridden only sixty kilometres before collapsing at the end, and our next leg would be twice the distance. Nic and I spent the morning going over the maps and yet again checking the total mileage we had to cover in Iran. We were faced with a real difficulty. In total we would have to cycle just under 3,000 kilometres to reach Pakistan. We had been granted a thirty-day visa, which should afford ample time. The problem was that lost days would simply have to be recovered elsewhere. Our nightmare scenario was that we might all fall ill at different times. If Sarah was sick for some days I would soon have to make a decision to get back on the road, and if necessary, that meant she would have to travel in the vehicle until her condition improved. I really hoped it wouldn't come to that, as Sarah, perhaps more than anyone on the team, deserved success by virtue of the work she had already put in. We just had to hope that she would get better quickly.

Things looked up in the afternoon, when the owner of the hotel suggested we should go to the spa. We were sceptical – we had seen few shops in the tiny town, so the idea of a spa seemed a little far-fetched. Twenty minutes later, and after a short taxi ride, we pulled up alongside an enormous round red-bricked building – a sort of Albert Hall in miniature. The driver pointed at the girls and then at the door. Confused at first, we then realised there were two separate entrances for men and women. He drove us boys around to the far side. Now separated, we paid our entrance fee of about 10,000 rials (about 50p).

Inside we entered the men's changing area, before passing through to a cavernous space and the main swimming pool. Around it were a number of plunge baths of varying temperature, all decorated in beautiful tiling and marbled motifs. Tall pillars rose to the ceiling and you could be forgiven for thinking we had stepped into a gentlemen's baths in Victorian London. Perhaps a dozen locals sat around chatting with their feet in the dubious-looking brown water, laughing and joking with each other. They greeted us warmly as if expecting us – news of our arrival in town had no doubt spread. We began with a fiercely hot sauna, sweating away all the grime of the last week's cycling. Afterwards Jamie and I jumped in the pool to swim a few lengths, but the locals were aghast, and we soon realised why. Very few of them could swim. It simply wasn't something they did routinely. A group of three young lads signalled to us that they wanted to learn and we spent an enjoyable half-hour trying to coax them to do a width, while Dickie and Nic amused themselves trying to outlast each other in the freezing plunge pool.

As we prepared to leave, a very sick young man arrived, so hunched and skeletal that he needed support to reach the edge of the pool. It was a touching sight as those around him leaped to their feet and assisted him with enormous tenderness. Yet again we were witnessing another facet of this complex country. The more I saw of Iran and its people, the more conflicting ideals seemed to emerge, but here we were witnessing true community spirit, a glimpse into a world that had until now remained hidden. The dress code of the female population in particular had only served to exclude us, but later the girls told us their experience was every bit as rewarding. Away from their men folk, the Iranian women were able to swim and relax freely, and had no hesitation in talking to Pauline and Ro. They failed to understand how the girls had secured permission from their husbands to embark on such a dangerous journey – and, much to their dismay, with unmarried men.

Back at base we ate the same meal yet again. The repetition was starting to wear thin but I forced down the chewy rice and gristly kebabs knowing there was nothing else on offer. We longed for the traditional *sabzi* we had eaten at our first meal. While a day off had been useful, even enjoyable, Sarah had improved only slightly and still had eaten nothing. After dinner we stayed in the restaurant where it seemed to be warmest. Ice was already forming on the insides of the windows and another guest explained with some pride that Bostanabad was the 'coldest town in Iran'. Although warm in bed, I had trouble sleeping, worrying about just how far we were falling behind. The lack of exercise hadn't helped, as by now we had grown used to falling into bed exhausted. It seemed unlikely that we would move again the following morning. As it turned out, it was just as well.

I woke to the smell of smoke and shouts outside. Scraping the sheet ice off the inside of the window I was met with a bizarre sight. Long lines of parked trucks were blocking the road, some with fires burning under the engines. The scene was like the aftermath of a medieval battle – black smoke, clouds of steam and huddles of men wrapped in blankets against the cold. I woke the others and we went down to have some breakfast. The owner scurried in and out of the restaurant with buckets of steaming water and it was some time before he served us. He tried to explain all the excitement.

'Night time . . . very, very cold. Twenty-nine!' he indicated that it had indeed plummeted to minus twenty-nine by pointing at the floor furiously. After breakfast we wrapped up warm and ventured outside. The sharpness of the cold stung our faces and took our breath away in huge steamy clouds. The lorry drivers had lit fires to try and thaw out their engines and presumably stop the oil from freezing. It was a disordered scene, but as we walked around we were greeted with friendly shouts and offers to come and warm our hands. Rather reluctantly we retreated back to the hotel and went to have a look at Martha. We had parked her behind the building and unfortunately down a steep ramp. The result was predictable and one turn of the key confirmed our suspicions with a morbid click. Absolutely nothing. It was no surprise, it had now been very cold for two nights and yesterday we hadn't moved. We really needed to get Martha out of the car park and up into the weak sunshine where the warmth might help a little. We heaved unsuccessfully for twenty minutes to push her up the ramp and only when we recruited a few locals did we finally make it.

Bostanabad was not short of mechanics, but they were all doing good trade that morning. When we did get hold of one he tried the key, unsuccessfully, the engine oil having turned to thick sludge in the conditions. He then calmly lit a gas burner, placed it under the sump of the engine, and assured us he would be back later. Worse was to come. As I put the gearbox back into neutral, the entire gearstick came off in my hand, the metal joint shearing at the base. It seemed the cold was finally getting the better of Martha and we were paying the price for our bargain Jordanian deal.

Jamie and I went to a local hardware store with the offending metal joint and after much rummaging on the rows of shelves behind, the owner produced a used, but almost identical piece. Feeling pleased with ourselves, we had it fitted before our mechanic even returned and he was none the wiser. Dickie was impressed and thought the gearstick felt a lot firmer than it had done previously. With the oil finally returned to normal she started after a short push, belching thick clouds of black diesel into our faces. Much relieved, Dickie and Nic decided to take her for a drive to get her warmed up properly and recharge the battery. There was certainly no rush. Although it was nearly midday, Sarah had just thrown up again after trying to eat something. It was obvious we were going to be here another day and realistically we also needed the conditions to improve. At these temperatures cycling could easily result in frostbite and we had to be cautious. Instead, Dickie and I spent a dull but useful afternoon going over the finances, which were now looking much healthier than they had in Turkey.

'Dickie, are you sure about this amount here?' I queried, pointing at a 10,000 rials bill for fuel. 'Absolutely,' replied Dickie. 'I couldn't believe it myself. That's about fifty pence to fill a van with diesel. Not bad!'

It was indeed a bargain and gave me a bright idea to stop Martha freezing again. 'I've got it! Why don't we leave the van running all night to keep it warm? It may use half a tank but at these prices what have we got to lose?' It wasn't the most environmentally friendly solution, but it would avoid a repeat performance of the morning. The van was behind gates again in the car park so at least it wasn't going to get pinched. As long as it didn't run out of fuel it would be warm and ready to go first thing.

The plan worked well and in the meantime Sarah was making a shaky recovery. She put a brave face on things, but by the following morning all she had eaten in two days was a piece of toast and Marmite. We decided to call a halt for a third day, reassured at least that she was on the mend. Privately I knew if she was not ready the following day we would have no choice but to press on. We had now done only three days' cycling in the six days we had spent in Iran and the clock was ticking. If she could get some more food inside her, she would hopefully have the strength to press on. Needless to say, the others were growing frustrated but there was little point in putting any pressure on Sarah. She knew as well as any of us that we were up against a deadline. She simply had to get well in her own time.

The next day we were up early, eager to get back on the bikes. Sarah was a lot better, but quite clearly nervous whether she would be able to keep up. Conditions had also taken a turn for the better, with the weak sun already warming the freezing road. Traffic was non-existent while we climbed very gently for the first leg, cresting a small pass about thirty kilometres outside town. Then we were on one of the longest downhill stretches I had ever encountered, almost seventy kilometres of sheer delight, following the path of a river through a beautiful landscape of snow-covered hills. Mount Sahand – according to our map nearly 4,000 metres high – dominated the view to the south. The gradient was not steep enough to allow us to freewheel but the cycling was almost effortless as we lost height ever so gradually.

We stayed in the compact little town of Miyaneh that night and found our cheapest accommodation yet, at only a pound a head. It was on the top floor of a rickety and fragile building, and although clean, the plaster on all four walls was heavily cracked. This would have been of little concern, except that the town had hit the headlines only three months earlier after a medium-sized earthquake. It was a restless night with bad dreams of toppling buildings and thoughts of being buried alive.

Outside our hotel the following morning sat an old man on a small stool, wrapped in a thick sheepskin coat which almost enveloped him. I felt for him, as it was bitterly cold. His woollen hat and each glove were all different colours and his feet were placed on a tiny sheepskin rug to protect them from the chill. He clutched a wooden walking stick in his bony hand and I thought at first he was begging. He stared silently at the ground ahead of him, lost in thought, before raising his head and smiling kindly at us. As we departed, the hotel owner brought him a steaming cup of black coffee and he clasped it tightly between his hands.

The sun warmed us when we escaped the shade of the narrow streets, and thanks to our lower altitude the snow was also disappearing. The highway followed an open gorge, hemmed in on both sides by steep rocky hillsides. It was quick going and thankfully the hard shoulder offered us some safety from the huge trucks that roared past us, blaring their horns in warning. We chickened out of cycling through a two-kilometre road tunnel.

The hard shoulder had all but disappeared and there was barely room for lorries to pass. Instead we followed the old road that wound around the hillside, which was wonderfully free of traffic. It followed the same course as the river and must have been in use until the tunnel was built as a short cut. The waters below us were fast flowing and choked with rafts of ice being swept along in the current. The weather was more like the ideal conditions in Syria three weeks earlier, and while Ro drove, we tempted Dickie on to one of the spare bikes for the afternoon.

Still twenty kilometres short of Zanjan, our destination for the night, things took a turn for the worse. A stiff headwind sprung up and our speed was instantly halved. It was too much for Sarah, who had put on a brave face all day. The effort to battle into the wind was immense and she was already running on empty. I could see she was on the verge of collapse. We stopped for a tea break next to an old ruined house, and I checked around, finding below and hidden from the road a perfect campsite. I could tell immediately that Nic was frustrated and he called me to one side.

'Look, Dom, I just think we should press on, we could be there in an hour. Sarah could climb in the van if necessary. If she wants to ride it tomorrow we could drive her back to this point.' Nic's plan had its merits but I also thought it would be discouraging for Sarah to get in the van and then repeat the section on her own. I valued his judgement enormously but for the first time we had to disagree. I was relieved that Sarah had cycled as far as she had, her strength was returning, and at least now lack of food not illness was the problem.

Sarah had been on the point of fainting when we stopped, but with her appetite returned she looked much stronger after a brew. Being so close to town, Dickie and Ro decided to do a quick shop, and while they were gone we squeezed in a game of volleyball, employing an old football and the washing line from Martha. An hour later they were back with mountains of carrots, onions and, best of all, tins of fruit. Our favourite dessert was any form of crumble, which tasted delicious from the Remoska cooker. We knew Sarah was on the mend when, much to our relief, she came back for seconds.

It was a delight to be camping again and we settled back into the old routine easily enough. The advantage of camping was the view. Across from the tent was a series of low striated ridges and in the distance a snow-capped horizon. In the setting sun they caught the light perfectly against the backdrop of a leaden sky. There seemed to be a storm on the way and sure enough it was a restless night as the tent was battered relentlessly by the wind.

The storm had if anything increased by the morning and packing away the tent was a real struggle. Typically the wind was in the wrong direction and we knew we were in for a difficult day ahead. Just an hour into the ride it began to snow again. It knocked our morale, just when we had thought the worst of the conditions were behind us. Out of desperation, we took shelter briefly in a concrete underpass beneath the road, but were soon shivering miserably. There was nothing for it but to press on through the conditions. For me the problem was really my feet, as my neoprene overshoes had long since expired. My cycling shoes in turn leaked badly and then the slushy water would freeze on the shoe itself. We longed for the powdery snow conditions of Turkey, where at least we had stayed dry. This was pure wet cold, simply the worst for sapping both energy and morale. We spoke little during the day, each of us wrapped against the cold and privately battling the conditions. We stopped in an unpromising-looking town, hungry and desperate for some warmth. We sheepishly entered a small café, dripping slush and leaving black oily footprints over the floor. The owner was unfazed and happily mopped up after us whenever we moved.

Inspection of the map revealed the next town to be Soltaniyeh, still some forty kilometres away and, according to our guidebook, famous for its enormous domed mausoleum. It seemed like a realistic and interesting target, despite being a few kilometres off the main road. We laboured for another unhappy hour before a weak sun put in an appearance. The bitter cold remained but the conditions were definitely easing and we began to dry out a little. Having agreed to call a halt at the turn-off for the town, I pulled up next to Jamie and Nic only for the wheels of the bike to slip from under me. With my feet still clipped into the pedals I went crashing to the ground. Jamie was far quicker with the camera than coming to my aid and they both enjoyed a good laugh at my expense. I had been ribbing them for weeks each time they had a mishap, and until now I had been the only member of the team not to have fallen, so they could barely contain their delight.

The girls joined us and with my pride dented we pressed on to the south, the dome of the mausoleum already dominating the skyline ahead. The wind dropped for the last few minutes of the ride, but so too did the temperature. It was an eerie, even ominous atmosphere, the landscape blanketed with snow and with no traffic at all, just an icy wintry stillness. This mausoleum had stood for the best part of 800 years and we were witnessing exactly what thousands of others had seen over the centuries.

The town of Soltaniyeh itself was tiny and consisted of just a few streets around the main site. We received a warm welcome in a small teashop and the owner ran off to investigate when we enquired about somewhere to stay. It appeared that tourists were rare despite the town's status as a World Heritage Site. Apparently the interior of the dome was being renovated and the painstaking work of restoring the decorative tiles would take years. When the owner returned, it was with some family members who continued to gawp at us as we made feeble attempts at conversation. We were all tired, very cold and urgently needed somewhere to get warm and changed.

After an hour had passed the constant assurances of 'no problem' were wearing a little thin. We took the initiative and got up as if to leave and get back on the road. They scurried into action and a small army escorted us along the street to the outside of a small shop. I felt guilty when I realised the cause for the delay. The shop was empty and being renovated. A couple of men were working hard, sweeping and cleaning, making it ready for us to use. They seemed concerned that it would be adequate for us, but we quickly reassured them that it was just perfect. In these situations we had to unpack for any spectators to realise just how comfortable we could make ourselves. They were completely unfamiliar with items like our self-inflating mats, which always drew admiring glances. Similarly with our sleeping bags and the cooker, we had the ability to be completely self-contained anywhere we stayed. One thing we did try to hide were the laptops, to avoid flaunting our means unnecessarily; also, it always resulted in having to go through hundreds of photos that our hospitable hosts wanted to see. On this occasion it was Jamie's turn to send pictures to the website, but it was dark before he retreated to the park opposite to upload through the satellite link. It was extremely cold and it could take the best part of twenty minutes for the connection to be made, so I went to give him some moral support. We hid behind a park bench, knee-deep in snow, and kept a lookout. Once the process had started it was difficult to stop and hide the equipment if anyone came along, but sure enough the shop owner's inquisitive son found us. Our efforts to be secretive were wasted on him, all the more so as he spoke excellent English.

'What is it you are doing?' he asked, looking over behind the bench.

'Oh nothing really. We'll come inside I think, it's too cold.' I did my best to sound bored.

'Ah, I see you are uploading your website via satellite, is that correct? What software will you be using? Is that a USB or fire wire connection?'

Back in the shop we had plugged in a small heater. The atmosphere was now thick with steam from our drying clothes and the smell of curry. Dickie was cooking for the first time and it promised to be delicious, but unfortunately like everything he did, it was taking a while. It was now nine o'clock and we hadn't eaten for eight hours. Nic had lost the will to live. He always went quiet when hungry and curled up on his mat in the foetal position. Needing something to do, he had already been to the barber's shop next door and had his head shaved all but completely. When Dickie finally produced his masterpiece it was worth the wait. An okra curry, cooked with local spices and mountains of rice, hit the spot after a wet, cold day. Exhausted and with full stomachs we all slept like kings that night.

We were relieved to see that the skies were clear in the morning, but the sun was not yet up and the cold was piercing. We had put the bikes under shelter overnight but they had frozen solid. Both front and rear derailleur gears refused to budge, cemented in a layer of thick ice. We used the cooker to heat pans of boiling water, which we then dribbled over the working parts, slowly coaxing them back to life. It delayed our departure by a good hour but even then, by the time we reached the main road, the derailleurs were already freezing up again. The girls looked on in dismay as us boys dropped the bikes, stood in a regimented line and urinated over the chains. Within seconds the parts sprang back to life amid clouds of acrid steam. Then the sun came out and with a breath of tailwind we seized our chance, racing through the morning and covering eighty kilometres in less than three hours. The only hiccup came when a police car pulled up next to me and frantically indicated back along the road.

'Hello, hello. Bicycle, problem, big problem.' My heart sank. This was the moment we had all been dreading – someone had injured themselves coming off the bike. I thanked them and returned down the road, soon realising the benefits of the tailwind we had enjoyed all morning. I was now battling against it, cursing and worried sick about what could have happened. It was eight kilometres before I caught site of Martha and, next to her, with bikes on the ground, Sarah and Pauline. They were just preparing to leave as I arrived.

'What's the problem?' I gasped hurriedly. 'Are you OK?'

Pauline glanced up. 'Oh we're fine, just a puncture, then we thought we might as well have a brew.' They climbed on to their bikes and headed off as I recovered my breath. I wasn't sure whether to be angry or relieved.

* * *

'Right. I know you all thought the shop was a bit different last night. Well, wait for this one. Tonight we're staying in a bank!'

It was indeed a bank, about two kilometres outside the small town of Shal, and complete with a huge foyer and several rooms off the back. It seemed to be disused, or at least mothballed. Keen to make some cash on the side, the surly caretaker in residence offered us a room, far larger than the previous night and even carpeted. We used the foyer to give the bikes some much-needed attention. Salt from the road had caked all the parts in crusty grime. Both Nic and I had also broken more spokes. Thankfully they were on the side that we could more easily mend, but it was clear the bikes had taken some punishment over the previous days. After covering 140 kilometres, we slept soundly knowing that we were starting to close the gap.

The following day we continued to lose altitude, albeit gently. The traffic was quiet, but occasionally we were passed by massive industrial loads that swamped the entire road. Usually they had a lead car driving ahead, lights flashing and an assistant in the back, madly waving a flag from the side window. At least it gave us a modicum of warning, but as they took up the hard shoulder, we had little choice but to get off the road completely. For hours we crossed a wide plain, scattered with the ancient remains of small volcanic cones, an ancient lava field, still windswept and desolate. Dickie, who was back on the bike for some training, described the landscape perfectly as monochrome, and the whole day was indeed devoid of colour. Our last ten kilometres into the city of Saveh was downhill and we sped along the straight road, even overtaking cars and startled drivers in our quest for food and a bed for the night. A good hotel beckoned after several nights roughing it, but we were out of luck.

It was exam time. Students from the surrounding area had come to the city to sit their papers and we were assured that every hotel would be full to the brim. Not to be put off, Dickie and I resorted to hiring a local taxi and asking the driver to find us somewhere. The technique had worked in the past and was our preferred option in a city where we didn't know our way around. It was a fruitless exercise, barring one hotel that wanted 100 dollars a night. After an hour the driver sensed our desperation and turned to us. 'Camping? Yes?'

'We can camp? Here in the city? Yes please . . .!' We weren't quite sure what he had in mind, but a few minutes later we met the others outside a gated complex of small buildings, barely a couple of minutes from where we had first started.

He jumped out and signalled to us with his palm down to the ground. 'Wait, please, wait.' He clearly knew the night watchman and they embarked on a long-winded discussion. When he returned it was with mixed news.

'No problem, no problem, sleeping here, yes. But for police passports.' He pointed at the taxi, and then back at Dickie. We took from this that Dickie was to go to the police station and register. Frustratingly, the nervous caretaker would not let us pass in the meantime. Instead we collected the bikes, which we had left nearby and waited. It was now eight o'clock and it had taken over two hours just to find somewhere to sleep.

'We have some new friends,' said Dickie from the taxi window when he turned up an hour later, trying to inject some enthusiasm. Even he looked worn out from negotiation.

'Oh my God, you must be joking,' muttered Jamie under his breath. Nic just sat with his head in his hands, as I too realised our chances of eating soon were dwindling.

'This is the Chief of Police and his wife Tamirah.' We shook hands politely while Tamirah explained that she was an English teacher, before introducing her husband and two young daughters. It was a relief to have someone to translate and I hoped we could be through in a couple of minutes. She exchanged conversation with her husband, the police officer, before turning to us.

'We hope very much that your group will come and eat with us this evening.' It was a generous offer but, feeling exhausted, I tried to find the words to decline politely.

Pauline, as ever, was there before me and responded enthusiastically. 'Fantastic, that sounds great – a traditional Iranian meal. We can talk girls' stuff!'

Leaving the bikes, we climbed into the convoy of vehicles, now including Martha, and made our way to a local restaurant. I was relieved we weren't visiting their home as leaving would have been all the more difficult and I just felt too tired for conversation with strangers. At least the boys shared my lack of enthusiasm, unlike the girls who had been waiting for this opportunity. They were always far better than us in social situations and were anxious to know what life was really like for an Iranian woman.

Pauline, of course, led the way with Tamirah. 'Now look – what about all this get-up?' she pointed at her own *hijab*. 'It must get you down sometimes – be honest. Don't you want to just rip it off!'

'Not at all. I am proud to wear it. I would feel . . . how do you say . . . naked . . . if I went out without it. Would you go outside naked in your country?' she laughed.

'Do you remove it at home?' Sarah asked.

'Certainly, yes. With my husband and my family, it is no problem. But if we have guests I must wear it.'

Ro pointed at Tamirah's girls, Naheed and Yasmin. They were impeccably polite and slightly in awe of meeting us strangers. 'At what age must your daughters wear a scarf?' she asked.

'Only when they reach seven years,' she explained, smiling at Naheed. 'She feels very grown up now, as she is eight years old.' Tamirah smiled fondly at them both. It was obvious they were a very close family. Yasmin was only four so had no need to wear a scarf in public, but her elder sister seemed proud of her *hijab*. Pauline was also curious to know how the opposite sexes met each other in the first place. There were no bars, or much in the way of nightlife, and with limited public entertainment it must make it awkward to meet a potential partner.

'How did you meet your husband?' Pauline enquired.

Tamirah grew increasingly shy and I wondered if we were being too intrusive. She patiently explained that their families already knew each other and had introduced them both.

'Was it an arranged marriage?' asked Pauline.

At this Tamirah seemed quite taken aback, even shocked. 'No, No. We don't do that in Iran. My family wanted me to choose whoever I wanted.'

While the girls did all the talking, we enjoyed listening and ate as much as we could. It had been a pleasant evening and certainly an informative one. The family had been welcoming and like everyone else in Iran extremely generous. We paid for the meal to indicate our thanks before returning to the gate and our bicycles. Tamirah explained that it was an empty police barracks, and her husband had said we were welcome to stay, for which there would be no charge. We posed for pictures before we retreated to our room. Only in the morning did we find that Tamirah and her daughters had stayed for another hour chatting in the girls' room. As an English graduate it was a rare opportunity for her to meet and talk to native speakers.

The previous two days had been very hard and the morning saw us reluctant to get moving. At least better weather conditions beckoned. Our hosts came to wave us off and we swiftly made our way out of Saveh in the bright sunshine. There was a chill in the air but nothing more. For the first time in a couple of weeks we were able to take our gloves off and even dispense with a layer. It was an enormous psychological boost. We flew through the first leg before facing a fifteen-kilometre ascent. At least the steady gradient made it easy to find a rhythm, while in every direction the view was breathtaking. We were still in an agricultural area and on both sides the wide cultivated valley gave way in the distance to steep mountains blanketed in snow. We stopped at the crest of the hill to gaze back at the huge distance we had travelled. Now we were truly heading south and with it we prayed that the cold weather was finally behind us. It was good to feel a bit of warmth again and the hill had exercised some unfamiliar muscles.

It was three o'clock before Martha caught us up. Dickie and Ro explained they had again been delayed by shopping for supplies, but that was the least of their worries, as Martha now appeared to be overheating. Sure enough we could hear the cooling system bubbling away and coolant was dripping from one of the hoses. This is all we need, I thought – just as we're starting to make progress. We decided they might as well press ahead, albeit slowly, to Delijan, our next stop about forty kilometres away. They had plenty of water so could easily keep her topped up en route. In the event we arrived not too far behind them.

The prognosis was not good. It seemed that the head gasket had gone, which I knew was a long and expensive job to fix. Furthermore, the garage in town couldn't replace it. It was a foreign van, which didn't help matters, as parts in Iran would be in short supply. Our best option was to get to Esfahan, our destination in a couple of days' time. A large city increased our chances of finding a well-equipped garage to carry out the repairs. It was a low point for us all. The trip was challenging enough without an extra difficulty like this. With the weather improving and Sarah's recovery, we had all turned a corner, but now we had a major problem on our hands and potentially more wasted days. At least the garage had a tow truck on which they could easily carry Martha to Esfahan the following day. Our plan then was for Dickie and Ro to travel ahead while the cyclists continued independently for two days. We packed rucksacks and sleeping bags, again preparing to fend for ourselves, as we had in Turkey. Hopefully by the time we arrived in Esfahan Martha would be fixed and ready to go. With the promise of a day off in the city there was still some flexibility for any delay.

We left Delijan under a darkened and threatening sky. A not-so-brief stop at the bank allowed us to change some more dollars. It wasn't a process they were used to and it took at least half an hour. For some reason they would accept only dollar bills printed after 1998, which required some major sifting on our part. No sooner had we left town than the storm arrived. We were battered with freezing rain and within minutes were thoroughly soaked. Now that we had climbed higher, the hard shoulder was again covered in snow, forcing us out into the middle of the road. The trucks made no effort to slow down in the poor visibility and sped past us with mere inches to spare. The conditions were truly miserable and I cursed myself for thinking that we had escaped the winter conditions. We stopped after the first leg and took shelter in a ruined house. We sat amongst the litter and broken glass, trying to escape the wind but there was no point resting. What little warmth we generated by cycling just ebbed away. Back on the bike my feet were icy cold and every passing lorry drenched us in the freezing slush. The only respite emerged after the second leg, with a small truck stop set back from the road. The room was tiny but in the centre stood an ancient wood-burning stove, belching out heat. The proprietor welcomed us, oblivious to our clothes dripping with mud and oily grime. A couple of lorry drivers stared open-mouthed, clearly incredulous that anyone would want to come to their country and cycle through these conditions.

We requisitioned the stove and soon had it covered with gloves, hats and, in Sarah's case, even socks. The rain and sleet continued to lash against the windows, the wind even blowing the door open on occasion. Unprompted, the owner brought us a huge bowl of warm pitta bread and a pot of black tea. We were expecting the usual kebabs, but instead we were served traditional *abgusht*. The steaming mix of lamb and vegetables was served in earthenware pots, together with a pestle. We hadn't seen this arrangement since our very first meal in Iran two weeks earlier and had grown used to carrying our own spoons, not only to make life easier, but in a bid to stop us getting ill again. The truck driver adjacent to us tutted in disgust and leaped to his feet. Lots of frantic miming ensued as he explained the correct process to us with his own meal. The bread was clearly needed to soak up the soup or juice on the surface. This left a dense mass of meat and vegetables in the pot. Our friend then grabbed his pestle and furiously ground away at the remaining mix, tilting it towards us so we could see the unappetising mush. He scooped this up with yet more bread, nodding eagerly to himself to demonstrate his satisfaction. We had seen the process before and actually preferred it just as it was.

When the storm eased it was replaced by freezing temperatures, but at least the source of our misery, the driving sleet, had disappeared. By cycling hard we kept warm, stopping only briefly to join up and check everyone was fine. We continued to ascend and a check of our altimeters indicated that we were now back at 2,000 metres. Our extended lunch stop meant that we arrived in the town of Meymeh soon after dark and we followed Pauline straight into another café with an enormous oil-fired heater. One look at her explained why she had pulled up so abruptly. She was literally blue with cold. Her top lip appeared frozen solid and she made even less sense than usual, trying to mutter between uncontrollable shivers.

We didn't go far that night and bedded down in an adjacent room. With no van to pack in the morning we were away sharply, our ascent the previous day paying dividends as we cruised a gentle downhill in fair conditions. The mountains bordering the road grew increasingly jagged and impressive as we approached the city. Just a few kilometres to our left and west of our position lay the town of Natanz. Here, housed deep underground, was the home of Iran's nuclear enrichment facility. Discussion of this was all over the news and the BBC website, with the West applying pressure on Iran to allow inspections. The Iranians were countering with the defence that all their nuclear facilities had been constructed with the sole aim of providing energy.

I knew Esfahan itself was at the heart of this nuclear programme. Rumour had it that huge investments were being made to construct a network of tunnels beneath the city to house the facilities. A cynic would point out that the government had selected a populated and culturally sensitive area on purpose. Deeply laid tunnels would require nothing less than a nuclear strike to destroy them – an unimaginable step against one of the world's most ancient cities, with a population of over a million. A city visited by the French poet Renier in the sixteenth century, who, overawed by its magnificence, dubbed it simply, 'the city that is half the world'.

Chapter 7

A City of Half the World – Iran

Esfahan was for centuries one of the most populated cities in the world, a major crossroads for traders passing from north to south and east to west. As the ancient capital of Persia it prospered steadily, but economic decline began during the eighteenth century when goods traded to the east started to be transported by ship. Nevertheless the city's rich heritage still endures today, most notably in the stunning examples of Islamic architecture. Even in the approaches to the city you can sense the gravitas of this special place, the immense cultural wealth clear in the wide boulevards, mosques and stone bridges. The mix of East and West is everywhere. For the first time, we saw cycle paths and even litter bins. Cafés and mobile phone shops were again in abundance and for once we were spoilt for a choice of hotels. We checked in at one recommended to us, the simple rooms centred on a small paved courtyard, ideal for storing and servicing the bikes.

Anxious to explore the sites, we headed straight back out and barely ten minutes later emerged through an ornate stone gateway into the Imam Square. The sheer size was breathtaking and caught me unawares. At over 500 metres in length, centuries ago the square had seen polo played in its confines, watched by the Shahs of the time; the marble goalposts still stood at each end. On all sides, the majestic buildings were serene, beautifully proportioned, and to the south the view was dominated by the Imam mosque, the elegant dome covered in exquisite blue painted tiles. From the enormous entrance portal, over thirty metres high, we could see through to the inner courtyard, angled subtly away from the entrance and towards Mecca.

Further along the western boundary of the square lay the Ali Qapu Palace. This was home to Shah Abbas the Great, the instigator of the Imam, and designed to be the 'jewel in the crown' of his new capital. The palace has an elevated terrace, affording views high across the square. Opposite and to the east is the Sheikh Lotfollah mosque. Considered by many to be the most beautiful in Iran, it was smaller and at first sight less ornate than the larger Imam. Appearances were deceptive, though. The softer, cream-coloured dome changed hue at every glance, catching the changing light as the sun fell lower in the sky.

It was a wonderful, even magical, place to just walk around and soak up the atmosphere. Later we sat by the fountains in the centre of the square as the daylight began to fade and floodlights illuminated the architecture around us. A few Iranian students strolling by stopped to ask us where we were from. Their English was good and they were visibly thrilled that we had come to visit their city. There were no other tourists in evidence, or even any of the trappings that so often accompany these great places. It felt as though one of the world's best-kept secrets had been opened for our private viewing. Feeling tired, and more than a little humbled, we headed back to the hotel relaxed and content.

Dickie and Ro soon brought us down to earth with news about Martha. She did indeed require a new head gasket, but now matters were even more complicated. There were no parts in Iran for our kind of van. That meant we could either order one from another country, at huge expense, or have one made here. Dickie, as always, appeared to have landed on his feet. After getting a tow into Esfahan, he had been directed by a local shopkeeper to a garage. They offered to repair the van and try to make the part – but all for free. I was usually sceptical of this kind of gesture, but it was proving typical of the generosity we had received in Iran. All being well it would be ready the following day, and in plenty of time for us to get back on the road.

The next morning we enjoyed a bit of a lie-in before getting down to a long list of jobs. The mountain phase of the expedition was also starting to become an issue, and I found myself having to liaise constantly with our agent in Kathmandu, who in turn was dealing with arrangements for the mountain and our permits. Of course, eight members of the climbing party were still in the UK, and with their departure looming they were bombarding me for details about the climb. Mostly I dealt with Seb, who was acting as coordinator of the remaining climbers back home. All were in good health, he assured me, and together they were beginning to sort their kit for the mountain, now just two months away. For us it seemed very premature to focus on the mountain as we were not yet halfway through the ride and there was still so much that could go wrong. I realised with some irritation that I hadn't even started one of the dozen reading books I had brought with me for the journey.

That afternoon we gave ourselves some space and decided to do our own thing. It was nice to cruise around on the bike with no pressure and no particular destination. Esfahan was a perfect city for cycling. The traffic was still busy but the roads were wide enough to feel safe. I headed due south down the Chahar Bagh, the street on which we were staying. The wide tree-lined cycle way ran straight for a couple of kilometres before reaching the river. Here the Si-o-Se crossing spanned the river in a series of thirty-three elegant arches. It seemed to be part bridge and part dam, holding the river water back before it cascaded across in a broad weir. The upper walkway was crowded with locals strolling in the afternoon sun between the open arches, while beneath were a host of smoky tea-houses and crowded stalls. I crossed to the far side of the river and kept cycling, looking for the Golestan e Shohoda, the cemetery for those who had lost their lives in the Iran–Iraq war. I had no idea why I wanted to see it or what I expected to find, but its mention in the guidebook had caught my attention. When I arrived, it was to discover that the entrance was being guarded by soldiers. I immediately felt out of place and had no business going inside, but there was little need. From where I was I could see the endless rows of headstones, on each a metal frame supporting a sad black and white photograph of the deceased. During the war, information had always been scarce with none of the frontline reporting we take for granted today. It was hard to believe the conflict had occurred barely twenty years ago, lasting eight long years from 1980 to 1988, during which time half a million men lost their lives on each side. One cannot escape the irony that the West supported Saddam Hussein and Iraq throughout, such was the American animosity towards Iran. History records it as a particularly brutal and vicious conflict, with gas and trench warfare used widely for the first time since the First World War. Iranian forces were organised on two levels. The more professional soldiers were known as the Revolutionary Guard, but the vast bulk of forces, or foot soldiers, were the Basij. The latter, including many child soldiers, suffered terrible casualties, pushed into battle with the promise of martyrdom. No one we talked to ever mentioned the war but many of the people we had met must have played their part.

I returned to some frustrating news back at the hotel. Martha had been fixed but a test drive had revealed further problems with the gearbox. We couldn't afford to be delayed, but were now committed to getting her back on the road. In any other country hiring a van and driver might have been an option but this facility wasn't readily available in Iran. There was also the fact that we had already invested a considerable amount of our overland budget buying her in the first place, so we really had to try and get our money's worth, at least until we were much closer to our destination. Dickie was doing wonders going back and forth between the garage and the hotel. He had also been pressed upon to visit the garage owner's house where, much to his surprise, he had even been offered wine with his meal and a bed for the night. He was experiencing a very different Iran to the one he had expected.

We decided to delay our departure the following morning, hoping that good news about the repairs was imminent. I was keen for us all to set off together again but that was starting to look like wishful thinking. While the morning slipped away, matters were soon taken out of our hands. It transpired that our hotel owner, ever the entrepreneur, had rung an Iranian TV station to tell them of our journey. We were descended upon, unannounced, by a film crew in the courtyard, who quickly arranged us around a table. The main presenter was charming and spoke reasonable English, but it was obvious from the start that he had little interest in the aim of our journey. After having us introduce ourselves on camera he asked a number of questions.

'Please. How do you find the people of Iran? They are very good, no?'

'Yes – we've received an amazing welcome. The Iranian people are very generous,' said Sarah diplomatically. Our interviewer persisted.

'Can you tell me how they have been kind to you? What has happened?'

I was keen to redirect the interview as much as possible so tried to step in. 'We have received many offers of food and places to stay. This has helped us very much in our aim of cycling to Everest. We are trying to be the first to go from Jordan . . . .

'Yes, yes. I understand. But please tell me what kind of foods you have been given?'

The interview continued in the same vein and in relaxed mood we were happy to give them what they needed. After all, we had experienced incredible generosity. Their motives were interesting, though, and I detected a deeply entrenched paranoia of how they were perceived by the outside world, and of course the West in particular. Most Iranians will never have met anyone from the West, such is the scarcity of tourists. They were clearly flattered that we were here to visit and our very presence showed that we weren't all bad. But they needed more – to know what we really thought of them and how they, our hosts, compared to other countries. What would we say to our friends when we got home? What other countries had we visited? Were they as generous as the Iranian people? The psychology was almost childlike and smacked of deep insecurity.

Just when we thought we had finished, the producer announced they needed some footage of us riding. We had by now resigned ourselves to another rest day anyway, so were happy to oblige. They filmed us cycling along the street and back to the bridge I had crossed the previous day. It was clearly a major tourist backdrop, and we did at least half a dozen takes, passing by in perfect convoy. Later that afternoon, as we sat in the courtyard drinking tea and awaiting news of Martha, our interviewer returned, but this time without the attached camera crew. He seemed embarrassed and introduced himself to Dickie and Ro, who he hadn't met earlier. He had with him a large bag of gifts, which he solemnly handed out to each of us in turn.

'For your journey,' he said. 'Thank you, thank you, from the people of Iran.'

We each received an ornate-looking box of *gaz*, nougat-like sweets, an Esfahan speciality. They tasted absolutely foul – but then as Jamie reminded us, it's the thought that counts.

Dickie reappeared that evening with a very clean-looking and functioning Martha. He rightly looked very pleased with himself, as he had been incredibly patient over the last three days. Ro had also played her part, but had grown frustrated at being sidelined in any discussion. Even though many assumed they were a married couple, most dialogue was inevitably directed at Dickie. The call of 'Mr Richard, please come this way' was all too familiar. At border crossings and garages she was often left stranded and had to wait obediently while decisions were taken around her.

It took two hours to escape the suburban sprawl of Esfahan, and we passed miles of faceless shops and warehouses, all the while weaving between buses spewing filthy diesel fumes. It was with some relief that we emerged again on to a desert highway in glorious winter sunshine. Gone were the jagged mountains of a couple of days ago. Instead, only low-lying hills in the distance offered welcome respite from the dull view. We assumed that much of the heavy traffic we had previously encountered was moving between Esfahan and Tehran, the capital. Now that we were moving into the remote south of the country, we expected traffic and population to decrease.

We climbed steadily all morning on a gentle gradient, barely noticing the effort, a tribute to the design of the Iranian roads. Only in the afternoon did we begin to tire and we were still some thirty kilometres away from Na'in, our destination for the night. Right on cue, we crested a small pass and began a fantastic descent all the way into town, even picking up speed, 'surfing' behind lorries, before using the momentum to whizz past the slower trucks. It was a thrilling end to the day, but it had been a long one, and the temperature was again plummeting as we entered town. Enquiries led us to a mosque, adjacent to which was a pilgrims' rest-house. Our host led us down some steep steps as if heading underground, only to emerge into the corner of a beautiful enclosed courtyard, surrounded by rooms on two levels. Everything was whitewashed and spotlessly clean, the caretaker even making us remove our shoes before entering the room. There was no furnishing, just a thin mattresses unrolled on the floor, and in the far corner of the courtyard a small kitchen. It was fantastic. Dickie and Ro had only just caught us up and the news was utterly disheartening. They had stopped again several times from overheating.

'Martha' was rapidly becoming a dirty word. Jamie and Nic had always referred to her simply as the van or the wagon, and now their emotional detachment was looking wise in the light of recent events. Dickie too had simply had enough. He had left the garage in Esfahan with much ceremony, even presenting the staff with a framed picture of the mechanics together. They too had given us gifts to send us on our way and charged us nothing for the repairs. It was all very final, yet now Dickie saw no choice but to go back and ask them to start all over again. It was clear that the new gasket simply wasn't working. With typical good humour, he accepted this as the only course of action.

To compound matters it started to snow again. This time it fell silently in gentle flakes and without a breath of wind. In the centre of the square was a tall fir tree that was soon coated in a soft white blanket. It was a beautiful sight and like children we gazed entranced, this time feeling relaxed about the weather. We were now heading back into the desert and it was warm enough to melt any snow. It felt instead like the winter's parting gift, a blessing to speed us on our way after all the rough weather we had endured. Despite being a month after Christmas, it was the first time we had felt the least bit festive. It was Dickie that seized the moment. 'Anyone fancy a carol?' He had a great singing voice and without further ado broke into the first verse of 'Silent Night', capturing the mood perfectly.

Even though the snow lay two inches thick the following morning, there was no repeat of the conditions a week earlier. In the morning sun it soon began to melt. After some negotiation, we had managed to hire a local taxi to accompany us. The idea was that Ro would travel in the taxi with our essential gear, some food and bike spares. The taxi also meant that Ro could bring along a simplified 'kitchen'. It didn't take much to ensure we could be comfortable away from Martha for a few days.

There was only one guesthouse on the main street of Arkadan and I entered the lobby to encounter a strange sight. On a long wooden table lay a very fat man with a bushy moustache, flat on his back. I assumed he was the owner but I wasn't sure whether to disturb him, as he was fast asleep and snoring loudly. I coughed, intentionally knocking into a chair in a bid to rouse him. It was a good minute before he twitched a few times, began to stir and dragged himself off the table. He glanced in my direction, then, after a moment's hesitation and without a word, beckoned me to follow him. The rooms were nicely furnished and there was even a decent hot shower. As he slowly came alive, he turned out to be quite jovial and introduced himself as Mohammed. He seemed to have a genuine interest in what we were doing but babbled away in Farsi, oblivious to my lack of understanding. He let us use his garage to store the bikes in before showing us the large roof terrace, where we settled down to watch the sunset. It was certainly getting warmer and Mohammed assured us, through sign language, that last night's snow was very unusual this far south.

The town seemed oddly placed in the desert but only later did I read that this was the result of the *qanat* system of irrigation channels. This is no ordinary way of bringing water across the desert. The nearby hills provide an aquifer that is higher than the surrounding desert, but rather than pump water up to the ground and then across the desert plain, tunnels are used instead. These begin in the local town and are excavated at a gentle gradient towards the mountains and the source. They are engineering marvels, often running in excess of five kilometres underground and all dug by hand. Once made, though, they may last for centuries, and deliver a reliable source of water to the community, immune to evaporation and fluctuations in rainfall.

Ro's taxi driver and our escort for the day had returned to Na'in where he lived, and so we needed a new driver for the following morning. Mohammed had assured us it would be arranged for eight o'clock. I had my doubts, but when we emerged into the street after breakfast, we saw Mohammed himself looking very smug and giving a final polish to his saloon car. Furthermore he had brought his wife, a doctor, along for the journey. Ro's previous driver had not spoken a word in their eight hours together, but today she was to have no such luck. Language was no barrier to Mohammed, who was happy chatting away irrespective of who was listening. The scenery and conditions were again perfect, the wide hard shoulder also allowing us to ride in relative safety for once. After fifty kilometres we met the car and enjoyed our first picnic lunch since the Syrian desert – bread and juicy green olives – which Mohammed tucked into readily after we invited him to join us. Mohammed's contribution was a box of natural-looking sugar lumps. They tasted delicious but we watched as he filled half his cup with them before pouring some black tea over the top and returning our gaze with a toothless grin. We noticed later that he had left his wife sitting in the car, obediently awaiting his return.

The small town of Mehriz appeared with little warning, a token mix of garages and truck stops lining the main road. At first we thought we had stumbled into a riot or demonstration of some kind, as a crowd of perhaps 200 men were shouting furiously at something in their midst. My inclination was to cycle past, but as we drew closer the crowd seemed less threatening, so we dismounted from our bikes and moved to the edge of the throng. Ahead of us the men were gesticulating frantically and thrusting through the crowd with saucepans and buckets held aloft. In the centre of the mêlée were two enormous black cast-iron cauldrons, and the men in charge were ladling out some kind of soup or stew in huge dollops to whoever was closest. We must have arrived at peak time, as it couldn't be served quickly enough. It was all quite a spectacle, and within a few minutes we got close enough to have a look in the simmering pot, our interest rewarded with paper bowls full of the steaming sludge forced into our hands. The lurid green didn't make it look too appetising but it was delicious and filling all the same. Jamie tucked into several portions, seizing the opportunity to grab a few calories. We were told later that this was the traditional dish of *ash-e-jo* or barley soup, rich with dried fruits and pistachios.

Everywhere we turned we were met with smiles, even handshakes, and always the same greetings. 'Welcome. Welcome to Iran. Welcome to our country.'

We spent much of the evening in Mehriz lounging at one of the tables in a nearby restaurant. Many of the roadside cafés we visited had now resorted to plastic tables and chairs, but the more traditional places still maintained low, carpeted tables. The owner, Farid, had accosted us at the soup festival and insisted we stay in his tiny café. With no sign of hotels we had accepted readily and Mohammed had said a quick farewell after looking ill at ease in a strange town. As in any Iranian restaurant, the form was to remove your shoes before sitting cross-legged in a circular fashion to eat the meal, often served from a large central dish. It seemed to be perfectly acceptable to relax and lie down afterwards. For a group such as ours, it was a sociable style of eating that suited us very well. After supper we wrote diaries and sorted some pictures before retreating upstairs for the night. It was little more than an open mezzanine above the restaurant and no sooner had we settled down, than Farid stuck his head through the curtain, looking apologetic but also very agitated.

'Please, please. Passports. Hurry, police!'

I gathered our seven passports together and suggested the others stay upstairs. Sitting with legs crossed and looking regal in the centre of the restaurant was a single bearded man. He had an authoritative air and wasn't smiling. All the other staff had retreated into the corner, clearly intimidated. He certainly didn't appear to be a policeman and wore no uniform. I stood opposite him, as he avoided eye contact, merely clicking his fingers in my direction. I handed over the passports and he began to deftly flick through each one. He extracted a notebook and pen and laboriously copied the details from our visas. To date, none of the policemen we had met were actually able to read our passports, beyond the Iranian visa itself. This man was clearly a lot more educated but gave nothing away. After a few minutes I tried to lighten the situation in my simplest English.

'Is everything good . . . with the passports? OK?' I asked.

He barked such a quick reply, and without even looking up, that it startled me. 'What are you doing here in Iran, in this town? I want to know, what is your business?'

I was taken aback at his fluency. 'We are cycling across Iran. We are going to Bam and then on to Pakistan,' I explained. I guessed he had little interest in our journey so I wasn't going to spin the whole story. Farid plucked up his courage and stepped forward, visibly shaking. What followed was a couple of minutes of discussion in Farsi, and I only hoped an explanation that would help us. Farid at least knew we had been unable to find somewhere to sleep for the night and also knew we were cyclists. The policeman chose to ignore his protestations and for the first time stared at me intensely. He had beady eyes and a look of total disgust.

'I do not understand. Why do you stay in this place? With women? This house is for eating . . . you must not sleep here. This is no place for your women!' He waved his hand dismissively at the surroundings to indicate it was all beneath him. Now he was angry and I thought at best we would be thrown out. He turned on the owner and gave him some sort of reprimand, after which he gathered his papers, got up and left abruptly.

I couldn't quite believe that was the end of it and turned to Farid.

'We must leave?' I said pointing to myself, then at the door.

'No, no problem.' He repeatedly tutted in the direction of the departing man. 'Mullah police,' he explained and tapped his head to indicate that he was mad. With that, he and his sons fell about laughing and the atmosphere relaxed considerably.

After all the coming and going we were never destined to have a good night's sleep. Only later did we realise that our hosts would normally sleep in the room we now occupied. Displaced downstairs, they lay on the tables talking, joking and farting their way through the night. It was too much for Sarah, normally the most patient of our party, unflappable in most circumstances. By two in the morning she finally snapped, sitting bolt upright, struggling desperately to emerge from her sleeping bag.

'That's it – I've just about had enough!' she shouted. 'Can't they understand we need some sleep? I'm going to sort them and have some words!'

Between sniggers Nic and I dived to restrain her, grateful that at least we had a bed for the night. We were hardly in a position to vote with our feet and head down the road. Begrudgingly Sarah climbed back into bed.

As if the night hadn't been late enough, our hosts were up and singing loudly by six o'clock. It got us out of bed and on the road, albeit feeling the worse for wear. We dragged ourselves on to the bikes, hoping it would be our one and only night staying in a kebab house. Just as we were about to depart, Sarah yelled and lashed out at the man standing behind her. Our first thought was that she was still tetchy after the lack of sleep, and the man retreated pretty rapidly, defensively raising his hands.

'He slapped my arse!' yelled Sarah, pointing at him. We rounded on the character, who continued to back away, protesting his innocence. He had been hanging around the restaurant the previous evening and had clearly misjudged things. It was one of the pitfalls of staying in a place such as this: Iranian men are not used to being in such close proximity to other women and seeing how they behave. In that respect at least, the Mullah had been correct. Despite Sarah covering her head, it was still obvious that she was blonde and this only increased their curiosity. I had little sympathy for the man, who had not realised she would react so forcefully. We had embarrassed him in front of his friends and the point was made. By now Farid had emerged and was extremely apologetic. I felt sorry for him as he had tried to help us. After the visit of the Mullah, and now this, he was mortified. We thought it best just to get out of town and bid him a rapid farewell.

Conditions were beautiful and we sped through the desert, soaking up the warm sunshine. Again the terrain was flat and featureless and we all donned our music players to help the time pass. Barely an hour into the ride and the gentle cross-breeze turned into more of a gale. I fell into the slipstream of a passing petrol tanker but the only place to shelter was on its leeside and that meant cycling in the middle of the road. My speed topped fifty kilometres per hour as I stayed as close as I dared to the large rumbling wheels. When something came from the opposite direction I had to drop back behind and then pedal furiously to regain my spot after its passing. It was a dangerous game but it made progress more rapid and helped to break the monotony for an hour or so.

Our taxi system was working well, although we were now on our third driver after Mohammed had retreated home. It was actually a relief not to worry about Martha disappearing for hours on end. Nearing our destination, we took the chance to wander around a new mosque still under construction. The decoration and workmanship were stunning. Even more impressive, I thought, was that Iran still had the means and wherewithal to build new structures like this. We all agreed that none of us had seen a new church being built back home. After lunch the wind became our friend again with an abrupt change of direction, and we raced through the last thirty kilometres to arrive in the small town of Anar.

The following morning was properly hot for the first time. It seemed unbelievable that only four days earlier we had been setting off in the snow. The road was blissfully flat for once and we made headway quickly. The view ahead would have been monotonous but for the constant backdrop of jagged peaks, the Zagros mountains. Much of our route through Iran actually ran parallel to the mountains and consequently we encountered few steep ascents. After lunch we began to see signs for 'green gold', while passing orchards of short pruned trees. They reminded us of French vineyards and ran impressively for miles into the distance. Nic and Jamie were a font of knowledge, having dropped into a local school the previous evening. They explained smugly that Rafsanjan, our destination, was in fact the world's capital of pistachio production. We made a mental note to stock up on supplies.

We thought it best to stay somewhere obvious where Dickie might easily find us. Latest reports indicated that Martha was truly fixed but it was nearly ten o'clock by the time he arrived, looking shattered after a marathon drive. By now he had seen enough of Esfahan to last him a lifetime, but the generosity of his hosts had remained unconditional. Martha appeared to be working, having just covered 700 kilometres without overheating, which boded well for the onward journey. It was a relief to have the whole team together again and for once with no problems on the horizon.

Fired with renewed motivation, we decided to head for the city of Bam in a long two-day push. This would require back-to-back 100 mile days, but we were beginning to find that sort of distance routine. A light headwind was not a good start but we pressed on, eating up the miles steadily, the mountains on each side becoming increasingly sculpted and jagged with every passing mile. All had a light dusting of snow, but thankfully at a much higher altitude. Our lunch break was brisk, as we didn't want to linger too long. Whenever we had cycled this distance in the past we had always finished in the dark and we were anxious not to get caught out again. It was still winter, of course, and the light would begin to fade soon after five, and by six it would be pitch black. I was feeling on superb form, and raced through the last thirty kilometres as fast as I could in the gathering gloom. Even Nic was taken aback by my newfound speed and I waited on the outskirts of Mahan for the others to catch up, slightly regretting my haste. The sun had dropped and it was a full half-hour before everyone arrived, by which time I was shivering violently.

The road to Bam gave us all time to reflect. It was just over two years since the devastating earthquake there and we had no idea what kind of welcome we would receive. I wasn't alone in feeling some trepidation. Pauline confided in me at lunchtime just how nervous she felt. 'How are you supposed to react when you visit a city where half the population have died?' Sarah felt the same, but her concern was coupled with anticipation. As a geologist she had studied Iran extensively and here was a chance to see at first-hand the devastating aftermath of an earthquake. Nic and Jamie were also very quiet. Nic, I knew, was sensitive and any form of suffering distressed him. Jamie's mood was sullen but he seemed at ease with himself, displaying a maturity far beyond his years. I had to remember that he had worked a lot in Romania and Kenya with orphans and was perhaps more prepared than any of us.

The empty landscape suited our mood and as the light fell in the afternoon an ominous wind sprang up from nowhere and blasted across the road, heavy with dust and sand. For an hour it was a struggle to keep the bikes on the road at all. To the west, the sunlight reflected on the rocky hills, while above, the sky fell into a menacing leaden blue. Then the cross-wind turned as if intent on pushing us into the city and we flew along at an incredible speed.

Darkness was falling by the time we arrived and with no streetlights we got hopelessly lost. I had expected even more devastation but at first glance the town seemed prosperous and everyone was industrious. Only on closer inspection could you detect the true magnitude of what had happened. Almost every other building had been destroyed, piles of bricks and rubble were on every street corner, even lengths of twisted metal. Many shops operated not out of buildings, but from steel shipping containers, the end doors thrown open to welcome customers. Everywhere was a cacophony of traffic, the hiss of welding and the rumble of generators. Building was going on manically, even well into the night, and all around we were surrounded by rigid steel frames, ready to be dressed with bricks, designed presumably to replace the mud-built buildings responsible for the devastating loss of life. The roadsides were packed, even at this hour, coffee stalls and fruit sellers all competing for every inch of space. Only later did I appreciate that with so few buildings there was little choice but to move on to the street.

The earthquake had struck at 5.30 a.m. local time on 26 December 2003, an estimated 6.6 on the Richter scale. While this is not of enormous strength, and there have been much bigger quakes, it was sufficient to destroy some 70 per cent of the modern city. The weak clay bricks simply collapsed under the shock wave and many thousands were buried in their sleep. Of the population of about 80,000, it is estimated that at least half died and many more were injured or made homeless. I had expected a desolate and sullen town, a shadow of its former glory, and although this wasn't the case, there was no denying that behind the façade were stories of immense tragedy.

It took us an hour to find Akbar's famous hostel through the maze of streets, the only indicator being the name hastily painted on a cracked brick wall. Akbar himself greeted us warmly when we arrived. He was perhaps sixty years old, with a neatly trimmed grey beard, glasses and an easy smile. He beckoned us in. 'Please, please . . . relax, and be happy in my humble home.'

Akbar was a legendary figure in the town and had done much to coordinate relief efforts. One of the principal reasons for his influence was that, as a former teacher, his English was fluent and in the aftermath of the disaster he had given countless interviews to foreign news crews. He had retired some years earlier to run his guesthouse, interested in meeting travellers and helping them to enjoy the sights of the city. He had spent years establishing his business before it was destroyed, like so much else, on the night of the earthquake. Not only had some of his guests died that night, but also several members of his family. For several days they had no option but to sleep in the streets until help began to arrive.

Akbar's guesthouse was still a pale imitation of the original, but adjacent to his new home were a series of three prefabricated buildings linked together – the new guest rooms. He had done his best to make it homely and, although basic, it was actually one of the most relaxed places in which we stayed. It was late by the time we got to bed but we slept well, knowing that there was to be no cycling the next day.

We had arranged an unusual guided tour for the following day. Our fundraising efforts back home had raised a considerable sum for local charities[8] and Jamie had made contact by email with Leila, an Iranian girl who worked with the relief effort. We were immediately taken with Leila; she had an effortless charm that had us hanging on every word. She explained that as an English student in nearby Kerman, she had graduated just days before the earthquake struck. With her ability to interpret she was in high demand to work with the NGOs that flooded into the area and she had remained ever since. As we drove a few miles out of the city, she described the plight of those injured in the disaster. One of them was Abdoulreza, our driver for the day, who had been buried, together with his family. For five hours he lay under the crushing weight of rubble, struggling for breath. He assumed his family must have been killed, but miraculously his wife and daughter were also pulled out alive. He suffered a broken wrist, his wife a broken leg, and his daughter a severe chest injury. Amid the confusion they were all sent to different hospitals and it was forty days before they were reunited as a family.

We spent the day touring small clinics and a project where new, and much stronger, houses were being constructed. The work being undertaken by all of the charities was impressive and seemed well coordinated. All had adopted simple and cost-effective solutions designed to restore some dignity and a normal way of life to the village people, many of whom were living half an hour's drive from the town. It was a stark reminder that the effect of the earthquake extended far beyond Bam city limits and consequently the true death toll will never be known. Everyone we met was overwhelmed at the level of support they had received from the West. In the aftermath of the disaster, aid had poured in from across the world. Although intended to save lives and rebuild the city, the long-term benefits ran much deeper. Foreigners, often demonised by the Iranian political machine, had shown compassion in their moment of need.

At sunset we retreated to the citadel, the old town of Bam, whose origins can be traced back to before Christ. As with so many other places we had visited, its very existence grew from necessity, as a trading crossroads between Europe and the Indian sub-continent. Marco Polo himself is said to have passed this way in the thirteenth century, en route to present-day Beijing. The citadel, the largest adobe structure in the world, was surrounded by a similarly constructed town. But now, the scene before us was one of utter devastation. Under the watchful eyes of some soldiers, we climbed a scaffolding tower, from where we could see the entire site. I had seen impressive pictures of the vast citadel structure, but now it lay in ruins, almost entirely collapsed. As one of the country's premier tourist destinations, it was a pitiful sight, but the government had already begun painstaking repairs to return the old city to its former glory. All around were towers of incongruous yellow scaffolding. A few workmen beavered away but the magnitude of their task looked overwhelming. Conservative estimates suggest that reconstruction may take as long as thirty years.

Back at Akbar's we felt emotionally exhausted, our visit again all too short, but rewarding just the same. The fortitude displayed by the people of Bam was quite incredible. As we left town the following morning, I felt strangely privileged to have visited such an inspiring place.

Akbar had warned us about the road south of Bam, through an area known as the Kavir Loot desert. This was remote country and few Iranians themselves ever ventured that way. There were frequent reports of bandits carrying out robberies along the main highway to Zahedan, itself the scene of several bomb attacks and anti-government demonstrations. It would be our last town in Iran and we estimated it was still four days' ride away. In fact we had little option, as our visas were due to expire in precisely four days' time.

Some fifty kilometres south of the city we pulled up outside a small roadside truck stop, the first habitation we had seen amid the desolate landscape. We were sitting and enjoying a warm Coke when an army jeep pulled alongside, clearly having driven from Bam. Inside were an officer and three other soldiers. They didn't seem at all surprised to see us and wandered over to introduce themselves. I wondered if Akbar had asked the Army to protect us, such was his concern. The officer spoke hardly any English but indicated that they would be accompanying us. Just as in Syria, there was little we could do. It would at least ensure our safety, but again our movements would be restricted.

The soldiers were a jovial lot and they examined the bikes closely while we finished our drinks. We were in no hurry, having had an early start, but they quickly grew restless. No sooner had we set off than they started to get bored and instead drove ahead at intervals to wait. Their frustration increased as they began to realise that we were cycling the whole distance, a fact they clearly hadn't appreciated at first. Occasionally they pointed at Martha with a shrug, clearly confused as to why we didn't just jump on board. By the afternoon the desert had become almost totally featureless, even the skyline offered little respite from the flat expanse. Our map indicated a settlement called Shur-e-Gaz in the heart of the desert and still some fifty kilometres away. We checked with our soldiers, who nodded eagerly when we repeated the name. It seemed like a sensible target and we pressed on through the fading heat.

Shur-e-Gaz turned out to be nothing more than a mud-built desert fort and remote army outpost. The front of the complex was piled high with the wreckage of crashed cars and a large bus. Our escorting officer held up eight fingers and shook his head, clearly the number who had died in the accident. Our guards obviously had friends here and soon disappeared. There was a stand-off while perhaps twenty soldiers emerged and looked us up and down, before we took the initiative and unloaded the tent from Martha. They soon got the drift and led us to a quiet spot behind the fort. It was a great setting, despite the complex being surrounded by barbed wire. Once in a while a soldier would amble round to see what we were up to, but generally they left us alone.

By the following morning the wind had embedded Martha up to her axles in sand. We borrowed a shovel from the soldiers and spent twenty minutes in vain trying to shift her, before resorting to a tow from a nearby jeep. The desert slowly became more undulating as the day wore on. At first, small sand dunes started to replace the flat scrub and frequently dead camels, killed by trucks, lay by the side of the road. But by mid-afternoon the dunes had become so impressive that we simply had to stop. Jamie and Pauline wasted no time in running to the peak of the highest one, before leaping their way back down in huge great bounds. The dunes appeared beautifully sculpted – only the very peaks caught the sun and already the dark shadows were quickly lengthening, as the sun dropped.

Back on the road the lunar landscape returned, the shattered remains of ancient lava flows scattered like wreckage, all utterly desolate, and except for the single road nothing to indicate any civilisation. Then we reached a line of hills glowing warm in the evening sun and at the base of which was parked a smart Mercedes police car. The officers seemed to be more senior than the soldiers and promptly took over the escort role while the others trailed behind. A blue flashing light now compromised what should have been a beautiful evening ride. As we passed through a series of tunnels on the steep mountainside, the police shouted encouragement and sang songs in Farsi through their speaker system, shattering any chance of reverence. They led us over a pass and down a steep hill to a formal-looking police post called Nosrat Abad. It was a forbidding spot, consisting of a single concrete building, some twenty metres long, and adjacent to it a huge tarmac area on which were parked a dozen lorries and buses. A barrier was down across the road and the vehicles were being inspected by customs officers moving between them to check the papers of passengers. Adjacent to one wall lay the mangled and burned-out wreckage of several vehicles. How many it was hard to tell.

Later, our police driver, who spoke a little English, explained the dreadful accident that had befallen Nosrat Abad the previous year. On the spot where we stood a petrol tanker had crashed into a line of public buses, waiting at the barrier. They were mostly full of Afghan and Pakistani refugees, awaiting onward passage into Iran. The ensuing explosion engulfed five buses, over ninety people were tragically burned alive, and many more injured.

Opposite the police station and on the far side of the road was a small mosque, and here the police, albeit reluctantly, allowed us to camp. They insisted we must call them if we had any trouble, as this was a dangerous area. And to emphasize the point one of them drew a finger across his throat. We locked the bikes, fearing for their safety as much as our own. To have them stolen now would be one of our worst nightmares. When we saw two characters huddled suspiciously behind the mosque we assumed the worst and fetched the police opposite. I felt guilty afterwards; they were young men and dressed in little more than rags. Goodness knows what hardships they had endured just to reach this pitiful spot. The police quickly arrived and arrested the men, carting them back to their building. 'Pakistani. Refugee,' the officer said, pointing at the men as they were led away.

The deaths of the previous year made for a wretched story. For people who already had little to live for, Nosrat Abad was a desperate place, its very location now attracting unwelcome attention from the West. It was utterly bizarre that international politics should manifest themselves here of all places, around such a dismal little concrete building, but with Pakistan less than 200 kilometres away and Afghanistan a similar distance to the north, we joked among ourselves that we were entering 'Bin Laden' territory. In Zahedan local people had recently vented their fury against Western intervention in Afghanistan and there could be no doubt where their sympathies lay. We were also at the centre of a flourishing opium trade, with this very road a popular route for overland smugglers en route to Europe. It was certainly a lawless area where borders are frequently abused – and why shouldn't they be? The local tribes had existed here for centuries before intervention by foreign powers decreed the limits to their territories, in the process often driving division through established regions. Now the surrounding desert and mountains offered a refuge from which it was difficult to dislodge those most wanted. Two years earlier, Iranian soldiers had seized a large drugs consignment but the traffickers had responded by kidnapping three Western cyclists. The two Germans and one Irishman were travelling much the same route as us, from Bam into Pakistan. They were eventually released unharmed, although there were conflicting rumours about whether or not the five-million-euro ransom was paid.

We agreed to meet the police on the road for a six o'clock departure. The early start was fine by us, as we were keen to move on as soon as possible. While we needed their protection, they seemed equally keen to dispatch us safely. We hadn't seen the dawn while cycling for some time, and within just a few minutes we felt the heat from the rising sun, an enormous yellow orb cresting the broken hills ahead. This time two police cars drove ahead, and a jeep accompanied us with six armed soldiers trailing behind. They were taking few chances, it seemed. We stopped infrequently as our companions grew restless, making the stops just long enough to drain water bottles and top up from the spares in Martha. One blessing was that she seemed to be behaving herself. Now was definitely not the time for a breakdown. By mid-morning we crested a spectacular rocky pass and far below could see the outline of Zahedan, the last and remotest town in Iran. Our escort grew ever larger and numbered half a dozen vehicles as we descended the steep mountain road.

We paused at a police post on the outskirts of town where a senior officer emerged and entered into a lengthy discussion with our escort driver. There was much gesticulating and occasionally a flippant gesture was directed towards us. No doubt they were discussing what to do with the crazy cyclists. How we were going to stay in Zahedan was my main concern. The border was still another day's ride away. I approached the officer, hoping to clarify the situation in my simplest English.

'Hello. Hotel in Zahedan? Yes? Tomorrow we will go to Pakistan,' I said pointing east. He shook his head defiantly. 'No hotel. No stay,' he said firmly with his palms raised.

With discussion suspended we responded in our usual way, by sitting down and having some lunch. These situations generally had a habit of resolving themselves. Sure enough, half an hour later the friendly lead driver gave us the nod and the convoy swung back into action. This time we entered town with blue lights flashing and the occasional blast of a siren. If we had had any chance of maintaining a low profile, it was already too late. We pulled over at the first sign of a hotel, at which point all the vehicles deserted us, leaving us with just two nervous outriders. I wasn't sure if it was a good or bad sign, but we felt dreadfully exposed.

I left the others and quickly ran up a narrow flight of stairs to a dimly lit hall and a bare reception desk. 'Sala'am. Do you have rooms? Can we stay here?' I held one finger up reassuringly to indicate a single night. The young man looked horrified and emerged from behind his desk only to scurry down the corridor. 'Ye shab' (one night), I persisted, shouting after him. I hoped he had gone to get the manager, but as he never returned I had to give up and go back to the others. An unsmiling and tense-looking crowd, perhaps numbering a hundred, already surrounded them. They had encircled the bikes completely and gone were the friendly Iranian faces we had grown accustomed to. These were clearly tribal people, their faces weathered and their eyes suspicious. Our two police guards were equally tense and paced up and down to keep the silent crowd from encroaching further.

A middle-aged and portly man broke through the front of the crowd and spoke to us in clear English. 'Hello sir, where are you coming from?'

'We're from England. We have cycled across Iran and we're going to Pakistan tomorrow.'

'I understand but you cannot stay here.' His voice dropped to a whisper. 'This is a very dangerous place for you. There are many bad people. Please, you must move from here. This town is not safe for you.' He spoke calmly but something in his manner indicated that he was being very serious.

'We need to stay in Zahedan for just one night. Is there a hotel?' The man hesitated, as if measuring our stubbornness, before turning to the policeman and speaking rapidly and seemingly with some authority.

'He will take you there, to a safe place. Please be careful.' I thanked the man and he melted away as quickly as he had appeared.

The policeman signalled and we followed at speed through quiet back streets before arriving at a formal-looking hotel on the far side of town. At first sight it appeared to be an office block, surrounded by a high steel fence, and with sentries posted at the gate. There was no doubt it was intended for businessmen and officials, not for overland travellers. Arrival at these places always meant that we suddenly felt ten times dirtier, but Dickie and I went to Reception anyway, suspecting it was way beyond our budget. They quoted us a ludicrous $100 a room, but within five minutes we managed to halve the rate. Still too expensive, we held our ground hoping for more, but both parties knew we had little choice.

'We're really staying here, in this posh place!' Pauline was incredulous. 'Yippee!' Within a couple of minutes she had introduced herself to the staff, handed her dirty laundry in and enquired about a manicure. She really was a consummate traveller.

'Guys, I just thought you might like to know that today we passed the 4,000 kilometre mark. We are officially halfway between the Dead Sea and Everest!' Nic announced.

It was indeed good news and I couldn't help but feel that the toughest section was behind us. We were heading into more familiar countries and the weather had already improved significantly. I was loath to speak too soon, so thought it best to keep that thought to myself.

Our outriders met us early the following morning and escorted us to the edge of town, where we sat at a roadblock for a frustrating hour. We awaited the arrival of yet more soldiers before heading out of town in a long convoy of bikes and vehicles. Iran had one last sting in the tail. Within half an hour we were met by a vicious headwind. In a bid to keep the pace up we decided to ride as a pack, taking it in turns to lead at the front for two kilometres at a time, before dropping back to swap with someone else. It was significantly easier in the slipstream and we worked like this furiously for two hours, making arduous but steady progress. When the small border settlement of Mirjaveh finally came into view we knew we were close. It seemed like the end of a major chapter in the expedition and an adventure in its own right. Iran was behind us and we had managed to cycle across a truly vast and unfamiliar country in less than thirty days. I felt sad to leave, but equally relieved that we were still in one piece. It was an enormous privilege to witness the country in the way that we did. My preconceptions had been shattered.

Once again, leaving the country was not going to be easy for Martha. She had to have her papers stamped by the police. Dickie had tried that morning to do it in Zahedan but was told instead to proceed straight to the border. Now he was being told to drive back the ninety kilometres to Zahedan. He was as angry as I've seen him, the sheer futility of the paperwork finally getting the better of him. There was no room for compromise and Nic valiantly offered to drive back with Dickie to Zahedan that afternoon while we waited. Reluctant to enter Pakistan without them, we set up camp in no man's land. By the time the others returned, the sky was awash with blue and orange as we were treated to our last Iranian sunset. We sat in the dirt road, exhausted but content, homeless between nations.

Chapter 8

A Nation Lost – Pakistan

A short walk led us across the dusty and litter-strewn no man's land into Immigration. Gone were the austere modern Iranian buildings, replaced instead by a gloomy mud-walled office. It wasn't long before we were beckoned into a small anteroom where a picture of President Musharraf in full military regalia hung on the wall. The portly official said nothing but motioned for us to sit down on white plastic chairs. His gruff demeanour evaporated when he saw our passports and he sat bolt upright, beaming with delight.

'But you are Britsh!' he exclaimed. 'Please, please, you must be having tea with me.' He shouted an order through the open window and a minute later a smiling boy appeared with a tin tray laden with small glasses of milky tea. Pauline was simply ecstatic.

'Milky tea! Oh, you lifesaver, what a gent.'

The official offered a confused laugh in return. For the last two months we had rarely found milk. This was creamy white, sweet, and a delicious change.

Somehow this remote outpost in a bleak desert seemed welcoming, almost familiar. We could have been in the nineteenth century, just about anywhere in the colonial world, the cramped office, well-spoken officials and piles of dust-laden documents all reminders of a bygone era. We were in cheery mood as we stepped into the sunshine to walk across to the customs building, but a dull thumping boom in the distance was enough to halt us in our tracks. We ran to the corner of the nearest building to get a better look. A tall plume of black smoke rose over the nearby town barely a kilometre away with nothing to indicate its origin.

We were ushered into the customs building with our newfound enthusiasm slightly dulled. The office was a hive of activity with at least twenty officials tapping away on typewriters and filing papers. Perhaps it was an everyday occurrence in these parts but they seemed oblivious to the explosion. We were shown to a desk where an official patiently listened to Dickie and I explain once more the purpose of our trip. The response was polite but devastating.

'What you are doing is simply not possible. It cannot be permitted.'

We were not easily put off, but when the answer was delivered formally and in perfect English, the impact was greater. A language barrier had allowed us to plead ignorance all too often. 'But we need to cycle across Pakistan as part of our journey,' I countered.

'I understand this. But to cycle through this country you would have to be very, very crazy.' He tapped the side of his head for extra effect. 'It has never been done before.'

I knew he must be wrong here. It was the only crossing between the two countries, so Gerry Winkler for one must have passed this way. Despite his enforced stopover he would be well into India by now.

'We have a friend,' I lied. 'He came this way only a few weeks ago on a bicycle. He is Austrian.'

He shrugged, still unimpressed. 'Maybe this is so. But it is out of the question for you to take your vehicle. We do not let cars through into Pakistan. You will have to leave it here.' At this he beckoned us to a side window adjacent to his desk. Outside were the remains of a red painted van and stencilled on the side in large white letters was 'Everest 2004'. We had noticed it on the way in.

'This gentleman was driving from Holland, I believe. He became sick and returned to his home. He has never come back.'

To me that was slightly different from not letting him pass and I said so.

'It may be possible for you to continue by bicycle but you would be very foolish.'

At last I felt we were making progress, chipping away at the official line. 'Could we pay a bond, a deposit for the vehicle? Every country has helped us on our journey so far. It would be sad if we had to stop here in Pakistan.'

At this he hesitated but chose not to take the bait. Instead he deftly chose to delay the decision. 'You must return here tomorrow. The senior officer, the Customs Chief, will meet you and he will decide.'

Frustrated at another delay, I asked him what time we could meet.

'Early. We will decide then. Do not worry, we will try to help you.'

At this we felt a little encouraged and thanked him before getting up to leave.

'You are free this afternoon?' he said. We nodded in reply. 'Then we will play cricket. You have a team, yes? We will meet at five o'clock. England against Pakistan!' he laughed.

We all rose and shook hands. Our journey was becoming more extraordinary by the day.

We moved into the nearby guesthouse, seemingly reserved for stranded travellers such as ourselves. It was dusty and hadn't been cleaned for years, but the manager was friendly and helped us to store the bikes. Later, we made our way back to the customs house at the appointed time, to find the officials already practising. Their pace and accuracy was quite frightening. Fortunately they took pity on us and we opted for mixed teams, otherwise they would have received little competition. There were few rules but they pointed out the boundary to us, with just one exception. A ball that hit the mosque resulted in instant dismissal.

'And if you hit the Mullah – you will never play again!' At this they fell about laughing, slapping each other on the back.

They were true gentlemen and happily bowled slowly for those of us less competent. Despite that I managed only a measly twelve runs before being bowled out. Dickie salvaged us some respect, later revealing that he had played county cricket as a boy. Against each other their bowling was truly unleashed and there was no doubt they were the stronger nation. We played for a couple of hours, revelling in the good company, and as the sun set a few spectators gathered, mostly truck drivers and traders. They were unsmiling and bewildered, their weather-beaten faces serving only to remind us of their isolation. Life for them must be incredibly tough, as well as dangerous. I knew our game of cricket was going to be a brief interlude before the next few days. Ahead lay 600 kilometres of empty and dangerous desert. Even the citizens of the nearby town kept to themselves.

After the game our hosts insisted we join them for supper. They lived in lodgings on the far side of the customs buildings. We sat on the tiled floor, while the carpet in the centre was loaded with a huge variety of curry dishes. The food was delicious and a welcome change from the staple kebabs and rice to which we had become accustomed. The officers were well read and informed about world events, a couple of them even having been to England. For the first time on our journey, someone refreshingly understood the magnitude of what we were attempting. Our conversation and debate continued late into the evening, Pauline and Sarah quizzing them about the role of women in their country. Like everyone we had met on our journey they seemed impressed that women could complete such a journey. But when Pauline suggested they should let their own wives go on such a trip, they were horrified.

It was a lonely posting and only once a month did they receive a few days' leave. Then they would travel the long road east to

Quetta, the nearest city and our next destination. Our hosts repeatedly warned us about the dangers of our journey. The road ran parallel to Afghanistan and there was limited supervision in the area. Army outposts were still manned, but the government was struggling to keep control in this lawless region. Despite feeling apprehensive, little could dampen our mood, and we retired to our beds the most content we had been in weeks. Tomorrow was still very much up in the air, but we knew we had done all we could to ingratiate ourselves.

The next day we enjoyed a breakfast with a difference. It was Nic's birthday and Sarah had been up since five o'clock, raiding Martha's larder to make a pineapple upside-down cake in his honour. She had mastered the art of whipping up the impossible from our modest little cooker. Even the '31' was tastefully arranged in pineapple chunks.

The atmosphere was not quite so jovial back in the customs house. There was a formality in the air, which left me feeling despondent. Frustratingly, there was no sign of the official to whom we had explained everything the previous day, and I suspected that we were back to square one. Ushered to chairs at the side, we waited for the Chief to give us some time. At least he had arrived from Quetta, as promised. He sat imperially at a large central desk while runners came and went, delivering various papers for signing and stamping. We were finally summoned over and he beckoned us to sit down while another official briefed him in Urdu. Occasionally the official asked us in English for certain details, and all the while the Chief sat and listened expressionless while continuing to sign papers. He was either paying no attention or was very adept at multi-tasking. I had no idea he too spoke English until the explanation finished. He put down his pen and spoke with immediate authority.

'We appreciate the magnitude of your journey but I cannot allow your vehicle to pass this border. It is possible that you could sell it in Pakistan and then it would have been imported.' He raised his hands to indicate the matter was closed.

'We are happy to pay a bond or guarantee. Other countries have let us do the same,' I countered, employing yesterday's argument.

'That will not be necessary. There is one solution I can suggest. We would like to help you in your great adventure.' We listened intently, detecting some leeway. 'A customs official can travel with you in the vehicle and therefore guarantee that it is not sold.'

'All the way to India!' Dickie and I exclaimed together.

'Of course. Then we will know it has been exported out of Pakistan. You must also give him the keys every night.' A smile of satisfaction indicated how pleased he was with the suggestion. It seemed like an over-complicated solution, but it was at least workable. This way we could get back on the road, and besides, we were in no position to argue.

'There is a problem,' he continued. 'You will have to pay the wages of the official for the duration of your journey. I cannot finance this extravagant exercise.' My heart fell. There always had to be a catch and the budget was already stretched.

'How much will it cost?' I asked with some exasperation.

'It very much depends. How long will your journey take?' he responded.

'Maybe seventeen or eighteen days,' I suggested optimistically. There was some discussion while the two officials talked in Urdu again. This was clearly uncharted territory.

'It will be very expensive for you. Maybe one hundred dollars.'

I panicked for a second thinking that he meant per day. Then I remembered with relief this was Pakistan; he meant for the whole journey. Dickie and I were thrilled. 'That sounds fine. When can we leave?'

While they found someone suitable to accompany us, we headed into the local village to get supplies. There wasn't much on offer but we did manage to refill our gas. It transpired that yesterday's explosion was no bomb, but the result of a faulty cylinder, which had blown apart. We stood well back as the shopkeeper attached our never-before-seen Syrian model to his ill-fitting Pakistani compressor. We also bought several hundred bottles of water, certain we would need several litres a day each in the hot conditions. We stacked them in boxes on the roof of Martha as the locals looked on aghast. Bottled water was an expensive luxury here and we were buying out the town supply. We attracted further curious glances as we walked around. Even in Iran local people would always stop and engage us in conversation, but like Zahedan and other border towns this had a lawless feel. Very few travellers ever came this way, and those that did would rarely stop. We were about to enter some very challenging desert for the next few hundred kilometres.

Back at customs we were introduced to our escort, Mr Nabad. He seemed pleasant enough but extremely shy. He wore a long black *kameez* or shirt and the black beret of the customs service. I was disappointed to see that he wasn't armed. It was explained to us that he was not there to offer us any protection, merely to accompany the vehicle. He travelled with Ro in the front of the van while Dickie bowed to Nic's persuasion to get on the bike for the day and join us for some training. We teased him that it would do him good to be chased by bandits for a few hours and Nic was in his element cajoling and encouraging him as we headed out into the desert.

It was again a classic desert road, running straight but undulating across a succession of rocky skylines, each more dramatic than the last. On each crest, the road had been blasted through the rock to form a deep cutting and ease the gradient. It was thrilling cycling. I continually scanned the horizon, looking for any evidence of the tribesmen we had been warned about, nerves tight with all the stories we had heard of highway robberies. As leader I had worried for months about cycling through this area. Nic, who had spent a lot of time researching the route, also shared my concerns. Our actions certainly bordered on the reckless, but there was no avoiding the very crux of our whole journey. Even the British, who had once governed this territory, managed a tenuous hold only by making regular payments to local warlords. They had tried to stamp their authority by imposing the 'Durand Line' in 1893,[9] which still forms the modern-day border between Pakistan and Afghanistan, some fifty kilometres to the north of the road we travelled. It drove a wedge, some say intentionally, between the Pashtun people. Of course they have always ignored the border and ever since have drifted freely back and forth. None of this was of much concern to the outside world until the events of 9/11. Suddenly, free movement and the lawless nature of the people drew the unwelcome attention of the West, with the region a possible hiding place for Osama bin Laden.

We took lunch at the first ramshackle check post. Randomly placed in the desert road, it didn't serve much of a purpose. A tattered length of rope was strung between a sentry hut and a small mud building. It was barely enough to stop a cyclist. An old man emerged and smiled, revealing hideously rotting teeth. He was friendly enough and even lent us a deflated football, which Jamie made full use of during lunch. Before we departed he ushered us inside to sign the passport register. I saw an opportunity and quickly flicked back a couple of pages. With only a few names a week, I didn't have to look far and beckoned to the others. 'Look, Gerry Winkler, went through on 21 December, the very day we left the Dead Sea.'

It was strange to see his name and signature in his own hand. Proof, if we needed it, that we were not alone in our quest. Jamie wasn't wasting any more time.

'Looks like we'd better get back on the bike. Gerry, here we come!'

I was surprised to see that we seemed to be following a railway. It ran parallel to the road, the two narrow rails almost obscured in places by the sand. Every ten kilometres or so stood a neat white building adjacent to the line, a remnant of a colonial past. Small pathways bounded by whitewashed stones ran from the front steps to the road. Some were in reasonable condition and had signs of life, but most had fallen into disrepair. It felt desolate and forlorn, even today, but for anyone posted here in the nineteenth century, it must have felt like the end of the world. I assumed the railway must be abandoned until we heard a train approach and saw it rumble slowly past with a long line of freight cars.

It was late afternoon when we pulled into the dusty settlement of Nukundi. For once, we had little trouble finding somewhere to stay. Mr Nabad directed us straight into the customs compound, attached to the local police station. Secure and surrounded by a high wall, we pitched our tent, while Mr Nabad settled into the customs house with Martha's keys. We still had plenty of curry leftovers from our hostel at the border, although the flies had been at them during the day. Unable to resist the change in diet, I probably ate too much and soon paid the price. I was up several times in the night, running to the stinking pit in the corner, diarrhoea pouring out of me like water.

By the time the sun rose I felt completely washed out. Fortunately, the terrain was much the same as the day before, with mile after mile of empty rolling desert and a few minor inclines. Loaded up with water, I concentrated on drinking continually. I had lost litres of fluid and knew that would be my undoing if I didn't replace it. By the afternoon I was fading quickly and feared I wasn't going to last. Nic detected my falling pace and pulled alongside, and in a welcome gesture silently handed me a ready-peeled orange. It tasted delicious, the sugar instantly hitting my bloodstream and seeing me through to the small outpost of Yakmach. We hadn't intended to stop here but the others appreciated that I was at my limit. At least we had still managed to travel a respectable 114 kilometres.

We were shown into a disused government rest-house at the side of the road, piled high with pre-war furniture. The ancient owner hovered while we inspected the facilities. Camping would have been far preferable if only it had been safe enough.

'Do you have any water? Toilet?' To both questions he simply raised his hands apologetically and shrugged. 'You like . . . yes?'

I collapsed on to an ancient settee, sending dust billowing into the room. I didn't care any more. I had a bottle of water and there was a bucket in the corner. It felt glorious and I didn't plan on moving anywhere for at least twelve hours.

When I woke, it was to sunlight streaming through the wooden shutters and catching the dust in the air. Unsure how long I had slept, I lay motionless in the gathering gloom, and realised with relief that it was still evening. I had another night ahead of me to rest. I pulled myself out of bed and headed outside to look for the others. I didn't have to go far. Behind the building was an enormous sandy football pitch and, true to form, they seemed to have drummed up another sporting fixture. There must have been at least forty players in total. So many in fact, that it was hard to identify teams, but this didn't stop Pauline, who ran round madly in circles, rarely touching the ball. Jamie was the most adept and seemed at the heart of the action. Nic was solid in defence, as was Dickie. Feeling weak, I was just happy to take photos and enjoy the spectacle. The local teacher came and introduced himself and together we chatted and laughed at the efforts on the pitch.

Our next destination was the town of Dalbandin, a relatively modest sixty kilometres away. I had still eaten nothing and by the time we rolled into town was again on my last legs. Thankfully, the short distance meant we were there for midday and the prospect of nearly twenty-four hours' rest beckoned. I sensed the others were becoming a little frustrated, but to their credit they were incredibly patient. The plan had always been that we would cycle this phase as quickly as possible. The longer we took, the more danger we were in.

A walled courtyard offered an ideal spot for the tent below the minarets of a small brightly painted mosque. On the opposite side and behind a low wall were a series of market stalls. Inquisitive children lined up on tiptoe to peer over, their chins resting on the wall as they grinned widely. We entertained them, and ourselves, for over an hour. Pauline taught them nursery rhymes and counting while I turned the camera on them before showing them the footage. They squealed with delight, pointing at their faces on the small screen. The afternoon also presented a good chance to service the bikes. Nic and Jamie did most of the work while I watched from the comfort of my sleeping mat. Strength was gradually returning and we resolved to do a full ride the following day.

As always, our best-laid plans were put to the test. The officials appeared tense first thing, and Mr Nabad particularly nervous. They revealed that a demonstration was in progress on the main street barely 200 yards away and we could already see the ominous sign of smoke above the rooftops. It was too dangerous to head outside, but equally staying put was not the best option. The customs house was likely to be a target if the protesters became aggrieved and needed to vent their anger. We waited as long as we could before venturing out, a reluctant Mr Nabad cowering between Dickie and Ro in the front seat. We had been assured that the protest was about lack of water rather than anti-Western in sentiment.[10]

We pedalled decisively into the small side street that led from the customs house up to the main road. Ahead I could hear the rising crescendo of shouting, but we pressed on regardless. All we needed was a bit of speed and we would be out of town in two minutes and back on the open road. We turned on to the main street with Martha close behind us in convoy, but directly ahead lay a line of burning tyres blocking the road. Thick noxious smoke belched from the fire, forming a black wall twenty metres wide and the detritus of thrown stones and broken glass lay all about. There was a small gap through the middle of the barrier but we were already too late. Now less than fifty metres away, a crowd suddenly erupted from behind the barrier, leaping over the tyres and sprinting in our direction. They were yelling and waving their arms furiously. There was little time to tell if they were just being friendly or not. I played safe and wheeled the bike around in an abrupt U-turn, yelling at the others to do the same.

Two minutes later, we were back in the relative security of our compound exactly where we had started. In all the excitement we had forgotten Dickie and Ro, left stranded in Martha with our entire supply of mineral water loaded on the roof. As lack of water was the source of the original protest, it hadn't been a good move on our part. We needn't have worried; Dickie soon arrived as unperturbed as ever. We put the kettle on, got the Frisbee out, and settled down to give the crowds time to disperse.

Just when we had started to accept we might be stranded for the night, Mr Nabad offered us an alternative. If we cycled back in yesterday's direction we would meet the ring road, which would then bring us around the town. It meant a detour of perhaps ten kilometres but we would bypass the ongoing riot completely. Why he hadn't mentioned this earlier we had no idea. Itching to get going, we were on the road within minutes. Our escape out of town attracted jeers and some curious glances, but we were soon back in open desert.

The ancient road narrowed steadily until it became a single-lane strip of potholed tarmac. Gone were the stony, faceless plains which had accompanied us much of the way. Now we were in beautiful picture-book desert. Rolling sand dunes came right up to the roadside, and far to our right a striking rocky escarpment rose out of the desert floor. Twice we saw camels sauntering across the road. By lunchtime, we were thirsty from the heat and pulled up in a tiny settlement of a handful of mud-walled homes. A few locals scurried away when they saw us, but some young boys stood at a distance, eyeing us suspiciously. We drained our water bottles before one of them came over and pointed to the nearby well. We went to have a look and stared into the inky blackness unable to detect the bottom. He smiled encouragingly, and to be polite we used the huge medieval wheel to haul up a bucket of stagnant water. We had no intention of drinking it, but refilled a couple of bottles to wash in later.

We drew ever closer to the mountains that had filled our view all day but just when it looked as though we were heading straight through them, the road dived to the left and we found ourselves cycling in their evening shadow and parallel to the range. It was another two hours before we pulled into an isolated army camp. Set back from the road were some barracks and in front of the officer's house a square of bright green grass, looking incongruous against the backdrop of stark desert. Mr Nabad told us we could stop here, but he seemed uneasy and out of sorts. Our last two nights had been spent with his colleagues at customs houses. Now with the Army the situation was less familiar, and just like us he was among strangers.

The scenery faded the next day, along with the quality of the road. Hot and dust-covered it was mid-afternoon by the time we approached the town of Nushki. We were now desperately remote, and I immediately sensed a deep suspicion of outsiders. We stopped for a Coke at the first stall we found, but it was handed to us silently as a small crowd gathered. Almost 200 years earlier this isolated town had been the launching point of the so-called 'Great Game'.[11] Two young British officers, Henry Pottinger and Charles Christie, had been dispatched on a secret mission from Bombay, the former having only just turned twenty years of age. Their mission was a dangerous one and they certainly would have been killed if the local Baluchis had detected their real purpose. Over the course of several months, they separated, making reconnaissance missions west and deep into Iran. When they finally met, it was in Esfahan, neither recognising the other for several minutes, such had been their hardships. They had both used enormous cunning and duplicity merely in order to survive. That they also collected a huge amount of intelligence was simply astounding. Officers from both sides repeated their efforts with similar endeavours over the course of the next century.

It was easy to believe that little had changed in the last 200 years. We chose to ignore Mr Nabad's protestations, and stopped outside a ramshackle house marked with a tattered 'Hotel' sign. It did have a nice garden though and we thought we might even be able to camp. The owner was having none of it and quickly informed us he was full, shooing us away for extra effect. It was clear that travellers, especially those who attracted attention, were not exactly welcome in these parts. I wondered to what extent history had left the population with an in-built distrust of outsiders – perhaps deservedly so.

We admitted defeat and followed Mr Nabad's directions to the local police station. Here we received a warmer welcome and were ushered into a small courtyard surrounded by cells. The few prisoners in residence stared vacantly back through the bars as we passed. We were shown into a large room in the back corner of the building. Having by now slept in a kebab restaurant, a disused garage and empty shops, a prison didn't faze us in the least. It was devoid of furniture but spotlessly clean and would do nicely for the night.

'How about we try and knock up a chocolate cake tonight? What do you all reckon?'

Pauline's suggestion was particularly odd as with little chance to shop in the last few days we were running very low on supplies.

'Look, Dickie and Ro, I'll join you guys and we'll head into town with Martha and get some stuff.' She was already on her feet.

'Yeah, OK, I suppose we might find something,' replied Dickie cautiously, while lying prostrate on his sleeping mat, hands across his belly.

I had to smile to myself. It was always a huge relief when Pauline offered to help. We had learned that Dickie and Ro could simply disappear for hours on end when given free rein. Both of them were easily distracted and had no concept of urgency. Pauline was more methodical and when she wanted something would cut straight to the chase.

Our hosts were aghast at the fact that we wanted to venture outside. They insisted that we must be accompanied, and two vehicles and a score of heavily armed police took them to the market. Despite the unusual surroundings, we managed a passable chocolate pudding and spent one of our most comfortable nights. The police, who had been gawping for hours, eventually left us alone and we even braved the shower in a corridor sandwiched between two cells. The pathetic trickle of freezing water was long overdue.

Quetta, we hoped, would offer us a welcome break and chance to escape the stranglehold of our escort. The plan was to book into a hotel, relax, and then meet Mr Nabad again after a couple of days. He had grown to trust us a little more and was already less rigorous about collecting Martha's keys every night. In the event, what we had hoped would be a simple day was full of surprises. The police roused us before dawn, concerned that another protest would endanger us. We were soon on our way, the road out of town delivering a punishing start as it wound in steep switchbacks up the mountainside. As the gradient eased we made better progress, but then another steep climb challenged us on the outskirts of the city and we crested a rocky pass after racing the last section to the top. It was a popular truck stop and we joined a small crowd of onlookers staring back at the wonderful view across the desert. The land was more fertile now and stunted fruit trees lined the way we had come, but beyond that, enveloped in a purplish haze, was the desert we had crossed without incident. Yet again, preconceptions had clouded our judgement. It had been incredibly remote and very beautiful. Under different circumstances, I could happily have explored further.

Even though we had reached the outskirts of the city, it was another thirty kilometres to the centre. The contrast to the previous day couldn't have been greater. Every conceivable form of transport was on the road: donkeys pulling rickety carts, filthy diesel buses, bicycles, and even yellow taxis. One cut in front of us with four small children peering out of the open boot. The hooting of horns and ringing of bicycle bells was incessant, as every vehicle vied for its patch of road. We were left trying to carve our way through the mayhem as well as keep sight of each other. We made our way to a small hotel that had been recommended to us. Hidden from the main road and with a large garden, it looked idyllic. The owner was not quite so willing and gave us a frosty reception.

'It is very difficult to have foreign guests with me at this time,' he explained, shaking his head forcefully. 'My hotel may be at risk ... you understand?'

We did our best to say we would only be a couple of nights and offered to pay the full rate. It was not a time to haggle.

'Why is it so dangerous?' I decided to press him further.

'Have you not seen our newspapers?' he looked incredulous. 'There are many pictures mocking Mohammed, printed in Europe, Danish people, I think. They make us Muslim people very angry.'

'But we are British. We know nothing of this.' I tried in vain to distance us from whatever was going on.

'Of course, of course. This I know because I am an educated man. But many poor Pakistani people will not know this. They have no education. To them, all Western people are the same. They may attack my hotel if they think you are staying here.' He seemed genuinely nervous, constantly looking over our shoulders and through the Reception window, lest we were spotted.

Again, we got our way through a combination of stubbornness and patience. He agreed to let us stay if we promised not to walk out on the street and advertise our presence. It seemed a fair compromise. The hotel had its own restaurant, so we had little reason to move anyway. We enjoyed our best hot shower in weeks, before Dickie answered a knock at the door. The young man introduced himself in hushed tones as Ahmed, the manager's son.

'Would you be liking some beer tonight, sir?'

Dickie rubbed his eyes in disbelief, hardly able to believe his luck. 'Beer, mate? Is the Pope Catholic? Let me get my wallet!'

Without beer, Dickie had suffered more than most, used to his sociable Oxford lifestyle of a few regular pints out with friends. The entirety of our journey had so far been in the Islamic world, throughout which alcohol was prohibited. Pakistan was no exception, but we heard that it was at least tolerated behind closed doors. Ahmed explained that he would have to cross town to buy the beer and would return in a couple of hours. We must on no account mention this to his father, who would be very angry if he found out.

In the end, we spent a relaxing three days at the hotel. In theory, the worst was behind us but the situation with the recent Danish cartoons was an unwelcome complication. Our timing was chronically bad no matter where we went. If it wasn't heavy snow or bird flu, it was riots or stone-throwing. For now, at least, the hotel was a welcome respite from the open road and afternoons were spent sipping tea in the garden amid the fading colonial splendour. Our evening deliveries of brown paper bags full of bottled Lahore lager continued seamlessly. I had never seen Dickie quite so happy. We ventured outside a few times to a small internet café around the corner and even further across town for a meal. The warnings we had received seemed to be an over-reaction and though the atmosphere was hardly welcoming, neither did we feel in any danger. However, on the evening before our departure we were summoned to Reception by the owner. Waiting for us was the young and immaculately dressed Chief of Police. He was very courteous and introduced himself before enquiring about our plans and more specifically our route. He seemed incredulous and shook his head continuously from side to side after we fetched the map. He could not even bring himself to look at it.

'You must be crazy . . . crazy,' he announced. 'You cannot bicycle through this country in the way you describe. It is not possible!'

'But we have already cycled through a third of it,' I countered. 'And we were told that was the most dangerous part.'

He continued to shake his head and tutted to himself continually. Eventually he threw his hands up in despair. 'Do you not value your lives?' he said directly. 'Quetta is a very civilised city. Here we are educated people. When you go to the mountains, the people are very poor. They will take your lives, it is very dangerous.'

The constant political hassle and red tape was getting tiresome. We had heard the dire warnings at the border and yet managed the most dangerous area without incident. We couldn't fully relax until we reached India, of course, but for that reason alone we simply needed to push on and the quicker the better. Speed, we had learned, was by far our best safety policy. As experienced travellers, we all shared the same gut feeling, and it mostly stemmed from the reaction of local people we had met. Generally speaking, the poorer the people, the better the reception. I was starting to suspect the police were paranoid.

With the Chief mellowing a little, he started to offer some constructive advice. I gladly left Nic to work through the details. His patience was spectacular in these situations and he could happily talk cricket for hours, a surefire way to make friends with any Pakistani. Once again his charm saw us through and together they came up with a workable plan. The Chief of Police would not only provide us with an armed escort but he would call ahead to all the local stations in his district. That way they would expect our arrival and we would have somewhere to stay. It was hardly the cycling freedom we yearned for, but the priority was simply to get back on the road.

It was a relief to be moving again, albeit in convoy with two police trucks and a dozen armed guards. It was still early and the wide streets of Quetta were eerily quiet. There was no visible sign of the recent riots of which we had heard so much and we stopped for an hour at the city limit to wait for a change of personnel and vehicles. It was infuriating as we had cycled only twenty kilometres and barely warmed up. Curious children smiled shyly at us, but every time they got too close our guards barked at them furiously and waved their long sticks until they scattered back into their homes. It was doing nothing to help our reputation and I had to wonder if being shadowed by the police was actually putting us in more danger.

Our destination was Ziarat, high in the local mountains. We were facing a tough day and a long ascent but at least the road was entirely free of traffic. To our delight, the steep hillsides became carpeted in juniper trees as we climbed higher. They were small and stunted, but the smell was heavenly and made for sharp contrast after weeks of bland desert. Our escort of armed vehicles had clearly grown bored and drifted back to the city, leaving us with just Mr Nabad and a lone policeman on a moped. His shopping was tied on in a yellow plastic crate and he wore an old Enfield rifle slung across his shoulder. Cycling behind him, I was alarmed when he screeched to a halt and whipped the weapon off his back. He fell to one knee and fired off two shots in quick succession. By this time I had jumped off the bike and hit the ground, fearing we were under some kind of attack. Across the valley, plumes of dust sprung up where his shots slammed into the hillside, followed by the crack of the rifle echoing around the hills. I caught sight of a desert fox bounding across the moraine unscathed. The policeman turned and offered me a gap-toothed smile, before jumping back on his moped.

It was a challenging climb but Ziarat was a welcome contrast to the lowlands. During the British occupation of Baluchistan, it had been a famous hill station for officials during the blisteringly hot summer. Now it was all but deserted. After a restless night in the police compound, we pressed on, the road leading higher still and the juniper becoming even more abundant. To our delight, all the climbing paid dividends as we enjoyed a gentle downhill stretch that lasted for miles, but with the loss in altitude also came the reappearance of the desert. We passed numerous small mud villages of simple one-room houses, a stark reminder of the poverty that still exists in Pakistan beyond the main cities. Reaching Loralai, we negotiated the bustling market streets in search of the police barracks. We found them easily enough and as an added bonus there was a beautiful patch of bright green grass in the centre of the square, just right for our tent.

* * *

No sooner had we fallen asleep that night than the heavens opened and the rain hammered on to the roof of the tent, flashes of lightning and endless peals of thunder keeping us awake until the early hours. At least we were warm and dry and had to be thankful that it hadn't occurred in the middle of the day. I drifted off eventually, vaguely aware of Nic and Jamie getting up to go outside and check the guy ropes. Then, at five in the morning a guard came and shouted into the tent through the driving rain. 'OK, OK?' he repeated, sounding overly concerned. Of course we're OK, I thought, just let us sleep. It was him we should feel sorry for, out in the cold and wet.

The first sign something was wrong was when Dickie uncharacteristically leaped to his feet a few minutes later. 'Shit, oh my God, quick, quick, we're flooding!'

He had barely issued the warning before I felt the first rush of chill water enter my sleeping bag. Within seconds, it was inches deep and still rising. I struggled half-naked out of the bag and tried to reach for some clothes.

'We have to get the computers!' I yelled at the others. 'And the generator!' I was in a spin trying to remember the important items we simply had to save. Clothes and sleeping bags would have to wait. Instinctively we formed a chain and passed everything from the tent door to the shelter of a nearby porch, some ten metres away. It was still pouring with rain but we had some light in the weak dawn. A few policemen started to gather and watched us curiously. With hindsight we now saw that it wasn't a great spot. Around the grass was a low mud wall, presumably to keep the water out. Once the flood had breached this, our pitch was flooded in seconds. The guard who had woken us had been trying to give us a warning.

Under the shelter we started to relax a little and even managed to laugh at our misfortune. There was no serious harm done, and all the valuable equipment was rescued. We had got into the habit of storing the computers in plastic crates and that alone had probably saved them. More ominous was the smell that came from our soaked clothes, now ingrained with a fine layer of silt. The overflow had issued from an open channel next to the main road about fifty metres away and would have carried sewage and all manner of effluent. There was a real danger that we could fall ill, so we resolved to wash everything as thoroughly as we could, no matter how long it took.

First came the cooking equipment. We boiled up the kettle and sterilised the cutlery and mugs in hot soapy water. We were quickly using up our precious supplies of bottled water, and although there was a nearby tap, the guards nearly doubled up with laughter when we tried it. We should have known better. By mid-morning the sun had come out and we raised a washing line. There were now at least a hundred bystanders, mostly the families of policemen. They were the same crowd that had watched us so efficiently pitching the tent and cleaning our bikes the previous evening. Now they gawped at us, partly with curiosity, but more in amusement at our incompetence. In a large town there might even have been a laundry service, but in this village there was no such luxury.

It was nearly one o'clock before we managed to head out of town, this time accompanied by a modest escort of a single jeep. We were immediately greeted by a spectacular backdrop, as we wound our way through a desert maze of cuttings and rocky outcrops, the low sun catching the relief of the landscape. Now the tarmac had gone and instead we negotiated a surface of smooth compacted mud and frequent potholes.

It was nearing eight o'clock and pitch-black before we arrived in the remote village of Mekhtar. We were in no position to camp and Mr Nabad would also require a bed for the night. Enquiries led us to what at first seemed a normal house, but was surrounded by a high brick wall. Two young officers in uniform welcomed us warmly and introduced themselves as members of the border police. They were clearly proud of their status and explained that their men were out on patrols. They generously offered us a room for the night and even access to a small kitchen. It was more than we needed, but no sooner had we eaten than they announced with great fanfare that the hot showers were ready. In turn, we each paraded through their private quarters to use the small bathroom. The shower turned out to be a steaming hot bucket filled from a tap on the wall, with the tank outside heated by an open fire. It was sheer bliss, pouring ladle after ladle of hot clean water over ourselves, clearing away the muck of the morning's flood. Despite our best efforts, the smell had lingered with us all day.

I talked later with Fawad, who seemed to be the more senior of the two officers. Like all Pakistanis, he was keen to talk politics and hear about the West. With great ceremony, he showed me his radio on which he listened to the World Service every night.

'This is the only news I can trust,' he explained. 'It helps me to learn so much about the world.' He was fiercely proud of his position and his brief to protect Pakistan's borders.

'But we are a long way from any border?' I queried.

'Our role is very varied, we have many jobs to do. We are very adaptable.'

As if on cue, there was a commotion outside. Soldiers came and went and two men were led inside, wearing handcuffs. They looked scared and shamefully hung their heads. It transpired that they had been chopping down juniper trees, which were protected by law. Fawad was keen to show me his moral stance on such activity.

'You will have heard of global warming, yes? By cutting these trees the men are committing an environmental crime. For this alone they must be punished. They are very poor and wish to burn the wood for cooking. But this cannot be allowed.' He wagged his finger vigorously as he spoke. 'There are many men in my position who would turn a blind eye' – his voice dropped to a whisper – 'or accept many rupees to release the men. Me, I would never do such a thing.' He stuck his chest out proudly with the last statement and I had no reason to doubt his integrity.

'What will you do with them?'

'They will be kept here tonight and tomorrow we will take them to the court in Quetta. They will be treated well, I am a fair man, but they must be punished.'

I decided not to ask what would become of the wood, which was already being unloaded. Stacked against the outside wall, it was conveniently placed for the officer's hot-water tank, easily sufficient for a year's worth of hot showers. But I was in no position to pass judgement. Global warming or not, it was the best wash I had enjoyed in weeks.

Fawad's information about the route ahead was very vague. He was desperate to help, but having come from Quetta himself, I suspected he had never travelled in the other direction. Anticipating muddier conditions, we changed from our 'slick' tyres to 'knobbly' ones, and it was a wise choice. Rain the previous night had turned the road to a quagmire in places and lorries had already ploughed deep channels through the surface. These were negotiable on a bike, but they were too much for Martha. On several occasions, she grounded and the only option was to push. Every time this happened, of course, we had to dismount the bikes and progress became painfully slow. It was hard to believe this was the only route for traffic across the mountains, but at midday we crested a low hill to find a queue of at least 100 lorries trying to ascend the far side. Their wheels spun hopelessly into the ruts, simply making the surface even worse. Despite the gridlock, the drivers laughed and smiled at us as we picked our way past. To them, negotiating these conditions was all part of the job and they seemed in no particular rush. Their lorries were works of art, painted elaborately in bright colours with pictures of Bollywood film stars, numerous mirrors, horns, and lengths of tinsel. Even in the mud, the proud drivers took every opportunity to polish their gleaming creations.

The mud was becoming tedious and much to our relief the dirt road met a main highway that afternoon. The sudden ease with which we freewheeled was a delight after hours of strenuous pedalling, but the heavens opened yet again in a short but vicious storm. It only served to make us press on regardless and within an hour we arrived on the outskirts of Rakni.

A rather formal roadblock and two sentries stopped us proceeding. Ahead was what appeared to be a military camp, rather than the town indicated on our sketchy map. It didn't look too hopeful, although the police chief in Quetta had promised that he would call ahead on our behalf. The girls arrived a couple of minutes after us, confusing the guards still further, but we needn't have worried. A more senior officer soon turned up, inviting us through the barrier and showing us to some basic but comfortable barracks. The camp commandant had requested that we join him for supper that evening, a timely invitation, as we actually had nothing in the way of food.

Later, the major in charge greeted us from the terrace of his bungalow. Salim was young for his position, perhaps in his early thirties, and he smiled warmly as we approached, his arms outstretched.

'Welcome my friends ... my friends from England. You are very welcome. Please eat with me. You must be hungry after your journey.' He shook us each by the hand as we introduced ourselves.

His bungalow was modest but comfortably furnished and he even had a small computer that allowed us to show him a few pictures of the journey. When supper arrived, it was tasty but woefully inadequate. My own stomach was still delicate so I was fine, but I could see Jamie and Nic fading rapidly. On these occasions, all the boys could think of was food, while true to form Pauline took the opportunity to grill Salim about every aspect of his life.

To his credit, he was remarkably forthcoming. Yes, he was engaged to be married, and yes, he did miss his girlfriend. Only when they were married would she able to live with him in his quarters, but he spoke to her every day on the phone. Pauline wanted to know how they spent their time together, but Salim was equally curious about our lives.

'In your country it is very different, no? Sex is very ... how do you say ... free?'

Dickie didn't miss a trick. 'Not usually, Salim. I often have to pay for it!'

Salim looked horrified, having missed the joke; I thought it better to change tack.

'Salim do you know anything about the road ahead?'

This time it was his turn to laugh. 'Why do you think I am feeding you as my guests? Tomorrow you have a very, very big mountain to climb. The road goes up for more than twenty kilometres without a break. But after that you will be going downhill all the way to the Indus river. It is a very good road the whole way.'

Salim looked disappointed when we politely declined his offer of breakfast the next morning, but we knew from past experience that we had to get away promptly. He promised instead to send us a breakfast delivery to our barracks. Generous to the end, he had been a superb host.

His description of the road was fairly accurate. Dickie was back on the bike, having picked quite a morning to start training again. The road meandered back and forth up the mountain in a relentless series of switchbacks. Nic and I led the way, enjoying the break of routine and the good surface, our fitness such that even a huge climb now presented little challenge. It wasn't so simple for Dickie. The sweat poured off his brow as he muttered and cursed his way up the climb. Nic encouraged him the whole way, while I kept a lookout for Jamie. He had fallen some way behind the girls, having complained of feeling rough the night before.

The climb seemed never-ending but the breathtaking scenery was ample compensation. Behind us lay the range of mountains we had been crossing since leaving Quetta, a succession of ridges and valleys, the further towards the horizon the more each diffused into the landscape. Our road passed over innumerable false summits and it was lunchtime before we were confident that the ascent was over. Ahead, and far below, the road snaked down for miles, dropping from the mountains to the lowlands where we would cross the mighty Indus river.

Jamie soon caught us up but collapsed, exhausted, on to the side of the road. At least the worst of the day was over. Our aim was to reach the town of Dera Ghazi Khan on the Indus river that night, and although fifty kilometres away, a rapid descent would soon eat up the distance. Brimming with confidence, we had no idea that things were about to take a definite turn for the worse.

The afternoon started badly when Nic hit a young girl in the road. The children had been trying to get out of the way, but we were flying down from the high pass where we had lunch. There was no harm done but I could see Nic was shaken at the prospect of what might have been. We pressed on, more cautiously, the narrow road hugging the cliff side precariously. It was exhilarating and we stopped on the corners to snap pictures of the huge drop-offs. Even on these narrow ledges cut into the rock side, the lorries were attempting to pass each other.

As the gradient eased, we found ourselves descending gently on a broad ridgeline. In every direction, the view was wonderful and by the time we arrived at a neat and whitewashed police station we were grinning from ear to ear. The road was improving and again we had conquered a remote and difficult region. Ahead lay larger towns where we could find decent hotels and better food. Or so we thought.

The local police chief marched out of his house, aghast that we had somehow managed to evade our escort and enter his domain. He knew that we were coming but was still far from impressed. Lots of tutting and finger-wagging ensued. 'You understand that this is the edge of Baluchistan. In a few miles you will be in the Punjab. There you will not get a good reception. In fact the police will not let you enter without very special permission.'

We had heard it all before, of course – the dire warnings about safety and routes being impossible to negotiate, especially by bicycle. As always, our policy was one of sheer stubbornness. Today of all days we were high on success and feeling confident that we would emerge from Pakistan unscathed. After a stalemate of an hour, the chief offered us an escort to the Punjabi border 'to see for ourselves'. We were on our way again, but this time with guards who were twitchy and nervous. At some point we must have passed out of Baluchistan, as our escort simply deserted and returned to their territory. Unchaperoned, we pressed on to Dera Ghazi Khan, reaching the edge of town as darkness descended. There was some kind of festival in progress, and caught in the gridlock the surrounding motorists were in high spirits. They leaned out off their truck cabs and car windows repeating the same greeting. 'Welcome to Pakistan, welcome to Pakistan! Where from? Where going?'

The warm welcome was short-lived as we turned a corner to be surrounded by police. They had boxed us in on all sides in a coordinated, and no doubt pre-planned effort. Our route ahead was completely barred and we were told to dismount from the bikes. The first request was for a list of our passport numbers and total confusion ensued. It was a familiar game, not helped by the language barrier. The numbers were always scrawled on a piece of paper and no doubt discarded later on. It was pointless officialdom. The officers had difficulty deciphering our passports, so it was usually easier to do it ourselves. It was now dark so Jamie crouched in the light of Martha's headlamp while I recited the numbers. Once done, we hoped that would be it but there was to be no such luck.

'No cycle! No permission! Multan,' the sergeant pointed vigorously to the east, in fact exactly where we were heading anyway. But Multan was still eighty-five kilometres away and it was supposed to be the following day's destination.

'Hotel here . . . Dera Ghazi?' I pointed at the ground to indicate we wanted to stay put. The policeman was getting angrier by the second and wagged his finger at me.

'No hotel . . . no hotel!' he barked. 'No tourist! Multan.'

It was our second stand-off of the day, but this time the role of naive tourist was not quite working. Clearly we were not welcome, but Multan was simply too far away for us to press on. We had already endured a demanding day, Jamie was ill, and it was now dark. We continued to argue for half an hour before another police car swept alongside and out climbed a fat but rather important-looking officer. At least his English was better, although he was hardly friendly. He barked reprimands at the other men before turning on us.

'What is the problem here? You know it will not be possible for you to stop in this city. It is closed to all foreigners.'

'I understand, of course. But we are on bicycles and we cannot reach Multan tonight.'

'Then you will put your bicycles in the jeeps and my men will drive you there.'

'There is a problem. We are on a long journey and have to cycle every metre through Pakistan. If we drive we will be cheating.' I pointed at the bicycles and the road for extra effect. The concept of an expedition, let alone one for good causes, was totally alien to everyone we met. This officer was no exception.

'I understand, but tomorrow you can continue your journey from Multan. We are helping you, yes . . . free lift!' At this he relaxed and chuckled to himself.

We had lost the argument for the first time on the trip. We were tired, not just from a long day in the saddle, but from the constant negotiations. I must have explained the idea of the trip fifty times that day alone and now for the first time I had to admit defeat. I had an idea and turned back to the officer after consulting the others. 'Tomorrow, will your men bring us back to this point?'

'Of course, of course. No problem.' I didn't believe a word of it. To emphasise the point I dragged my foot through the dirt at the side of the road, marking a line to exactly indicate our progress, all the while keeping eye contact with the officer.

The ride into Multan was miserable. For the first time on the journey, we were heading forward by vehicle and not by bike. It was a wretched feeling and we sat in silence for most of the hour-long trip, with Martha following close behind. We pulled into an enormous army barracks but no one seemed to know what to do with us. Mr Nabad also looked ill at ease but we had little sympathy for him. He'd proved to be of no help in all our negotiations, preferring not to get involved.

Too tired to care, we pulled the tent out of Martha and pitched it right on the front lawn next to the parade square. It was the lowest moment of the trip so far. The tent still stank of the sewage from two nights earlier, the bikes needed a service and we had absolutely nothing to eat. We desperately needed showers and our sleeping bags were still ingrained with immovable fine silt. We fell on to our mats and as we tried to sleep flies settled on us continually in the warm foetid air. I sweated all night and felt dirtier than I had in weeks. I also knew the cycle journey, in fact the entire expedition, was now under threat. If only we could manage that section we would be through the worst and in India in just a few days.

There was little chance of a lie-in, as the adjacent parade square was being used to good effect at six o'clock. I unzipped the main door, clad only in Lycra shorts and no cycling top. About three to four hundred police were lined up, facing square on to the tent. I waved casually while they stared back in amazement. 'Just wait till you see the others,' I thought.

Dickie and I wasted no time in visiting the camp headquarters, while the others tried to rustle up some breakfast. We resolved to be as stubborn as ever and were fully prepared for a long haul. Without any discussion, we all knew that continuing with the trip having missed a section was simply not an option. It might only be eighty-five kilometres out of 8,000, but it was the principle. It would have knocked the heart out of our efforts.

At first sight, the camp headquarters was as chaotic as anywhere else in Pakistan; we were offered tea and ushered to seats while officials scurried to and fro. It was midday before we got to meet the top man, and like everyone else, he clearly thought us crazy. Despite that, he was ready to support us and, subject to sufficient manpower being available, we might be able to secure an escort back to Dera Ghazi Khan.

'Will it be possible to go there this afternoon?' I pleaded, tapping my watch.

'Of course. Of course. There is no "*Inshallah*" here. We are

Pakistani!' he said proudly. All of the staff laughed in unison to keep the boss happy.

Within the hour, the same two police trucks arrived, and we loaded the bikes and ourselves back on. Our escort was clearly aggrieved that they were having to drive us eighty-five kilometres, merely for us to cycle back again. I had to sympathise: from their point of view the exercise must have appeared futile. In Pakistan, it is only the poor who ride bicycles and then from necessity. I regretted that we didn't have a map of the whole route with us.

We sped through the city before coming to a grinding halt on the outskirts. Here the police were adamant they could go no further. We would have to wait for an additional escort from the other direction. Again our hopes were dashed. The chances of the police chief in Multan having rung through to arrange this were minimal. Every break in communication simply added to our difficulties. Making it worse was the fact that we could do nothing, now stranded by the roadside, adjacent to a shack of a police station. Dickie and I pressed them to make a call but we were shooed away.

We needn't have worried as just after two o'clock a convoy of heavily armed jeeps swung into view. My hopes were raised as they had at least come from the right direction and were evidently a different class of soldier. They wore tracksuits and baseball caps, both marked with 'Panther'. They could have been a basketball team, but instead were armed to the teeth with heavy-duty machine guns and bandoliers of ammunition. Their vehicles were clearly of a much higher standard as well. They barked orders at our now second-rate escort in a bid to determine what was happening. It was not looking good until the leader turned to us and smiled broadly.

'Bicycling? Come on, let's go!'

We wasted no time in squeezing on to their jeeps. Although better, they were much smaller, so we hung the bikes precariously over the side and did our best to hold on. The drivers commanded some serious road presence, and we swept back along the highway at top speed, carts and traffic of any description having no choice but to dive for the side of the road. Within less than an hour, we were back at the abandoned roundabout, and with great satisfaction I found the line in the sand from the previous night. The Panthers looked on with total bewilderment as we lined up very precisely behind it. They had just given us a lift here. Why on earth would we want to cycle back the way we had come?

We soon crossed the long bridge across the Indus, which looked as though it had seen better days. Potholes went all the way through, giving us a view of the muddy brown waters below. It was half a mile wide at this point and barely flowing, stinking with its cargo. With the river came a massive increase in population. Crops were grown right up to the roadside, water buffalo grazed, and children carried vegetables back to their homes through the throng of traffic. Even camels pulled carts laden with produce. We hadn't seen activity like this for weeks, desert and mountains having become our everyday existence. It was a welcome change, but there was a catch – and it was a depressing one. Crossing the Indus, I looked at my altimeter to see we were now less than fifty metres above sea level. The same height we had been barely two hours from the Dead Sea. After two months of work, the real climbing was yet to begin. We still had another 8,800 metres of ascent to the summit of Everest.

By mileage standards, it was an easy ride, but we were flagging after the efforts of the previous day and little food in the last twenty-four hours was having its effect. We stopped only once to buy a drink in a busy market, but the Panthers leaped into action, pointing their loaded and cocked machine guns at bystanders while we haggled for a Coke. It seemed easier just to press on. With barely ten kilometres to go, the sky became ever more threatening to the left of the road. A soaking was inevitable but we were perhaps only half an hour away and so pressed on. When I next looked, it was because of an eerie darkness, encroaching on us by the second.

There was little warning of what happened next as a tree fifty metres away was bent double by an invisible force. Then the force was upon us within a second. The wind slammed into us, almost plucking us off the bikes while the sand blasted our heads. Pulling our shirts over our heads, we dived for the cover of a nearby wall and crouched down as the vicious sandstorm swept overhead. It lasted some ten minutes before the wind abated, but in its place began a steady downpour, and we huddled together, seeking out what little shelter there was. We had to laugh at the timing. The last forty-eight hours had been the most demanding of the whole trip. At every twist and turn something had arrived to block our progress. Then barely ten kilometres from safety, with all officialdom conquered, we had to negotiate the worst storm yet. There simply wasn't much left to throw at us.

Yet the storm turned out to be a blessing. In the confusion, our escort had abandoned us, scurrying for safety themselves. We pressed on to find Multan inches deep in floodwater from the storm. As we surged through, I felt the urge to celebrate and make up for the last couple of days. 'Why don't we stay in a decent hotel?' I shouted over my shoulder. 'We've lost the escort and it's perfectly safe. What do you think?'

The others needed little persuading. I had seen a small but modern-looking hotel on the way out that morning. Our tent was still pitched at the barracks but we could always fetch that in the morning – along with Mr Nabad, who would be panicking at our absence.

Despite our horrific appearance, we were welcomed with open arms. The tension we had witnessed in Quetta a week earlier was non-existent. A hot shower and a chance to do some laundry were also long overdue. We were all shattered and not just physically. The whole trip had hung in the balance for the last twenty-four hours and psychologically it had been quite a scare.[12]

Over the next three days, the traffic became our biggest headache but it was nothing to the trials we had undergone in the previous days. From Multan, the roads, food and weather all improved and we made quick headway. Oranges grew in abundance at the side of the road and made for a refreshing snack whenever we stopped. Occasionally, we were accompanied by local police and we spent much of the time in a game of cat and mouse, trying to shake them off. They were invariably friendly but we were growing tired of the constant scrutiny. Mr Nabad was no trouble, but he too was becoming restless and was more than ready to head home. Pakistan had run its course and India could not come soon enough.

By the time we reached the outskirts of Lahore we were high on anticipation. Not only was it to be our last night in Pakistan, but we had also promised ourselves the best meal we could find. With Amritsar, in India, just twenty kilometres away, the next day also promised to be an easy one. We cycled along the wide boulevards lined by canals, still used but decaying into disrepair. A hundred years earlier and they would have been magnificent, the avenues of trees offering shade against the summer heat. We stopped to watch a herd of water buffalo cooling themselves and drifting gently with the stream. All of Lahore's faded splendour now took second place to a burgeoning population and incessant traffic. Grand colonial structures were much in evidence, crumbling mansions set back from the road a testament to what must have been a beautiful city. Instead, Lahore was now racing headlong to catch up with the Western world.

After deciding to give the bikes a rest, we headed for the old city in a couple of rickshaws. It was a decision we instantly regretted. It was now rush hour and the two drivers vied with each other by racing at breakneck speed. They dived and weaved the fragile machines through the traffic as we clung on for dear life, only removing their hands from the throttle a second at a time and then to whack the horn. On more than a couple of occasions we scraped against cars, but judging by all the dents that was just an occupational hazard in Lahore. Throughout, our driver maintained a running commentary by turning around to talk to us while tearing headlong down the road. I had been in rickshaws before but never anything like this. By the time we pulled up at the old fort my grip was cemented on the handrail and we knew

Ahmed's entire life story, even the details of his sister's forthcoming wedding. We tipped both drivers generously but they howled in protest and threw their arms up in mock disgust. It was a performance worthy of an Oscar.

'No mister, no. We very poor people. Petrol very expensive in Pakistan. Many children to feed . . .' The tirade continued as we walked away and through the old fort.

The setting of the old fort was magnificent, a blissful contrast to the chaos in the city outside. Not since Esfahan had I seen anything quite so beautiful and we ambled past the floodlit walls before making our way to the adjoining Badshahi mosque. Here we left our shoes and stepped through the enormous portal to the central square, a space that can hold 50,000 worshippers but was now almost deserted. We gazed up, silenced by the beautifully lit minarets and elegant domes. The marbled tiles felt cool underfoot, the effect instantly soothing. It was natural that we found our own space, and for an hour I wandered in contented silence. The last week had been so hectic; now I just felt my worries ebbing away.

On the far side of the square were a series of archways, similar to medieval cloisters, which led to the prayer chambers. A modest line of perhaps twenty men knelt in unison and I watched at a respectful distance. Their call to prayer could have been a monastic chant, the setting a cathedral. Majestic and solemn, it was a fitting end to our last night in the Islamic world.

We had heard the reputation of a restaurant called Cooco's Den. It was nearby and squeezed into a tall traditional brick-built house over several floors. The owner was Iqbal Hussain, one of Lahore's most famous artists. His subjects were the girls of the surrounding Heera Mandi, or red light district, and the walls were plastered with his lurid art. The ground floor was also crammed with antiquities and sculptures, even the doors were ancient and intricately carved. We climbed the steep stairwell and emerged on to the lower of several terraces. Before us was the most magnificent view of the fort and mosque, a panorama that would have cost a fortune in the West. Most of the meals were cooked on the street below, then loaded into copper pans and a loud bell rung. The waiters hauled on long metal chains and then, with great theatricality, swung the steaming dishes across the heads of the diners. A restaurant like no other, it made for a magical evening.

We emerged in high spirits to be hailed by Ahmed, the rickshaw driver. Clearly, we hadn't short-changed him. He had been lying in wait for hours.

'Hey, England! My friends! Here is best rickshaw in Lahore. Special for you I wait. Please please . . .'

Chapter 9

A River of Life – India and Nepal

We weren't sorry to see the last of Mr Nabad. The feeling was reciprocated when he announced he would not come to the border, and instead bid us an abrupt farewell in the hotel courtyard. We weren't quite so fortunate with the police. Again they were out in force, our escort numbering at least a dozen officers in two vehicles. They showed off in the narrow back streets, making their presence felt and brandishing their wooden canes at anyone who stepped too close. At least it made route-finding easier and within an hour we pulled into Wagah and what promised to be the end of police scrutiny.

Once a small village, Wagah was declared the only crossing point between India and Pakistan when Partition[13] dictated that the new border would pass straight through its midst. No vehicle traffic is allowed through the grand arch, and instead the meagre amount of trade relies on a colourful system. We stood on the Pakistani side, next to a long line of porters dressed in red and green waiting obediently for loads, while ahead we could see the Indian line, equally regimented but this time with blue-shirted porters with boxes balanced on their turbaned heads. Each Indian took his turn to offload his crate to his opposite number, for him to return with the imported goods into Pakistan. It was a simple but reliable arrangement. That was until we began to cross the border itself, wheeling our bikes through the transition area beneath the enormous arch. Amid the commotion a huge crate of tomatoes was dropped and splattered at our feet. Whistles shrieked and soldiers came running, all jostling for position to deal with the minor mishap. Anxious to avoid a diplomatic incident we promptly did a runner, forcing our way through the crowds to the relative calm of Indian customs.

Most government offices in India are a hive of activity, with countless officials scurrying around, piles of paper and endless rubber stamps. Not so customs, presumably because without letting anything pass, there was no work to do. I knew the news was not good when I saw Dickie and Ro sitting forlorn on plastic chairs in the far corner. Even Martha had a look of quiet resignation about her. Dickie explained that the decision was final; not even his negotiating skills or the offer of a 'customs fee' was going to get us through. There was simply no vehicle traffic between the two countries and Martha was staying put. I had long feared this would be the case and although it was certainly a setback it wasn't the end of the world. Martha had cost less than 3,000 thousand dollars and served us well through the worst of the weather. In truth, we were lucky she had made it this far. I was confident that now in India we would be able to hire something better, perhaps with a driver, for the ten days it would take to cross the country. Once in Nepal it was barely four days to Kathmandu and again we could make a similar arrangement.

While Dickie and Ro stayed behind to salvage what they could from Martha, we pressed ahead into Amritsar. We found a little hotel in the centre of town and that evening strolled along to the famous Golden Temple. As Sikhs traditionally wear turbans, custom dictated that we borrow a square of cloth outside the main gate. We placed it over our heads before washing our feet under the huge vaulted entrance. Stepping inside, away from the frenzy of the streets, it could have been a different world. Hundreds of people strolled along a white marbled avenue around a vast lake. It was peaceful, even calming, a place where you could only feel at ease. Many sat alone in silent meditation, heads bowed, as the crowds drifted by. The constant recital of prayer issued from the Golden Temple itself; at the centre of the lake and connected by a narrow causeway, it is the most sacred and holiest shrine of Sikhism. It was difficult not to be impressed. We watched as the sun set and the temple, entirely covered in gold leaf, took on an ethereal glow, as if floating lightly on the water's surface. Sikhism dictates that all temples and holy sites should be open to any individual, irrespective of race or creed. The generosity of the religion extends even further, as anyone can eat and sleep at the temple for no charge, the huge infrastructure supported by volunteers from across the world.

For the first time on the journey we heard British voices, and we chatted to a Sikh family from London. Their journey was a special pilgrimage, a chance to visit the very heart of their religion. They were aghast at the enormity of our expedition and promised to follow our progress over the coming weeks. It all felt like a world away from the rigours of Pakistan. For the last two weeks, progress had been faltering, but much to our relief the end of the cycling was in sight.

We were ready for departure early the next morning as our new van and driver arrived. His name was unpronounceable, so we promptly named him Mr P. He was as well turned out as his polished Mercedes van, immaculately dressed, and incredibly polite. He leaped into action when we began to load the bags and couldn't do enough to help. The plan was for Dickie to get back on the bike for some training, while Ro rode in the van, before they swapped later in the day.

We had hoped the early start would beat the traffic but there was to be no such luck. Our proposed route was to follow the line of the Grand Trunk Road, the main artery across northern India that originally connected Lahore and Delhi to the east. Our intention of camping was swiftly dismissed. There was simply no such thing as open countryside, with every square inch put to good use. Fields ripe with sugar cane were being harvested and to carry the crop every possible means of transport was employed. Lumbering oxen pulled heavily laden carts, sometimes with a dozen people aloft for good measure. They shared the road with lorries so overloaded they bulged to twice their intended width, and oncoming traffic was forced to swerve for cover. The very poor merely carried their loads on their heads and backs, risking their lives on the perilous road edge. Wherever you turned there was something to see, but less enticing was the constant wall of sound that prevailed. Indians love their horns even more than the Pakistanis, and invitations on the backs of buses call for you to 'honk if you're happy', as if more bedlam were really needed. The result was an incessant blanket of noise, impossible to escape.

Between the fields of sugar cane and the roadside lies a narrow belt in which people live and work. Every possible activity and business was in full swing as we passed. Women dressed in colourful saris collected dung from their oxen and carried it to the roadside, where elaborate pyramids several metres high dried in the sun. Barbers trimmed beards under the shade of trees, while truck stops vied for custom with hawkers in the middle of the road, and bicycle traders stopped to sell precariously loaded piles of oranges. Even laundry was being washed in filthy open drains and next to fly-ridden restaurants. It was dirty and overcrowded but we all loved it. Perhaps it had been the weeks of desert, or just the lifting of tension, but now the sights, sounds and smells were all intoxicating. There was no need to go in search of photos. Anyone standing on a street corner for half an hour would witness every possible aspect of life.

The main benefit was obvious within just a few miles. The roadside stops all had refrigerators from which we could buy cheap cold water and Cokes. It was a luxury we weren't used to, having depended on bottled water and tepid black tea. Now, during our breaks, we lounged on plastic chairs in the shade, feeling as though a huge weight had been lifted. Nic and Dickie made it their mission to spot the cafés that had a television in the corner. A test match between England and India was just starting and as avid sports fans they could happily have sat and watched it all day.

The pressure had eased but the atmosphere between us was increasingly subdued – I sensed a general edginess. It wasn't that we were growing tired of each other's company, we were getting on as well as ever, but now we were drawing to the end of a challenge that had occupied us for months. Thoughts were inevitably turning to the daunting prospect of the mountain and on a personal level we each needed to take stock. In another month we would be climbing the slopes of Everest.

There was another growing malaise in the team. All of us were feeling run-down and appetites were suffering. I had now lost twelve kilos, or two stone, since the start. Some of that was very welcome, but I also needed some reserves for the mountain and I couldn't afford to lose much more. Lunchtime stops, although relaxing, were not the most hygienic. There was always some form of dhal or curry on offer, but the open dishes were more often than not covered in flies and served with grubby hands and cutlery. There were few restaurants to speak of and without Martha we had lost our only cooking facility. The sole advantage of not cooking for ourselves was that we no longer needed to shop. Of course, it also meant that either Dickie or Ro could cycle with us. They too were starting to feel the pressure, knowing they had their own target of the North Col on the mountain and a lot of work to do.

Our route cut east straight across the Punjab in the direction of Delhi. Staying on the Grand Trunk Road would take us direct to Delhi itself, but we needed to head further south, and bypassing the capital would save time. With great excitement the following morning, we left the main highway and negotiated the back roads. To begin with, the route and scenery were a delight, the long avenues lined by tall shisham trees with whitewashed trunks, the regimented lines stretching far into the distance. They had been planted in the days of the Raj to offer shade to passing travellers against the fierce summer heat. Above us was the constant chatter of monkeys. They skipped through the trees and crossed the road high above where the branches had arched into a canopy. Sometimes they descended and were even bold enough to pinch food from your hands if you glanced away.

Soon the road surface deteriorated and we found ourselves on a potholed dirt track. Friendly passers-by assured us that we were heading in the right direction, although we had our doubts. The bordering fields were still being harvested, almost exclusively by hand, before the lengths of sugar cane were carried to the nearest threshing machine. Every few miles we came across them at the roadside. They chugged away repetitively while a spinning flywheel and belt chewed the cane fed into the machine. The resulting juice was collected in vats and tins before being piled high for collection. As the light fell late that afternoon I stopped to take a photograph of a family in a freshly cut field. The fine dust from the crop was suspended in the evening light, and the air glowed with a yellow iridescence. A small boy played alone in the middle of the field while his parents piled up the harvest. Unnoticed, a shaft of sun cut through the trees, and he too shone as if caught by a spotlight on a stage.

The next two days were bone-shaking. We made reasonable progress but by the end of each day were feeling battered by the endless potholes. The constant traffic was also getting us down. The lorries in particular were far too big and fast for the narrow roads. Gone were the long desert highways where we plugged into our music and found a rhythm for an hour at a time. Now we needed our wits about us at every turn, and the effort was draining. With some relief we arrived in Amoha to find a hotel with a large front garden and a tatty advert for cheap rooms. The owner was less keen and firmly turned us away. 'No mister . . . full, sorry, very full. Sorry.'

Unlike in Pakistan, there was no reason why foreigners should be turned away so we stood our ground. The place was vast and there had to be space. At our insistence, we were eventually given two adjacent rooms overlooking the central courtyard and only then did the penny drop. Final preparations were in place for what promised to be an enormous wedding that night. A few minutes later there was a knock at the door. The timid best man shyly introduced himself and invited us to the celebrations that night. We were dreadfully embarrassed, we didn't want to gatecrash. We declined politely, but the best man returned, this time with the short, smiling father of the bride. He tilted his head to one side and clasped his hands together as if in prayer.

'Please, please. You will be our very honoured guests. It is our very big pleasure if you will join our celebration.'

I might have been embarrassed but Pauline and Dickie were quite the opposite. They threw themselves into the party with all the enthusiasm they could muster. The guests treated us like long-lost friends, thrusting food and drinks at us all evening. I retired before twelve, unable to repeat the story of our expedition one more time, but there was no hope of sleep. The thudding Indian techno music started after the disco had finished – India is not the land of noise restrictions. It was nearly daybreak before sheer exhaustion got the better of me. Even then, a nightmare ensued in which I was kidnapped by Indian bandits and married off to the ugly daughter of a family in the mountains – all to the soundtrack of a Bollywood epic.

I woke feeling nauseous and exhausted. Another day of loud horns and bumpy roads beckoned, hardly the antidote for a hangover and a headache. Mr P. always slept in his van and he emerged looking as refreshed as ever, having had by far the better deal. We passed a succession of identical small towns and villages, and numerous small schools, mostly for younger children and with supposedly inspiring names. We saw the 'Blue Sky' school, the 'New English School' and even the 'Happy School'. All were advertised with brightly painted billboards, complete with smiling children clutching schoolbooks and satchels.

The highlight of the day was our arrival in a village square where we came across an enchanting sight. Hundreds of women sat on woven mats, chatting as they worked, sorting thousands of red chillies into baskets. The sweet fiery smell was intoxicating and the dropping sun lit the vivid carpet of red against their colourful saris. The sound of laughter rang across the square. It was unlikely that Westerners had ever travelled this way and we were witnessing something special, a common bond between people that our own society had lost generations ago. At first the ladies were shy of us taking photos, but Pauline soon won them round as only she could. They smiled warmly as we tried, hopelessly, to capture the scene, and giggled when we showed them their pictures.

Over the following two days, we made a big push towards Lucknow. We had thought the level of development might improve, but if anything the poverty actually increased. The roadside cottage industries continued unabated. The soil on each side was now of bright red clay and we passed numerous factories and kilns where it was being fired into bricks. Sadly, the workforce was becoming steadily younger. Children of six and seven dodged the traffic to sell anything from fresh fruit to cold drinks and samosas. The litter got worse, collecting in large piles that clogged the drains and sewers. Dogs and even people picked their way through the detritus, looking for goodness knows what. The most house-proud lit small fires in an effort to keep the rubbish at bay; they swept their area clean but in doing so made the mess someone else's problem. As we neared the city, we passed more and more gated communities, large signs advertising guaranteed electricity and water behind the high walls. It was an indication that the new wealth of India could not wait for a weak infrastructure to catch up. It was a widely reported problem. The young entrepreneurs and graduates that were driving the economy forward felt frustration, even embarrassment, that India was still a developing country. The solution was the vast apartment and villa complexes, effectively self-sufficient in their needs and security, but creating a barrier between rich and poor.

Being escorted to school by Da'Maria on my earliest form of transport.

Arriving at Everest base camp in September 1988, three months after leaving K2 and crossing the Himalayas from west to east.

The team about to leave the Dead Sea on 21 December 2005. From left to right are Pauline, Sarah, Nic and Jamie. The altitude is 420m below sea level. *PHOTO: Dominic Faulkner*

A lunchtime stop in Syria. As a talented artist, Ro took every opportunity to record the scene. *PHOTO: Dominic Faulkner*

Roman ruins in the desert oasis of Palmyra. The remote outpost in the Syrian desert was once the easternmost point of the Roman Empire. PHOTO: *Nic Clarke*

A winter picnic as the team enter the mountains of eastern Turkey.
PHOTO: *Dominic Faulkner*

Nic on the open road in Iran. Most Iranian roads are well made and allow for a generous hard shoulder. PHOTO: *Dominic Faulkner*

Nearing the Pakistani border, Pauline takes time out to enjoy the desert dunes of southern Iran. PHOTO: *Jamie Rouan*

Nic despairs at the flooded tent in Loralai, central Pakistan. The picture doesn't convey the smell that was to linger for weeks. *PHOTO: Sarah Lyle*

Sharing photographs with local children in India. *PHOTO: Pauline Sanderson*

Local women sorting chillies in northern India. The cyclists followed a remote route and tourists were a rare sight in the small villages.

PHOTO: *Dominic Faulkner*

Children in Nepal celebrate Holi, the traditional Hindu spring festival.

PHOTO: *Pauline Sanderson*

Negotiating the strong Tibetan winds and dirt roads at a height of 5,400m.

PHOTO: *Dominic Faulkner*

Nic and Jamie on one of the few downhill stretches in Tibet.

PHOTO: *Dickie Walters*

Tibetan girls near Tingri with EVERESTMAX stickers. *PHOTO: Sarah Lyle*

After 8,000km, the team cycle the last stretch into base camp on 12 April 2006.
PHOTO: Dickie Walters

Drinking tea and waiting for the weather to change in the dining tent at advanced base camp (6,400m). PHOTO: *André Zlattinger*

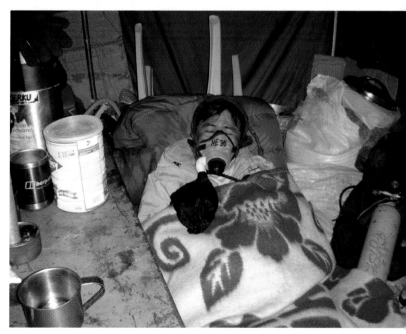

A dangerously ill Pemba was put on oxygen in order to save his life.
PHOTO: *André Zlattinger*

Departing the North Col for the summit. From left to right are Andrew, Sarah, Jamie and me. News had just come through of Jacques's death.
PHOTO: Pauline Sanderson

Jamie at a height of about 7,500m, climbing to Camp II, with Sarah in the background. *PHOTO: Andrew Sutherland*

Prayer flags were strung between our tents at Camp III (8,000m).
PHOTO: *Andrew Sutherland*

The view through the tent door at Camp III, showing the steepness of the
north face. PHOTO: *Andrew Sutherland*

Just below the summit on 21 May 2006. PHOTO: *Andrew Sutherland*

With Andrew (centre) and Sonam (right), safely down from the summit.
PHOTO: *Nic Clarke*

The traffic now increased in volume and ferocity. A slow ox or flat tyre would cause utter mayhem. There were never any traffic jams as such – everyone seemed to find a way through – but we witnessed the aftermath of some dreadful collisions. Twisted piles of metal were dragged to the side of the road only for the cargo to be picked through within minutes. But children were well fed and smiled at us wherever we went, and a warm welcome awaited us at every truck stop. We made our first 100-mile day in India, no mean feat amid the traffic and less than ideal roads.

Lucknow was every bit as hectic as we expected. We had experienced enough mayhem to know that cycling through the centre would be tantamount to suicide. We opted instead for the first hotel on the outskirts. It was a bit above our price range, but clean and comfortable, with a much-needed laundry service. The initial job was to deal with the tent. Since the sewage incident a couple of weeks earlier, we had slept in it for only one night and it had smelt so unpleasant that we nearly threw it away. I was keen to salvage it if we could, thinking it might prove useful on the mountain, if only for storage. We borrowed a hosepipe from the hotel gardener, but with Pauline in control we were soon soaked through while the bemused hotel staff looked on. It took another two hours to scrub it clean.

Lucknow had little to recommend it and by Indian standards was expensive. For the first time we witnessed young Indian professionals and the burgeoning effect of Western culture: fast-food outlets and American labels were everywhere. We even spotted a Marks and Spencer's store in a Western-style mall. We gave it a wide berth, anxious not to be reminded too much of home. Gone now were the oxen and carts of the countryside; instead, thousands of mopeds, modern cars and 'tut-tuts' vied for road space. Every second shop sold pirate DVDs or mobile phones. It was an explosion of everything technological in a desperate bid to keep up. I felt dismayed at the huge gulf in wealth we had already witnessed.

Now in the industrial heartland of northern India, we made quick time – there seemed no point in stopping for long. When we did, it simply attracted enormous crowds who stood and stared at us, the bizarre bicycling spectacle. Jamie began doing magic tricks, after admitting it was likely to be the largest audience he would ever get. Even our routine drinks stops had to be well chosen to avoid the gaze of onlookers. There seemed to be so many people with little to do, happy to stop and stare vacantly without a glimmer of expression.

Our mood lifted on the final night in India. Our stop for the night was Gorkhapur, a holy city on the banks of the Ghaghara river, a tributary of the Ganges and therefore our fourth and final river crossing. That alone filled me with pride: crossing the Euphrates in the Middle East, almost a different continent, seemed like a lifetime ago. We stopped on a bridge and gazed down at the pilgrims below, bathing and casting floral offerings into the muddy brown water. We found a small hotel on a busy street and wandered out later for some food. The street was thronged with a passing wedding parade, the groom being carried aloft on the shoulders of the revellers. Sparklers and firecrackers, horns and trumpets, all added to the spectacle as the cavalcade passed.

Our destination was Birethanti on the border with Nepal. Pauline especially could barely contain herself with excitement. She and her husband Phil had worked in Nepal for many years and she had a lot to catch up on. For mile after mile, we passed roadside vendors selling brightly coloured paints in preparation for Holi,[14] the vivid purples and lurid yellows spilling out of the open sacks before being weighed. We had timed it nicely for once. The actual festival was the following day, which, all being well, would be our first in Nepal.

With no Martha in tow, crossing the border was straightforward. Our hotel was modern and welcoming and much to Sarah's delight even had a bath, our first for three months. She had cherished a small bottle of bubble bath for the entire journey and promptly made herself scarce. The boys quickly began a full-scale assault on the menu. The food in India had been good but this was more varied, better cooked, and for once without flies hovering in attendance. An enormous plate of vegetable rice just wasn't enough. Soon our table was groaning with plates of chips and fried noodles, chased down by an inch-thick pancake with honey for dessert.

We quickly realised that our timing hadn't been so good after all, as we had arrived in the middle of a domestic Maoist strike. It was not unusual for Nepal. Political tension had been increasing steadily since 2001 and the massacre in the Royal Palace, when Crown Prince Dipendra committed patricide against the much-respected king and ruler of the country. He attempted to take his own life, but although mortally injured didn't die for another three days, during which period he was bizarrely elected King himself. His uncle then assumed power, but he failed to enjoy the popularity of his brother, the former king, and so the Maoists seized the chance to recruit the ever-more alienated population. A year earlier, the response of the new king had been to suspend parliament, such was his determination to tackle the Maoist uprising. Their favoured policy, in retaliation, was the occasional declaration of national strikes. These could last for days, and in fear of reprisals, no local people would dream of travelling during such a period. We were assured that cycling would be fine – in fact without motorised traffic even easier – but there was no way Dickie and Ro would be able to hire any kind of transport to shift the gear.

There was no real choice but to take a rest day and as it was Holi, local children were out in force throwing paint at anyone and everyone. The others went out to enjoy the festivities but I seized the chance to do some work. The mountain was drawing ever closer and there was no end of administration to sort out. The other climbers would begin flying out in just ten days' time, and would be anxious to see everything in place. I had updated the accounts and sent a load of emails by the time the others returned. Plastered from head to toe in powder paint, they really looked quite frightening.

Dickie had come up with an alternative and workable plan, albeit an expensive one. Flights were still operating despite the strike, so he and Ro could fly with the luggage direct from the nearby local airport to Kathmandu, leaving us cyclists to make our own way. We would need very little for a few days on our own, having done it enough times before. The weather was also warm and we would be staying in guesthouses each night. The plan would cost us several hundred dollars in freight, but we would make considerable savings by not having to hire a van and driver. The only downside was that Ro and Dickie, neither of whom had been to Nepal, would miss four days of wonderful scenery. As always, they happily resigned themselves to the new plan and we decided to cycle on the following morning, leaving them with the more onerous task.

With no traffic to contend with, cycling was sheer bliss. For the first time in weeks we could ride abreast of each other without any fear of being run down. We were still crossing the so-called 'Terai', a tropical plain of rich farmland continuous with northern India. We had been assured that the region was only about thirty kilometres wide in the south of Nepal and the hills would soon be upon us. One would think that a mountain chain as large as the Himalayas would begin gradually, even subtly, but this couldn't have been further from the truth. We stopped in the small village of Butwal for a drink, and then, within a minute of leaving, we were in the mountains. The first hill for weeks began so abruptly it was almost comical. This was the very boundary of the world's largest mountain chain, where sixty-five million years ago the Indian continental shelf had smashed into Asia and the Himalayan chain was born. After three weeks of cycling on the flat, at near sea-level, the change couldn't have been more pronounced. Our journey over the next couple of weeks would take us through the entire 'collision zone',[15] until we reached the high Tibetan plateau, the adjacent and enormous landmass pulled skywards by the tectonic uplift of the neighbouring mountains.

I rounded a corner to find Sarah surrounded by excited children. The others were ahead, but like me she was revelling in the scenery and had been stopping every few minutes to take photos. 'It's more beautiful than I ever thought possible. The people are just so lovely as well.'

She had to shout to be heard above the squeals of the children, all stretching high to try and touch her and see the camera. Their mothers looked on from the nearby terraces and before long we were offered milk tea and settled down to watch a game of football in the main street. Sarah was as happy as I had ever seen her. She had graduated in Geology just a few months earlier, and for her coming to the Himalayas for the first time was nothing short of a pilgrimage.

The mountains also presented a welcome change in the cycling, the steep inclines not fazing us in the least. We loved every minute, sweeping around precipitous corners, high above mountain streams, before coasting through villages and banana groves where the children cheered and chased us after us. Every few minutes we were greeted with a different view. It was everything a wonderful day's cycling should be. Our ascent for the day was almost a thousand metres, our biggest single climb since the day we left the Dead Sea, and at last we had something to show for our efforts.

We arrived in the small village of Bartung as darkness was falling. Many Nepalese villages offer guesthouse accommodation, but here we were well away from any tourist route. Instead, we made for a little teashop where we ordered some supper and enquired about somewhere to stay. The lady of the house fetched her smiling daughter, Prabina, who, it transpired, was a teacher and spoke good English. She immediately took charge and insisted that we stay with their family as guests, which had not been our intention. It was a generous offer, but if anything our embarrassment increased after we went upstairs. They had just one well-furnished room, meaning the family would have to sleep downstairs in the restaurant, half open to the elements. We proposed swapping but they would have none of it, making us as comfortable as possible.

We woke in the morning to the sound of children reading outside our door. It was only 6.30 but Prabina was already hard at work tutoring her young pupils. They were practising their English by reading old science books, and she later explained that they had to use whatever was to hand. We enjoyed a Nepalese fry-up in the café downstairs and prepared mentally for a tough day. Conditions were great but there were almost a hundred miles of steep mountain roads between us and Pokhara, our intended destination.

The day started well as we emerged from the village on to a sharp ridge which the road was contoured along. We were in the sun and, far below, the morning mist had settled like a pale blue sea into the deep valleys. Everywhere there was birdsong and the deep green foliage and heady scents that had been denied to us for so long. We crested a small pass and did a double take at the view before us. To the north, some fifty miles distant, rose the peaks of the mighty Himalayas. Half-hidden by the rising haze, the hundreds of mountains stretched impossibly high. It was a sign we were nearing our destination, but also a timely reminder of just how high we had to climb. These were small Himalayan peaks, and the biggest one of all still lay hidden from view, hundreds of miles away. It was hard to comprehend that we were going to climb that high.

We began a massive descent, coasting around gentle curves on the hillsides and through villages of mud-walled homes with thatched roofs. Children called to us continually, 'Namasté, what is your name ... where are you going?' The pleasant smell of smoke hit us in each village from the cooking fires – and, a minute later, we would be back in the cool air with overhanging trees and the scent of wild garlic enveloping us again. Always the valley side dropped far below as we descended ever lower towards a river at the bottom. For once, we could be carefree about traffic, and with the road to ourselves we took each turn at speed, safe in the knowledge that nothing was approaching.

After an hour of unchecked descent, we pulled into a riverside village next to the Kali Gandaki, one of Nepal's biggest rivers. It looked serene, but I knew that upstream it was ferocious; its waters had carved one of the deepest gorges in the world, between the peaks of Annapurna and Dhalagiri. There was no sign of Sarah, so we ordered some tea from a roadside stall and sat in the sunshine. The river below us was low in its channel and on the shoreline a funeral pyre was being lit, the shrouded body barely visible beneath the regimented pile of branches. A small crowd of people stood and paid their respects as a man advanced and a tendril of grey smoke snaked upwards. The cool breeze quickly whipped the flames and soon the crowd stepped back from the fierce heat. Others came and went on the shoreline, barely noticing the ceremony.

It was an hour before Sarah finally arrived. Her front brake cable had snapped and she had decided not to risk cycling the steep road. She had run the last five miles, missing the only downhill we'd had for weeks. Fixing the bike gave us another excuse to put off the inevitable ascent. We had to climb the valley on the far side and when we began it was relentless. Now cycling in the heat of the afternoon, the sweat poured off us and every turn brought yet another blind summit with no end in sight. In fact, it never did arrive. The day continued in a series of short, steep downhills, and for each one we had to climb the deficit and more. By late afternoon we were exhausted, but still needed to press on.

We saw little evidence of Maoist activity until we were about twenty kilometres from our destination. We took a turn in the road, only to be blocked by a felled tree and piles of stones in a hastily erected barricade. On the far side were the remains of a burned-out and still smouldering car. It wasn't difficult to pick our way through but it was a sign that the local people were not tolerating any passing traffic. We hastily grabbed a drink from a roadside stall to test the atmosphere, but it was frosty.

As we left the stall, the first ominous peels of thunder echoed around the hillsides. We pressed on regardless, but still the road climbed and dropped across an endless succession of ridges. We were cycling hard – now as fit as we could be – but we began to tire as the 100-mile distance took its toll. The air was charged with static, and although there was no rain, I could feel the prickliness on my exposed arms and the hairs on my head, high with electricity. Only when we reached the summit in the encroaching darkness and saw the lights of Pokhara far below did the storm really start.

It began gently, huge splats of rain that landed every few seconds. Then, within a minute, the heavens opened and torrents of water sluiced down from above. We were soaked to the skin in seconds, and there was little point in looking for shelter or even wearing a jacket. Then the lightning began, jagged blue forks dancing along the ridges above as we fought to keep control of the bikes on the flooded road. Our speed quickened as we dropped into the valley, but in the fading light we had to take extra care. If anything, the rain intensified and we lost sight of each other, doing all we could just to look after ourselves.

Clusters of houses began to appear as we neared Pokhara and I saw Jamie and Nic ahead, pulled up outside a tin-roofed house. The rain had eased off a bit but a small crowd of people stood around a man in some distress. He was pale and very clearly in pain. A local man was explaining to Nic that his friend had fallen from the roof in the storm, and on landing had broken his leg. They were anxious for us to phone the police so we headed off again, promising to do what we could.

Another fifteen minutes took us to the edge of Pokhara and a small roadside café. We paused to regroup and Nic tried to phone for help, but the best we could get was a vague response that they would pick the man up. We were fooling ourselves that they would do much about it and now we had another problem on our hands. We had waited a good twenty minutes, growing steadily colder, but Sarah was still to appear. Our wet clothes were chilling us and I began to shiver uncontrollably and could do nothing to get warm. By the time she appeared the rain had eased but it was fully dark. In her second mishap of the day, she had suffered a double puncture in the storm and wisely decided to take shelter. Tired and hungry we made our way into the eerily quiet town and found a hotel. It had been our greatest ascent to date, well over 2,000 metres, but the huge descent into town meant that we were at the same height as when we had started that morning. The real climbing was yet to begin.

Only on reaching Pokhara did we realise how few Westerners we had seen en route. In fact, we had counted barely a dozen since our encounter with German cyclists in Syria three months earlier. Now white faces were frequent in the bars and cafés and we felt reassuringly anonymous. We had grown used to being the most exciting event in the local people's lives, and while that had its merits, it could also be tiresome. At first we did little but eat and drink and enjoy the benefits of a decent email connection. Perfectly situated between lake and mountains, Pokhara was also the launching point for many treks in Nepal. The restaurants competed for hungry trekkers and the Western palate by serving lasagne, chocolate cake, pizza, and even imported wine. After the privations of the last few weeks it was delicious. We rounded off our second day at Pokhara's smartest hotel, drinking tea on the lawn and gazing at the view.

Jamie and Sarah had gone to pick up test results from the doctor, as neither of them had shaken off the stomach complaint that had bugged them for weeks. When they arrived it wasn't great news.

'Looks like Giardia, for both of us,' said Jamie, looking distinctly unimpressed.

'A full two weeks of antibiotics should clear it up,' added Sarah. 'At least we found out now, before we get on to the mountain.'

Both Pauline and I had also suffered and although she too had been tested, it had come up negative. Stubborn as ever, and much to Pauline's dismay, I had decided to take a chance and wait. I was feeling strong and, although losing weight, I intended to fatten up as much as I could in the coming week.

At least it was a relief to know that we were back on schedule and now Kathmandu was just two days' ride away. Of course we still had to reach base camp, in what was certain to be a very hard ten days, but that would be very different. The dynamics of our group were about to change dramatically. The climbers would begin arriving in just a few days and, for better or worse, the team would never be the same again. For now, I was just grateful that we had risen to the challenge and worked superbly as a team. Apart from the illness, we had also emerged intact and injury-free. There had been barely a harsh word spoken in three months and that was also no mean feat.

We could have happily stayed in Pokhara indefinitely, but after two days off were back in the saddle, for what promised to be a difficult couple of days. Now we were at a lower altitude, the forest canopy had all but gone and we found ourselves in an agricultural heartland. Paddy fields grew adjacent to the road and women worked in sociable groups, plucking the rice stems in what must have been back-breaking work. They never ceased to greet us with a cheery wave and shouts of 'Namasté'. The men worked alongside in charge of the oxen, attached to medieval-style ploughs, shouting brusque commands to turn the animals in the narrow strips. We crossed a succession of small rivers on iron bridges, built to withstand the monsoon floods, while high above, the paddies and terraces clung tenuously to the steep hillsides. Some were centuries old but they looked fragile enough to be swept away in an instant.

By the time we stopped in the small town of Mugling that afternoon our altimeters depressingly revealed that we had dropped over 400 metres since leaving Pokhara. Hard to believe, as we had been climbing for much of the day and it meant the final leg to Kathmandu was punishing. Every ascent was frustratingly followed by a sharp downhill, and our overall altitude increased only in tiny increments. Having travelled the road before, I knew there was a nasty sting in the tail. The pass into Kathmandu valley lay much higher than the city itself and from miles away we could see the road snaking in tight switchbacks up the mountainside. The gradient was steady but lorries and buses groaned their way around the corners, their engines straining at the effort of the ascent. The result was clouds of black fumes that smothered our efforts. It was a grinding ascent for us as well, and by the time we reached the clear air of the summit it was early evening and the light was fading.

At least Kathmandu was downhill, and now we were just ten kilometres and half an hour away from the centre. We needed to head for Thamel, the tourist quarter, but it proved elusive. Instead we found ourselves caught in rush-hour traffic on the manic ringroad. In desperation we resorted to hiring a taxi to lead us in the right direction.

'Thamel … hotel … we follow you.' Nic pointed in the general direction.

The utterly confused driver beckoned us into the back of the taxi.

'No, No. We will bicycle! You drive.' A few notes did the trick and the driver headed off, bemused at his first paying customers who didn't actually need a lift.

We knew Dickie and Ro had flown in the previous day and sure enough they were there to welcome us. Our 'EVERESTMAX' banner was even strung across the hotel entrance. With no Martha, they had done a brilliant job of moving all the freight through the Maoist strike. The trickiest part had been getting to the airport itself with half a tonne of gear. With no motorised transport, they had hired a fleet of rickshaws right up to the hold of the small plane. Now everything was safely stored in the hotel cellar. Three months to the day after setting off from the Dead Sea, we were once again a team.

Chapter 10

The Roof of the World – Tibet

Our first night in Kathmandu began with an impromptu party. Across from the hotel lay one of the city's most popular restaurants, Fire and Ice, serving all things Italian. We had been dreaming up pizza concoctions all day and wasted no time showering. As if we weren't excited enough, there was a surprise in store. No sooner had we stepped inside than Pauline's husband Phil greeted us with a shout from the far corner. Needless to say she was ecstatic, flinging herself towards him from some distance and sending a waiter flying. The evening soon became a double celebration. We had known Phil was out in Nepal already – his plan had always been to come out early and do some climbing – but he hadn't been due in Kathmandu for another few days. Pauline was uncharacteristically speechless.

It was the first time I had seen Phil since our meeting in Scotland almost six months earlier, but I was thrilled he was on board. I had a plan for integrating him even further into the team, which I had already discussed with Pauline. This was simply to ask him to be deputy leader of the climbing effort. He was the most experienced mountaineer amongst us and it would give him a worthwhile role in the grand scheme of things.

The details could wait and for now we gorged ourselves on fresh pizza and Italian ice cream, safe in the knowledge that we would not be cycling for at least a week. This was the hiatus in the whole expedition, a chance to prepare ourselves for the mountain, both logistically and mentally. Over the next few days, the other climbers would arrive and then together we would depart for the Tibetan border. We would continue cycling while the others enjoyed the luxury of travelling by jeep.

The following morning we took a taxi to the headquarters of Thamserku, the company that would provide us with logistical support on the mountain. They employed the four Sherpas who would be equipping our high camps, as well as providing cooks for base camp and advanced base camp (ABC). They were a reputable firm with a huge amount of Everest experience, but we still needed to check and double-check arrangements. Ours was no elaborate commercial expedition with hundreds of staff and unlimited oxygen and Thamserku were very much at the cheap end of the market.

I was pleased to see they had meticulously laid out in the garden everything that would be needed. We examined the dining tent, even the toilet tent, and of course some of the food that we would consume over the next two months. The Sherpas were terrifically friendly, shaking us warmly by the hand and we were soon introduced to our sirdar,[16] Sonam, a perpetually smiling character who couldn't do enough to help. At forty-three years of age, he had twenty years of Everest experience behind him and had summitted from both south and north sides. His English was faltering but he introduced us to his son, Tshering, who would also be joining us. He had already summitted the mountain once from the south, despite being only twenty-one. Like his father, he had an easy smile and a rock-solid handshake.

We retired from the garden to the company's main office where we met another Sonam, the boss of Thamserku and no stranger to Everest himself. His wife, the first Nepalese woman to climb Everest in 1993, had died on the descent. Her memory is still venerated in Nepal where she is regarded as a true heroine. With Sonam and Mr Rai, his assistant, we worked through every aspect of the operation. Most crucial of all was the number of available oxygen cylinders, and then confirmation of its quality.[17] Then there was the issue of tents and ensuring sufficient spaces for a team that now numbered fifteen. Lastly, we settled the final payment in a bill that came to well over $100,000. This would cover our permit to climb as well as the base camp support and wages for the Sherpas.

The meeting had gone well, but there was a long list of outstanding tasks. The support of Thamserku extended only as far as ABC and above that we would have to equip ourselves. This included the high-altitude tents, which would prove crucial to our success, and several hundred 'boil in the bag' meals, the food we would consume at altitude. Ropes, ice axes and spares all added to the freight that we collected from the airport. We spent a day unpacking and sorting, but much to our relief everything was intact. Then we repacked every item in labelled blue barrels that would later be carried up to ABC by yaks.

Modern-day Kathmandu now has numerous climbing shops dedicated to supplying the mountaineering industry. Only a few years earlier there had been none, but the Nepalese adapted quickly and it is now possible to acquire almost anything. Much of the kit was second-hand, offloaded by departing expeditions, and there were some great bargains. Nic and Jamie searched tirelessly for the best deal on a few gas cookers and 200 matching cylinders. It was probably more than we would need but any excess could be resold easily enough on our descent.

Nic and I also took the time to go and meet with two legends of the Everest climbing world, Russell Brice and Henry Todd. They had kindly agreed to meet us over a beer and offer some welcome advice. We waited nervously in a posh hotel bar, far nicer than anything we had stepped into for several months. I had met Russell a few years earlier when he had been of great help during our SAS expedition in 2000. He had summitted Everest twice himself, and famously surmounted the feared pinnacles of the North-east Ridge.[18] Now in his fifties, he ran the most successful commercial operation on the mountain, always on the north side, charging clients $40,000 to scale the mountain in a guided ascent – exactly eight times the amount we were paying. He was a no-nonsense Kiwi, but he warmed to us gradually and even broke into an occasional smile.

Henry Todd was an equally colourful character. He too was a commercial leader, but worked on the south side of the mountain and had not actually summitted himself. Extensive trafficking of LSD in the 1970s had funded his burgeoning climbing career, which was put on hold when he was caught and sentenced to fifteen years in prison. His reputation was less solid than Russell's, at the cheaper end of the scale, and he had even been accused of gross negligence with regard to his clients and equipment. Nevertheless, the so-called 'Todfather' of the south side was never short of clients on his trips.

Nic and I made good use of the evening, asking plenty of questions and getting all the advice we could. Top of my list of concerns were the weather and oxygen. The former could be an expensive problem as a decent weather forecast was critical to the safety of the team. Accurate forecasts for Everest were not freely available and the most reliable came from commercial sources in Europe. For a fee of several thousand dollars they could fax or email through regular updates on the nature of the jet stream at altitude. Commercial teams such as Russell's could afford this, but it was a luxury way beyond our budget. Henry did at least give us an idea for a more affordable solution – basically, be nice to lots of people and pick up what you could.

Oxygen was another difficult issue. Through Thamserku I had bought just thirty bottles, enough in theory to get six of us to the summit. The problem would arise, ironically, if the whole team were fit and keen for the top. At nearly $400 a bottle, our modest budget couldn't stretch to further supplies, although we all had some cash reserves of our own. For this, Russell offered a very welcome solution.

'Look, mate. I always take far more than I need. See how you're getting on and if you need some more, just pop over and see us in base camp. I'll do you a fair price but it'll have to be in dollars. There's only one currency on this mountain.'

'What if we don't use it all and have some left over?' I said.

'No worries. I'll buy it back. I'll always use it in the end. You guys don't want to be stuck with it.'

It was a generous gesture from Russell, who was after all under no obligation to help us. Amateur teams such as our own could be a thorn in the side for the big commercial operators. I sensed a grudging respect from Russell, who had been impressed on hearing the story of our ride. We wished each other well, knowing that the next time we met would be on the mountain. Nic and I left, feeling reassured that we had done all that we could to put things in place.

There was a welcome surprise at the hotel on our return. André Zlattinger and Chris Owen had arrived, together with Patrick Worthington and Nigel Lyle, the latest additions to the team. Pat had been a guest at our farewell dinner months earlier. He was no climber but had expressed an interest in just 'tagging along' and was happy to pay his way. With an awful taste in shirts and an Elvis-style quiff, he seemed an unlikely candidate for Everest. He was also a part-time comedian and promised to kick-start some base camp entertainment. I wasn't sure how it would work out, but the extra pair of hands would certainly prove useful.

Nigel was another latecomer, but his pedigree was more assured. He happened to be Sarah's uncle and had followed the progress of the trip closely. At fifty-three, Nigel would be the oldest member of the team and he was also a single amputee, having lost his leg climbing over thirty years earlier. A large block had crushed his foot while climbing on the Dru, high above Chamonix, leaving him trapped for two days. In one of the most daring and dramatic helicopter rescues in the Alps, he was swung 1,000 metres into space and hence to the safety of the valley. Gangrene had unfortunately removed any possibility of saving his foot. Fortunately, with the aid of modern prosthetics and the support of his climbing contemporaries, he was back rock- and ice-climbing within a few months. His passion for climbing, and even skiing, has continued until the present day.

It was great to see them all, but I was especially grateful to André. His fundraising efforts had continued long after our departure from the Dead Sea and made a real difference to the expedition. His enthusiasm for the climb was undiminished, despite the months of waiting, and he was eager to get started. Chris was a fairly late addition to the team and we still had a huge amount to catch up on, having lost touch almost ten years earlier. I knew from our numerous trips together that he had a wicked sense of humour. We had once cycled across Morocco as students and found ourselves stranded in a remote mountain village for the day. Spotted by the local teacher, we were pressed to give an English lesson. Chris happily obliged and decided to teach the names of body parts. I cringed while he pointed to his head and shouted loudly 'penis'! The kids and their teacher happily repeated in unison, while I could only pray that they never came to England.

The following day, Seb Bullock and Andrew Sutherland arrived. I knew Seb had been training, not that he really needed to. Like Chris, he was phenomenally strong and would be very quick on the mountain. It was a relief to have Andrew, our team doctor, with us as well. His schedule was such that he was the most likely candidate not to have made it, but I needn't have worried. Having just made the flight from a medical conference, he arrived looking frantic, but clutching bags of medical gear and free drugs. He hadn't let us down.

No sooner was the team in place than we had to go our separate ways. It was a two-day ride to the border, but for the others in jeeps it would take just a few hours and they could afford another day in Kathmandu. We planned to spend the night at Sukete Beach, a rafting station up in the mountains, but what I hoped would be a straightforward ride turned out to be just the opposite.

An upset stomach the night before had left me feeling weak and dehydrated. The fumes from the traffic added to my misery and I felt wretched. The few days off had done me no favours, and now I felt my fitness had all but deserted me.

Once in open country, the air improved and again the scenery was magnificent. Depressingly, though, we lost height yet again and the following morning were faced with an enormous climb. To make matters worse, the tarmac also disappeared and we found ourselves negotiating deep ruts and potholes. We had to get used to it. From that point on it would be dirt road all the way to Everest.

Our route carved its way up an impressive gorge and across the debris of numerous landslides, before bringing us to the roadside town of Kodari. It was a bustling but decrepit place. Ramshackle wooden buildings lined the filthy street while all manner of trade passed by and scrawny dogs picked through the litter. The main street finished in a dead end, only a rusty piece of corrugated iron and a pile of sandbags marking the end of Nepal. Behind them sat a teenage soldier playing with his helmet, the muzzle of his rifle resting under his chin. The defence of the nation was clearly in safe hands.

A few yards further on and the road swung to the right where we could plainly see the white concrete arch of the Friendship Bridge, the only crossing between Nepal and Chinese Tibet. Just like the border between Pakistan and India, no traffic was allowed to pass and a porter system was again in use. But this time there was no regimented colour-coded system. Instead, hundreds of Nepalese stood patiently in crowds waiting to pick up anything, a climber's expedition bag, plastic furniture, or a crate of food. The arrival of a lorry triggered an undignified rush and a long line formed behind the tailgate. More often than not there was insufficient freight and most were disappointed. Individuals carried a simple woven harness, which could be wrapped tightly around the load, before it was hoisted up and suspended from their heads. It must have been back-breaking work and we were told they would receive only a few rupees for each journey. To earn more they would simply head back to the start and queue for the next delivery. We watched with bemusement, and a little shame, at the many children working and even women with newborn babies. They had the added burden of carrying a child, usually in a makeshift shawl, in addition to their allocated load.

The others soon arrived and were in fine form. It was good to see them getting on so well and I noticed Pat already had the measure of everyone. All that remained now was to try and integrate 'us' and 'them' as a team. After all, in a few days' time the overland journey would be behind us and we would share a common objective.

The formalities at the crossing were straightforward and for a few minutes we stood on the high bridge suspended in no man's land. Looking back down the gorge at Kodari, we could see the wooden shacks that were the teashops, ominously propped up by stilts on the unstable side of the gorge. Such a volume of litter had been discarded into the valley below that it was hard to make out the river beneath.

To our left it was a very different view, our first of China and what used to be an independent Tibet. The very name conjures up romantic images of hidden peaks and windswept mountain passes, but this was definitely China – and China at its worst. The customs building was a modern three-storey block decorated in mass-produced white tiles, and could not have been less in keeping with the surroundings. Although more modern and better built than Kodari, less than a hundred metres away, it was every bit as ugly. At the far end of the bridge, an officious, uniformed soldier in a peaked cap checked our passports. Then, as a last defence against the SARS epidemic, our temperatures were recorded with a forehead thermometer.

It was by far our toughest no man's land. Passport formalities would not be complete until we reached the border town of Zhangmu, so high above us on the valley side that we had to crane our necks to see it. The road wound tightly in switchbacks for the

700-metre ascent, and although intimidating, it came easily enough, thanks to the steady gradient. We stopped a few times on the exposed corners to admire the drop into the gorge below, the bridge soon looking tiny against the enormity of the surrounding mountains.

Zhangmu is an ugly, officious-looking frontier town. What must have started centuries ago as a key trading post was now a bastion of Chinese officialdom, strung along a narrow winding street that snakes its way up the mountainside. There were no side streets, the terrain simply wouldn't allow for it. The roadside buildings reached several storeys high, with electric wires and tatty banners strung between windows, leaving the road below in perpetual shadow. Traders operated from ground-floor shops selling Chinese hardware and foodstuffs, while the higher floors were reserved for hotels, apartments and so-called karaoke bars. The bars are a favourite of the Chinese and the frontier demand for prostitution meant that many doubled as brothels, blaring out screeching Chinese pop music from tinny speakers.

Formalities at the passport office took another hour, but I was hugely relieved that we were through with the bikes. Independent cycling in Tibet is still illegal and I had prepared myself for the worst. My contingency plan had been to put the bikes on the lorry following behind, and then simply walk until clear of the guards' scrutiny. For now, though, it didn't seem to be a problem and the officials barely gave us a second glance. We had at last negotiated our final border crossing and I felt a little smug as we entered country number eight.

Having ascended by jeep, the others were already ensconced comfortably in our hotel. They mocked us as we approached, bottles of beer in their hands. 'What took you so long? I thought you guys were fit!' Spirits were high that night and we ate together for the first time with the Sherpa team. Sonam introduced us to the other climbing Sherpas, Dorjee and Karma. Dorjee wasn't much over five foot tall but with a barrel-shaped chest and thick climber's arms. His weathered face looked serious but at any time in mid-conversation he could suddenly break into a wide grin.

Karma was a very different character; handsome and smooth, he was the most Westernised of the team. He wore expensive sunglasses, smarter clothes, and didn't have the weathered appearance of the others. Much to my relief, he also spoke near perfect English, which I knew would be a huge asset. Inevitably it meant that we were already directing questions to him rather than Sonam, whose English was adequate but limited.

In the morning we were envious of the climbers who proudly climbed into smart Toyota Land Cruisers, provided as part of the Chinese permit we had paid to climb on Everest. There was no such luxury for us; instead we were back on the bikes for a mammoth climb. By following the gorge and the route of the Bhote Khosi river, now running far below, we would be able to cross the Himalayan range from south to north. If everything went well, we would emerge in a couple of days on to the Tibetan plateau. At least the distance was modest, barely thirty kilometres to our destination, Nyalam, a Tibetan village frequented by climbers on their way to the north side of Everest. At a height of 3,800 metres we would – for the first time on the expedition – be challenged by altitude. Once there, we intended to stop for two nights and allow ourselves some time to acclimatise.

It took an hour to leave Zhangmu. There can be few towns that are quite as long and thin. If anything the architecture became uglier, concrete and even glass buildings desperately out of place amid the mountain scenery, and tucked between them the sad-looking homes and shops of the original Tibetan inhabitants. It was soulless. Bouts of mist swept down through the gorge, swirling around the higher buildings and cliffs above.

I must have been distracted, as I noticed too late a toddler playing in the road and directly in my path. I swerved sharply to my left to avoid him and the bike jack-knifed, sending me crashing to the ground. With my feet clipped into the pedals, there was no way I could have escaped in time. Knowing a lorry was close behind, I rolled over only to see the enormous front wheels bearing down on me. He made no effort to stop and I threw myself – with bike still attached – into the gutter as the wheels rumbled past with inches to spare. I was convinced the lorry driver would have happily run me over. The bewildered child looked at me helplessly while I sat with my heart thumping in my chest. It was the closest I had come to a serious accident on the bike and I had been travelling at little more than walking pace. Infuriated but relieved, I hauled myself up, muttering at my loss of concentration. 'How annoying would it be to get run over by a truck in this crappy Chinese town . . .'

By the afternoon we were fading, despite the modest distance. The weather closed in and we were carrying little in the way of warm clothes, let alone food. We were running on empty by the time we reached the cosy 'Nyalam Hilton', cheekily nicknamed by Pat, who had arrived by jeep some hours earlier. At first sight it was perfectly acceptable, but the thick Tibetan rugs on the beds had never been cleaned and the open toilet could be smelt across the entire first floor. Lying alone in my sleeping bag that evening I heard the ominous scratching of rats beneath my bed. Thankfully we were eating our meals at the restaurant across the street.

The rats weren't the only problem. Howling dogs serenaded us through the night and a nagging headache from the altitude gain made for a fitful night's sleep. As our residence was lacking any kind of washing facilities, we were obliged to go in search of a shower the next morning. A Chinese shop owner hailed us and promptly led us down into his basement. Here he had installed Western-style 'wetrooms', complete with enormous tubs, and in one room even a jacuzzi. His enterprise was quite astounding and he knew it. He announced with a grin that the price was an exorbitant $5 for an hour. At two or three times the daily Tibetan wage it was daylight robbery – but worth every penny.

Afterwards, scrubbed and clean, we went for a walk through the village. The facial differences between the Chinese and Tibetans were very obvious, a sign that the Chinese desire to dilute the population was yet to be realised. Our hotel owner was very Chinese, with a longer leaner face and an officious manner to match. The Tibetans seemed friendly, with their squat frames and round smiling faces. Even the children were obviously different, the locals having the characteristic rosy cheeks which result from living at altitude. The efforts of the Chinese government to integrate Han Chinese into the local population have been fairly disastrous. Reports suggest that miscarriages among the immigrant population are far higher than with the locals. It would seem that the Tibetans have adapted to every aspect of living at altitude.

Although it was a rest day, some of the team chose to go for a walk on the ridges above the village. Phil had already acclimatised from his climbing over the last month and Seb was just as keen to push himself higher. André, Nigel and Chris also headed off and seemed to have formed a small working team. Nigel's disability didn't seem to be holding him back in the least and he was clearly in good shape. Those of us still cycling had enough on our plate without more exercise and instead chose to relax.

After lunch, the fifteen of us squeezed into one of the upstairs rooms for our first meeting and I used a large sketchpad to outline my plan of the climb. It was a nervous moment, one of my trickiest as leader, and one I had been mentally rehearsing for weeks. I had to earn my authority and convince them of my ability to lead the expedition over the next two months. I could be under no illusion – in the team were some very driven individuals and high achievers. Almost everyone in the room was in a position of authority back home and telling them what do was not going to be easy. It was fine when things were going swimmingly and there were few issues to be resolved. What about when there were arguments or, God forbid, debate about who should go to the summit first? Our expedition was unique and personally I was in an unusual position. Most teams on Everest were either of a very regimented structure with an obvious leader, or a loose amalgamation of climbers with no one particular in charge. Either arrangement might have been preferable.

Having thought long and hard, I had developed what I hoped would be a workable plan. I explained that the emphasis was very much on the individual to prove himself or herself on the mountain, before they could consider themselves ready for the summit. We would adopt the same model that I knew many of the commercial teams employed. In effect every member would have to overcome a succession of 'hurdles' to prove their ability, not only for the sake of their team mates but also for their own peace of mind. Everyone first needed to reach ABC at 6,400 metres – quite a challenge in itself – and later climb the North Col at 7,000 metres. The latter was the staging post for the upper reaches of the mountain and we also had to prove we could sleep there comfortably. The last test was to reach Camp 2 at 7,500 metres. Although there was a higher camp (Camp 3 at 8,000 metres) to get there we would be climbing on oxygen. There was therefore little point in training above Camp 2; in fact it would only waste our precious oxygen resources if we did so. It was a compromise plan but I felt confident that it would keep us more than occupied. Individuals could now push themselves as hard as they liked, and at their own pace, while at the same time we could measure our progress against each other. There was little point in being more prescriptive. I knew from previous experiences that plenty would happen in the next few weeks to take events out of our hands.

I was also careful to explain that my decision would have to be final if there was a dispute about who went to the summit. I simply could not afford to have a free-for-all, and I was relying here on people's better nature. If we were to be a close-knit team there was no room for anyone who harboured a competitive urge to be first. I waited at this point for a murmur of consent – and then paused again. We had to be certain of everyone's loyalty to each other.

There was a more likely scenario that also had to be dealt with. The chances were high that not everyone on the team would last the course, for whatever reason. Again I warned everyone present that if either myself, or Andrew as the doctor, deemed that someone should descend, then that decision would be final. Such occurrences have caused friction on previous expeditions. The symptoms of altitude sickness frequently mask themselves, and it is common for a sick climber to persuade themselves they merely have a stomach upset or a chest infection. We had to rely here on Andrew's experience – but Andrew also had a more immediate concern.

'Dom, bearing in mind that one of you cyclists needs to get to the top, does that mean you guys will be first in line for the summit?'

It was a fair question and I was glad Andrew had raised it.

'Not at all. You're right that if the expedition is going to meet its original objective then one of us at least has to summit – but as far as I'm concerned we behave as one team. If only for safety alone we have to put forward those who are fittest and strongest. If that happens to be a cyclist, then that's an added bonus.'

The only setback came later that day with some bad news from Pauline. Phil had decided not to accept my offer of being deputy leader after all, and Pauline apologised on his behalf. It was a blow, albeit a small one, but more worryingly I felt he must be sceptical about our chances as a team. I guessed this was his way of distancing himself from us all, in case of any mishap or failure on the mountain. He was playing safe, and while he had every right to do so, it put him immediately back on the margins of the team, something I had wanted to avoid.

The others left in the Land Cruisers early the following morning with three of the Sherpas, and again us cyclists found ourselves alone. Karma remained with Pemba, one of our two cooks and together they would drive ahead of us in a small jeep to make camp and hopefully stay with us all the way to base camp. We continued to follow the upper reaches of the Bhote Khosi, but now it had receded to little more than a trickle. Even at this modest height, habitation was scarce, just the occasional homestead, usually a squat building, whitewashed, and with a flat roof of dry grass. A vertical wand was always planted outside, carrying the five traditional prayer flag colours, bleached thin by the searing light. Yak dung was often piled high, drying in the sun to be used for fuel, and high walls surrounded the houses for protection against the fierce dust-laden winds. We took it slowly, stopping often for photographs. The ride was not about speed now, or even distance, but about staying healthy and letting our bodies adapt as effortlessly as possible.

It was a wonderful ride but I was anxious to check our progress before we tired too much. By the time we found the camp on the outskirts of a village, we had climbed well over 600 metres. We dropped to the ground, too exhausted to talk. We had barely cycled fifty kilometres, but in the rarefied atmosphere it had been tough-going. It didn't take long to recover after Pemba brought us some tea and biscuits, but already my head was pounding with the increased altitude.

We set off in the morning at a steady crawl. Already at a height of 4,200 metres we had to climb another 1,000 metres to cross the Thang La. Even higher than base camp, it would be the highest point of the entire cycle ride. Thankfully we would not be there long and would descend a little on to the plateau itself. We were back into working seamlessly as a team. After our time apart it seemed more natural to cycle close to each other, something we had done rarely on the overland journey. Caution was the watchword of the day and Nic and I set a steady pace of just seven kilometres an hour. It was no faster than a brisk walk but a rhythm was essential to maintain some progress. The road meandered its way up the mountainside in wide sweeps, keeping the gradient gentle for the lorries that travelled to and from the border. It was Tibet as it should be, desolate and bleak and in the distance always the backdrop of towering white peaks, punctuated by fluffy white clouds.

At the top we stopped for photos under a myriad of prayer flags, snapping in the gusts of wind that blasted up from the valley. We could see Shisapangma and Cho Oyu, two of the world's highest mountains, and numerous lesser but still enormous summits. It was a magnificent place to be and we were rightly proud of ourselves.

'We're 400 metres higher than Mont Blanc summit . . . and we cycled here!' Jamie had to shout to be heard through the wind.

An hour below the pass we found Karma sitting by a tiny Tibetan shack. Much to our relief, he beckoned us in and instantly the howling noise of the wind died away. The lady of the house smiled warmly and indicated the carpeted seats that lined the edge of the room. She was making butter tea, a mixture of tea leaves, yak butter and salt. The concoction had already been poured into a piece of hollow bamboo and now she used a long plunger to mix the tea to a frothy consistency. When it was ready, I declined, knowing it to taste foul and instead relied on Dickie, always our stalwart for local cuisine. Karma told us that although he enjoyed the occasional taste, some Tibetans drink thirty cups a day, a figure that filled me with horror. Instead, we enjoyed the more familiar Nepalese milk tea, made with bland powdered milk and a tonne of sugar. It tasted delicious and we savoured every sip. The mood was subdued as our appetites were already suffering, but we nibbled at a lunch of sweet Tibetan bread, yak cheese and a boiled egg.

It was downhill after lunch and the drop in altitude was a relief. We had crossed the Himalayas and before us lay a wide valley, devoid of vegetation, the desert of the Tibetan plateau. The road clung to a cliff edge and descended in spectacular fashion, the vista before us becoming more breathtaking by the minute. It was the most beautiful cycling we had done. The majestic surroundings were quite timely; we had entered a different world, the beginning of our next challenge. On this side of the Himalayas even the climate was different, the faces of the people more rugged, and the scale greater than anything we had witnessed to date.

At the base of the pass, the road eased and we cycled adjacent to a winding river for another thirty kilometres. Camp was again in a beautiful spot and Karma and Pemba made a real effort, scurrying around and attending to our every need. Even so, I slept badly and knew the altitude was beginning to catch up with me.

Not ascending slowly had been my undoing in the past but now we were frustratingly close. At least the following day would entail little climbing, as we now had to traverse east across the plateau and parallel to the mountains. The next day would also bring the moment we had worked very hard for.

It was mid-morning before we caught sight of Everest. We turned a simple bend in the road and there it was, looming on the horizon, majestic and serene. In the clear air it looked close enough to touch but we knew better – it would be at least another two days' ride. All being well the others would just be arriving there and hopefully setting up camp. We chatted and took photos but I walked off for a few minutes to be alone and take in the view. It was the first moment on the journey that I had felt the least bit sentimental about our objective. This was, after all, the mountain that had dominated my life for the past few years. My last view had been much the same, but that time I had been leaving it behind, despondent at my failure. Seeing it now made the magnitude of our task very real, greater than I could have imagined. Suddenly I felt very out of my depth.

Plastered in the dust that billowed up from the dry road surface we pulled into Tingri, second only to Zhangmu for grimness. Tingri was a dive of a place, a one-street town perched astride the main road. Vicious stray dogs wandered through the litter on the side of the road where every possible convenience was on offer. Open-air pool tables, piles of plastic Chinese goods, and even a portable butcher's with sorry-looking slabs of fly-encrusted meat. We watched a dog nibble at a piece of yak, hanging for sale, before turning to bark at a rival. It was a modern-day Wild West, a frontier town where a gunfight could have broken out at any moment and no one would have given it a second thought.

I was relieved to hear that Karma knew a good camping spot and he led us another three kilometres outside town. Here the road took an abrupt right turn – in fact our final junction. From this point it would be another sixty kilometres of steep mountain road. We were drawing ever closer and I was even starting to feel comfortable with the altitude. We braved a wash in the freezing waters of the nearby stream and Jamie and Nic celebrated with a haircut, shaving their heads one millimetre short, just as they had at the start of the cycle. Nic's mantra of 'look good – feel good' clearly hadn't deserted him. I went to sleep feeling confident that with two days to go not only were we going to make it, but with relative ease. My judgement couldn't have been worse.

Things started to go wrong soon after we left camp. We were following the road less travelled to base camp, one of two possible variations to get us close to the mountain. While it was more direct, the road surface was the poorest yet. The fine gravel we had experienced up until now had turned to large cobbles, and we fought to ride the bikes at all. The road was designed only for rugged four-wheel drives and frequently disappeared altogether. As if that wasn't struggle enough, within an hour we encountered the strongest wind of the journey. It blasted down relentlessly off the hillside, sweeping up clouds of dust and sand to sting our faces and halt our progress. We took shelter for a few minutes but it was no random sandstorm. In Pakistan the sandstorm we had experienced lasted barely ten minutes. This simply wasn't going to ease up. This was Tibet.

It was the only day of the entire journey that I thought I might not finish. The wind reached such ferocity that it became easier to walk, but my strength was failing rapidly and my throat was choked with dust. The road wound around the hillside, sometimes climbing, only to descend again, until it became interminable. I longed for sight of the tents but nothing appeared. In the desert we had ticked off twenty-five-kilometre legs with routine ease, even monotony. Now I focused on the next turn in the road – one step at a time. I would happily have traded an hour of desert highway for one minute of the effort required that afternoon. When the camp finally came into view, it started to snow.

'I can't believe you made it through that. I only had to walk one kilometre today and I can tell you that was gruelling enough,' Dickie shook his head. 'It's the strongest wind I've ever seen, even at sea.'

We had found a sheltered spot but Dickie still had to raise his voice to be heard above the gusts and the flapping of the tent fabric. We were despondent, even a little in shock. A bewildered Karma came in to say he had never seen conditions like it. After three months we thought we had seen it all, but, that day we had cycled just twenty-nine kilometres in eight hard hours of relentless effort. I was shattered.

I slept well through sheer exhaustion, and the next morning was relatively windless with a clear blue sky. It was piercingly cold, though, and for the first time in weeks we had to don hats and gloves in a bid to keep warm. It was a beautiful ride but it soon became obvious that we would not be reaching base camp that night. With few reserves left, we climbed for three hours to crest another bleak pass. I had always measured my progress against Nic and Jamie and now I could tell they too were fading. The girls were slower but as solid as ever and never far behind the three of us. I reached the pass ahead of the others, but only because I had pressed on through the last break. I collapsed, exhausted, to the ground, praying that all the climbing was behind us.

I needn't have worried. What followed was sheer bliss as we dropped gently for the next twenty kilometres into the Rongbuk Valley. We didn't have to pedal once and the channel of the road was eroded deep into the ground. We used the banked corners, like a bobsleigh in a chute, barely needing our brakes as we followed the natural line. It was a just reward after our efforts of the last two days.

We camped only twenty kilometres from Everest, but with the mountain further up the valley and around a corner there was little to see. At least we knew we would definitely make it the following day. It was no surprise when a gale was blowing the next morning, but we decided to try and cycle as far as we could. The effort was enormous, just to keep the bike at a steady four kilometres an hour, barely a slow walking pace. My scarf was wrapped tight around my face in an effort to keep the dust out of my lungs and I wore a full duvet jacket. Despite the sunshine, the air was now cold and we needed the warmth. The wind was from the side, and although that made progress easier we were blown across the road with every gust.

A strange thing happened as we rounded a curve in the road and faced due south. The wind died and we found ourselves in the shelter of the Upper Rongbuk Valley, besieged by tall mountains and an eerie silence. There before us soared Everest, every feature of the north face clear to see – even the summit looked perfect and serene. It was an emotional moment. Mother Nature had finally accepted us, having thrown all she could at us, and now admitted defeat in quiet resignation.

We took a rest at the Rongbuk Monastery, just six kilometres away from base camp and the last habitation. Over a milk tea we sat and chatted, realising it was soon to be over. We had worked together superbly for the last few months and I couldn't have asked for a better team. That we had all cycled so far and emerged unscathed was nothing short of remarkable. The mood was subdued and I too had mixed feelings. Despite the previous few days, cycling in good company across the world, taking what life throws at you, is as good as it gets. We all knew that we would probably never relive such a successful trip. Happiness came from sharing a common experience and whatever happened on the mountain, no one could now take that success away from us.

We contentedly wasted an hour before climbing back on the bikes for the last time. There was no escaping our next objective. It loomed bold and enormous, filling our view. We were on the flat for a while and then the last two kilometres began to climb in switchbacks. I heard a shout high on the rocks above and saw an arm waving.

'Dom! You're nearly there . . .' The voice echoed off the rocks. It was Andrew, offering some last-minute encouragement. The road flattened and we paused to regroup, savouring the last 400 yards. The climbers had done a great job. They had bought our sponsor flags down and even constructed a finish line. We punched our arms in the air as we approached, before collapsing off the bikes. There was laughter, hugs all round, and a few tears shed. Stage one was in the bag.

Chapter 11

The Eyes Have It

Spirits were high in base camp that first night. We squeezed shoulder to shoulder in the thin yellow dining tent and I thanked everyone, before making a toast to the climb ahead.

'Best of luck everybody and remember to stay safe!'

Andrew came back with a subtle dig. 'And remember we're one team now!'

We all laughed, buoyed by the success of the day. Pemba had been joined by Nat, our other cook, and in constant relay they brought us prawn crackers and soup, followed by a hearty pasta and sauce.

Although we teased the climbers about their easy ascent in comparison to our own, it transpired that things hadn't gone entirely smoothly. Chris had been quite ill for the first couple of days and the others had also endured splitting headaches. Arriving in jeeps was a mixed blessing. The speedy ascent didn't allow the body sufficient time to acclimatise to the increasing altitude. Phil appeared immune to all of this, having already climbed to 6,000 metres on the ridge above camp. The advantages of having come to Nepal a few weeks ahead of the main party were obvious.

Base camp itself was tucked under the steep terminal moraine of the Rongbuk glacier. The ice had long since retreated, at least a kilometre up the valley, and in its wake left an enormous pile of detritus some fifty metres deep. The moraine obscured any view of Everest and to see the mountain you actually had to walk about a hundred metres in the opposite direction before the magnificent vista revealed itself. As the crow flies, the summit was about fifteen kilometres away, framed beautifully by the long ridges high above us. Their craggy tops rose a thousand metres above the valley floor, their summits dusted with snow from the retreating winter.

A friendly Catalan expedition were our nearest neighbours, barely fifty metres away, and behind them was a huge Russian expedition who kept very much to themselves. Their complex of long interconnecting tunnel tents branched off each other like an alien spaceship. Across the valley floor I could see at least half a dozen other camps, some small clusters, others numbering over a dozen tents. In all, base camp probably described an area of at least a square kilometre across the moraine, but it didn't feel the least bit crowded and the distribution of camps was perfect, close enough to visit other teams, but far enough apart to have some independence. I had heard stories of teams on the congested south side of Everest coming to blows over lack of space.

It was a tired but contented group of cyclists that headed to bed that night. My own sleeping tent was about fifty metres away and I was shivering violently by the time I unzipped the door. The temperature had plummeted and I clutched two bottles of hot water, filled from the flasks provided by Pemba. Sliding into my luxuriously warm bag was a relief from the cold. I had planned to read but instead lay still and cocooned, watching the pattern from my head torch on the ceiling above.

Despite my exhaustion I woke at least twice during the night. I was trying to drink plenty but there was a price to pay. All climbers at this height were used to taking a 'pee bottle' to bed, to avoid having to get up and dressed before stepping outside in the cold merely to empty their bladder. But, unfortunately, even using a pee bottle wasn't simple: the process was a highly delicate manoeuvre and involved propping yourself up on one arm while grasping the bottle at the correct angle with the other. A spillage at this early stage of the trip would have been disastrous with no means of washing the sleeping bag for two months. The procedure was sufficiently complicated that it couldn't be done in a half-sleep. By the time you were finished you were fully awake, but at least relieved.

The following morning, our first at base camp, was stingingly cold. I lay in, warm as toast and feeling little urgency to tackle the cold and venture outside.

'Tea, Nigel? How do you want it?' André's voice cut the silence outside and I realised he was doing the rounds. By the time he reached me it was barely tepid, but it was a nice touch on his part. A few minutes later and the sun rose above the ridge and the heat struck the roof of the tent. The effect was instant and soon the inside had become uncomfortably warm. Unzipping the door I pulled a couple of layers on, before reaching for my shoes. Emptying the now frozen slush that was my full pee bottle was a priority before stumbling over the snowy moraine towards breakfast.

My appetite had never been good on mountains and breakfast was my worst meal. Porridge was a popular choice for most but I couldn't face it at the best of times. Altitude does strange and unpredictable things to one's taste buds. Our second cook, Nat, also produced pancakes, which, when smothered in cheap plastic jam, were quite edible. I contented myself with plenty of sweet tea, knowing that for once I wouldn't really need many calories. We had a day's grace before the yaks would arrive for the big move up to advanced base camp. It was actually great timing as there was plenty to do and we discussed tasks over breakfast.

Our Sherpas had brought an enormous and brand-new dome tent in which we could all sit if necessary. It was impressively comfortable and we covered the floor in foam mats, which made it even cosier. We designated it as Andrew's medical area and it also doubled up as a good place to store the laptops and satellite phone. Also pitched was the large green tent we had used on the cycle journey. It was a little the worse for wear now and ripped in places but it would make a great store tent. First in were the now redundant bikes, to be stacked in the corner. I had to laugh when Nic gave his a good clean and polish first. Much to his mock disgust, I flung mine in with little ceremony.

The main event of the day was to be the Puja ceremony, at which we would be blessed before setting foot on the mountain. This elaborate ritual was to be conducted by the Lama from the local Rongbuk Monastery and tradition dictated that we each chip in ten dollars. This allowed for the purchase of beer and whisky, which were stacked up around the makeshift shrine in the middle of our camp. Seated amongst us, the Lama began his chanting. In one hand he held his traditional string of prayer beads, 108 in total. I was sitting next to him and could see they were worn, eroded by the years of shuffling through his crooked fingers. In his other hand was a small brass bell, which he rang at intervals during the hour-long prayers. Although the service had far less meaning for us than for the Sherpas, it was hard not to be moved by the occasion, and soon we all became immersed in our own thoughts. For me it was time to reflect on everything we had gone through and to speculate on the coming weeks. We had just heard that Russell Brice's team, camped a few hundred metres away, had lost their cook. He had died a couple of days earlier from altitude sickness and for Russell it was a devastating loss – an early reminder, if we needed it, that just living here was dangerous enough.

After the ceremony the Sherpas were in a jubilant mood. They began to demolish the huge quantity of alcohol we had assembled, chased down with warm chang, the traditional beer. The Lama also seemed more than happy to partake in this part of the ceremony, before departing with the remains of the whisky secreted under his robes. The warm sweet smell of burning juniper added to the heady atmosphere. We encircled the shrine and flung rice on to the stones before Karma assembled the streamers of colourful prayer flags. These radiated out from a tall post not dissimilar to a maypole, stretching high above our tents. Each of the five bright colours symbolised one of the elements: sky, water, fire, air and earth. They whipped around sharply in the chill wind, the movement sending our prayers to heaven and blessing us in the process; things were looking promising.

The other main event planned for the day was a team photo. Strangely, it was possibly the one and only time we would be together. Having arrived earlier than us, some of the others would tomorrow head up the mountain. After that we would probably never all be in one place, with some at ABC and others here at BC. We headed across the moraine and away from the tents, in order to frame the mountain in our picture. It was the first occasion I realised that all was not well. The distance of just a hundred metres suddenly seemed daunting and for a moment I was worried about making it. I said nothing to the others, rather naively putting it down to tiredness from the previous day. It was all I could do to stand for the duration of the picture before dragging myself back to the comfort of the tent. I relaxed all afternoon and felt slightly better, but I knew that yet again the altitude was catching up with me. I could happily have missed dinner but made the effort, despite eating next to nothing. Things worsened in the night and I could hear gurgling in my lungs. Each intake of breath drew a sound like blowing bubbles through a straw. This was a worrying sign that I knew indicated high-altitude pulmonary oedema, or HAPE for short.[19]

I had a restless night and knew in the morning that descent was inevitable. My morale was dented as much as anything. It was an exact repeat of what had happened to me six years earlier. This time the stakes were a bit higher. We were already some ten days behind schedule in comparison to my previous trip. Any recovery on my part would have to be rapid in order to keep up with the others. It also compromised my position as leader of the party considerably. I had little doubt that things would run smoothly in my absence, but it would be immensely frustrating to leave at this stage.

After breakfast Andrew measured my oxygen saturations and seemed startled at the results. The pulse oximeter slides over your finger and the reading indicates the oxygen saturation in your blood as a percentage. Back home, one would expect to record close to 100 per cent most of the time. Mine measured in the low sixties, which was a little alarming. Andrew remarked wryly that if I were in a hospital back home I would be heading for intensive care. We talked at length about the various options. He suggested that in the short term I head down to the Rongbuk Monastery where we had stopped for tea only two days earlier. It was barely 200 metres lower in altitude but even that might make enough difference for my lungs to clear. It seemed like a good plan to me. I would be close enough to get back to base camp easily if I improved and I wouldn't feel too out of touch. There was also a Tibetan tea-house there, which meant I could get a bed and even a meal if I felt up to it.

We arranged for a driver down in the village to give us a lift. Andrew kindly offered to come down with me and make sure I was comfortable. Pauline helped me gather a few things together, the effort of which left me breathless and exhausted. Climbing into a vehicle was surreal after so much time on the bike. The jeep's soft suspension had us gliding over the dirt road and within half an hour we pulled up outside the Rongbuk Monastery. The tea-house surprisingly was full and instead we headed over to a faceless and ugly concrete building a hundred metres away. This was the new hotel that the Chinese had imposed on the small village to cater for visiting tourists. It required a monumental effort on my part just to walk there and Andrew waited patiently. We entered a cavernous lobby, a world away from the nearby smoky and warm Tibetan tea-house. Little wonder that was full and this was clearly empty. It took a couple of minutes before a bewildered Chinese girl appeared. I asked about a room before she scurried off and returned with another young woman and a man. They too looked equally amazed that someone would actually want to stay here. They spoke little English but after agreeing an extortionate rate of $30 I was shown to a room off the ground-floor corridor. It was spartan, freezing cold and musty. I made myself comfortable and climbed straight into my sleeping bag, not risking the damp sheets.

The room was deathly still after Andrew left. I couldn't help but feel I had checked into some sort of institution and I would never escape. He had left me with an oxygen bottle and suggested I use it for an hour or so to help clear my lungs. For now I felt comfortable enough and was reluctant to use oxygen unnecessarily, as we were already short on supplies. I lay in the stillness for hours, not even summoning the energy to reach for my book that lay on the shelf beside me. It was mid-afternoon before I had to get myself up to go to the toilet. It was tucked away up two flights of stairs; the sheer effort involved was exhausting. I clutched the handrail like a frail old lady, gasping for breath while my morale deserted me. I was supposed to be summitting the mountain in a month's time and I could barely climb a flight of stairs. I managed to buy some bottled water from the expressionless Chinese girl and returned to sleep all afternoon.

Too weak to make the stairs again, I used my pee bottle in the night and tipped the contents out of the window. That will teach them to make a hotel here, I thought. It was a miserable twenty-four hours and I was relieved when Andrew returned the following day. This time he had cycled down on Jamie's bike, shocked at the effort required.

'I had no idea you guys had worked so hard. And that was downhill!' Again he measured my 'sats', but I could have told him the result.

'It's not great, Dom. Really very little improvement, if any.'

'I guessed as much . . . Do you think I can still get better here?'

Andrew was insistent that I really had to descend further. Initially reluctant, I knew it made sense. Recovery here would be very slow and might not occur at all. If I descended properly, I would probably feel better overnight and would regain my strength a lot quicker. But that was much easier said than done.

Although the same Chinese drivers that bring climbers to base camp hang around for just such eventualities, the going rate for the twelve-hour trip to the border was no less than $800. They were ruthless and happy to exploit sick climbers, knowing they were flush with emergency cash.

The ideal destination would be Tingri, where we had stopped earlier, or the nearby town of Shegar. This was about three hours' drive away and crucially another thousand metres lower. There were guesthouses in both places and it should be low enough to kick-start a proper recovery. As it turned out, we had a stroke of good fortune. Andrew rushed outside and accosted a couple of jeeps, just about to head away from the Rongbuk. Unusually, the leading one carried just a single passenger. He was a gruff elderly American and reluctantly he agreed to offer me a lift if I was happy to tip the driver. Furthermore they were heading directly back to their hotel in Shegar. It was a lucky find and I climbed into the back seat after a rapid farewell to Andrew.

It was devastating to be leaving the mountain, but my condition was far more serious than I first realised. I knew within a few days I would make a recovery but would be at least a week behind the others in terms of acclimatisation. I had also eaten next to nothing in the last three days, barring a few boiled sweets. The weight was dropping off me quickly and I could feel my strength just ebbing away. I had to be realistic; my chances of reaching the summit were rapidly evaporating.

We sat in a comfortable silence for half an hour as the jeep bounced its way down the mountain, leaving a thick dust trail in our wake. Every few minutes we passed traffic coming in the opposite direction. Most climbers would now be at base camp, but there was a steady flow of tourists heading up to the monastery to catch a glimpse of the mountain. I tried to engage our passenger in conversation and introduced myself. His initial frostiness soon melted and he told me his name was Roy. He was actually a tour guide and ran small but exclusive Tibetan tours for elderly Americans. He explained that in the jeep behind were two elderly ladies, both in their seventies, whom he had been escorting up to the Rongbuk to see Everest. His other clients were too fragile to come up to this height so had remained behind in the hotel. He clearly had a love for the country and my respect for him grew when he explained he had led more than twenty trips here. We stopped for a break at the summit of the Pang La Pass, at an almost identical height to base camp. I had to stagger out of the jeep, but the views back to the mountain were magnificent. Roy offered to introduce me to his clients, impressed that I was a mountaineer, albeit a sick one. Out of the second jeep were climbing two of the most bizarre-looking ladies. The first was black and dressed in a full-length leopard skin coat. On her head she wore a wide-brimmed purple felt hat and enormous sunglasses. The second lady was tiny and wore copious amounts of jewellery. Her skin was stretched taut, probably from numerous face-lifts.

'Hey, Cheryl, will you take a look at that? Oh my gosh, isn't that just soooo awesome!' said the little lady.

'Oh my Gaad! That's just so big . . .' replied the black lady.

They were actually very friendly and were already enthusing at the prospect of our next stop, a visit to a real Tibetan home, 'to see how these people live'.

During the descent from the pass, Roy explained that he had been friendly with a local family for many years and had been supporting their son through school. When we arrived, the mother was there to greet us, but her son was nowhere to be seen. Roy was clearly disappointed but the boy soon appeared when summoned from the fields. He smiled shyly and looked very awkward when Roy gave him an affectionate hug. The whole situation was a bit peculiar but the American ladies loved it. They had seen 'real Tibet people' they drawled as we climbed back into the jeeps. I had to pinch myself to believe I had landed in such company in the space of just a few hours.

As we descended further, a cloud of dust appeared far on the horizon. Convinced it must be a mini-tornado or dust storm I watched curiously as it progressed determinedly towards us. Only after a few minutes did its true identity reveal itself. A band of perhaps twenty horsemen were racing across the plain. Above the galloping hooves we could see the riders dressed in all their finery. Stirrups glinted in the sun and atop their brightly coloured jackets they wore bearskin-like hats. They eased their pace as they passed and stared intently, their weather-beaten faces alone revealing the hard life they led.

An hour later we were in Shegar. The hotel we entered was just as characterless as the last one. Chinese-built and managed, it catered to the trickle of Western and Chinese tour groups that passed through. The sheer effort of the journey had finished me off. I booked a room, which again was freezing, and headed for bed, armed with bottles of water. Every breath required a fresh effort of will and I stared longingly at the oxygen bottle next to me. When darkness fell, I grew scared, thinking I might not survive the night. I had no means of summoning help and instead tried to cough up regularly the clear fluid from my lungs. Exhaustion got the better of me but I woke to more bad news. The familiar smudges from bleeding had appeared in my vision again, this time in my right eye. My spirits hit an even deeper low, if that was possible. So much effort had gone into the expedition, only to land up here, half-blind in a lonely hotel room.

The next three days passed in a daze of sleep, broken by bouts of difficult reading through one eye. It didn't take long to finish the two books I had brought. Only on the third day did I venture outside and walk for five minutes into the small village. I felt a little more human but pathetically weak. Returning to the hotel, I knew that I simply had to eat something before I wasted away. I couldn't face more Chinese food but luckily the restaurant did chips and I managed a plateful, washed down by a Coke. It certainly gave me some energy and I resolved that it was time to think about heading back up the mountain. It was not worth going home, I thought. I still had a role as leader of the expedition. For the sake of another six weeks, I might as well stay here and try and see someone to the summit, perhaps even one of the cyclists. That way the expedition would still be a success and I could return home with some pride intact.

Getting back to the mountain was not going to be easy. Everyone in Tibet is supposed to travel on a permit and within the confines of a tour group. I had already broken the rules by actually leaving the mountain unaccompanied. I would now have to pass back through several checkpoints in order to return. A couple of tour groups passed through the hotel, but they were very regimented and I didn't really want to impose myself on someone again. Instead, the manager suggested I head into the village square where I might be able to hitch a lift back in the right direction.

At least the walk was easier than the previous day, despite carrying my rucksack again. Traditional Tibetan houses surrounded the central square of the village but in the middle sat a petrol station in bright yellow plastic, complete with kiosk. There were no vehicles around and the wind was bitterly cold, sweeping in off the barren plateau. A small tea-house offered a good view of the forecourt and I settled in for a wait. After a couple of fruitless attempts, I was beginning to lose hope. Several cups of tea and a few hours later, a battered jeep pulled up and I spied a rucksack in the back. It looked promising. I made my way over to the driver as he was filling up. He was Chinese rather than Tibetan and wore an American flying jacket with Elvis emblazoned on the back. His jet-black hair was shaped into a limp quiff, presumably in an attempt to emulate his hero.

'Are you driving to base camp?' I asked. He shrugged and clearly couldn't understand a word. 'To Everest?' I pointed. He waved his hand as if to indicate maybe. 'Passum?' At this he nodded vigorously. 'Shi, shi.' He beckoned me to the passenger seat. At least this was across the pass and over halfway. From there, any traffic passing would be heading up the mountain. I had planned to tip him later, but he rather seized the initiative. 'Fifty dollar!' he barked. His English wasn't so bad after all. This was daylight robbery but he clearly knew the cost of transport in these parts. He also detected that I was fairly desperate.

I accepted – the alternative of another night in the hotel was just too much. With more cash he went back to top up the petrol before I flung my rucksack in the back and we both climbed in. He pointed to himself and said 'Chongu'. I replied in similar manner. 'Dom.' He then reached into the glove box and extracted a pair of thin white gloves. He slowly drew them on to his hands with magician-like precision. I wasn't prepared for what happened next. He sat still for a few seconds, gazing trance-like at the road ahead. Then with an aggression bordering on fury, he stamped the floor with all the force he could muster. I was thrown back in the seat as we flew screeching out of the petrol station and hit the road.

Chongu was on a mission. He was a lethal combination of repressed rally driver and Elvis 'wannabe'. Aside from the language barrier there was no chance of conversation. A tape of Chinese Elvis covers blared out through the cheap speakers. Things became considerably scarier when we reached the pass. He snapped and jerked at the gearstick, his cornering technique being to accelerate into the hairpins with inches to spare on the outside edge. We left long dust trails in our wake, as he showed no sign of slowing up. I wondered fleetingly if I could become his agent and enter him for rally competitions back home. He would have been a definite winner. I took to pulling my scarf over my mouth and nose to hold out the dust that was building up in the cabin, as well as hide my fear. I laughed inwardly at the irony that I might die in a traffic accident on the way to Everest before I even set foot on the mountain. The one blessing of his driving was that we pulled into Passum in barely two hours, less than half the time I had taken with Roy and the American ladies. I had hoped he might travel further, but he was stopping here and so I too checked into the local Tibetan guesthouse.

Unlike the Chinese hotels, this was a hive of activity. The huge open kitchen took up the whole of the earthen ground floor.

Around the edge of the room were low benches spread liberally with rugs and cushions. Local drivers and traders idly lounged around, their drinks and food constantly replenished. In the middle was the iron range, fed from a tall pile of dried yak dung. The smoke and smell were strong, but the atmosphere warm and friendly. I was offered a whole flask of nourishing milk tea, which tasted delicious. The gristly yak soup was a struggle but at least I was eating again.

It looked like I would be stuck for the night but there was no harm in that. As in Shegar I was still at a height of about 4,000 metres, so was recovering all the time. I slept much better and the following morning even went for a stroll above the village. Littered everywhere were the remains of ancient fortifications and ruined monasteries, some balanced precariously on rocky crags. It was starkly beautiful and I went exploring for hours – a sure sign that my condition and strength were improving. It was time to get back on the mountain.

In the event it was mid-afternoon before the owner of the guesthouse secured me a lift back up to base camp. Other drivers had been reluctant, presumably knowing that they could land themselves in trouble. The two Chinese I travelled with were attached to their own climbing team, so seemed familiar with my predicament. Within an hour we pulled into the village of tents below base camp and I tipped the driver, who unusually had asked for no money. I was really looking forward to seeing the others and felt like jogging across the moraine to camp. Caution got the better of me when I remembered that I had ascended 1,000 metres today. I was going to have to take it easy to avoid getting ill again. Seb was the first person I spotted at the edge of camp and he strode over to meet me, looking relieved that I was in one piece. Andrew, too, was over the moon that I had recovered, but urged me to take things easy for a few days.

For once it was a pleasure to go to dinner. I even had a small appetite and Nat had produced a 'yak steak sizzler' to celebrate my return. Nat's helper was a tall lean Tibetan boy called Guillet.

It was his job to serve the food and continually fetch the water for cooking and drinking. The water came from a small lake, fifty metres up on the moraine. Such was our thirst, he must have made the trip twenty times a day. Guillet was shy but beamed with delight when he saw how much we appreciated the food. It was the first meal I had enjoyed in over two weeks and I felt a little strength returning. Pemba, our chef during the cycle ride, had now ascended to ABC and was set to remain there for the duration. It was with some surprise therefore when Nat came running in after dinner with uncharacteristic urgency.

'Sorry, sir. Pemba sick. Doctor Andrew please.' He pointed at the kitchen tent next door. We hastened outside in time to see Pemba being lowered from a yak. His eyes were half closed and he looked dreadful. Nat and Karma helped him into the cook's tent, which was the warmest area.

'We have to get him into the altitude chamber,' Andrew insisted. Jamie and I headed off to the dome tent and gathered the necessary stuff. The portable altitude chamber was basically a coffin-sized inflatable tube large enough for one person. Sealing it and inflating it under pressure could simulate a descent of over 1,000 metres. Of course, while it could save someone's life, it was only a temporary solution. It was a well-practised routine but Pemba was incoherent as he was slid into the chamber. It transpired that he had felt ill at ABC and was soon beyond the point where he could descend on his own. I didn't envy him, knowing a little how it felt. It had taken seven hours for the yak to descend the entire twenty-two kilometres down the glacier. The moraine and scree were hard to negotiate at the best of times but on the back of a yak the journey would have been a nightmare. We had every reason to be concerned for Pemba. After all, Russell had lost his cook only a few days earlier. We spent the next couple of hours taking it in turns to pump air into the bag. It had to be constantly circulated to keep the person inside alive and the bag pressurised.

There didn't seem to be any visible improvement in his condition and by midnight Andrew insisted we put Pemba on oxygen. He had a clear case of HAPE and it would be the best way of getting him back to normal quickly. The only disadvantage was that our oxygen supplies were very limited and the cylinders were an expensive luxury. But in this situation we had little choice and there could be no hesitation when a life was at stake.

After just a few minutes with the mask on, the change in Pemba was dramatic. His eyes opened and between breaths he could talk a little. Half an hour later and he managed to sip some soup. The colour was returning to his face and then he cracked his wide smile, a sure sign that he was getting back to normal. He recounted that, during his journey he had fallen off the yak three times, barely summoning the strength to climb back on. His story must have been colourful as the other Sherpas started to cry with laughter. The translation from Karma was amusing enough. The rest of us gradually headed for bed, safe in the knowledge that he would be fine. For the second night in a row Andrew stayed up late. I was starting to realise that a doctor's lot was not an easy one.

Chapter 12

Oxygen Bother

There was a mass exodus the following morning. Phil and Pauline set off together to interim camp, closely followed by Seb, André, Jamie and Andrew. The full ascent up to ABC is twenty-two kilometres and at this altitude is an enormous undertaking. Most expeditions, ourselves included, had established a small camp en route, hence the name 'interim'. This broke the journey into two legs of about three hours, far more manageable than trying to do it in a single day. The camp was nothing elaborate – just two small tents, and an alarmingly leaky gas cooker. For Jamie and Pauline, this would be their first ascent up to ABC. The others had already made one foray and were now looking to head higher up the mountain, ideally to the North Col itself.

I spent much of the day trying to get through on the satellite phone to Kathmandu. Nat was worried that we would not have enough cooking gas to last the duration of the expedition. This seemed like a fairly basic error on their part and I decided to press Thamserku early to resupply us. There was also the oxygen we had used for Pemba. In the end he had needed two bottles, or about $800 worth. When I did eventually get through, the news from Kathmandu was alarming. Mr Rai, our agent, reported that there were widespread strikes and even riots in the city. The

243

Maoist rebellion, it seemed, was finally reaching a climax. Roadblocks were in force and there was little hope of being resupplied on the mountain. It wasn't good news but at least we had three or four weeks before we needed to get the oxygen in place and he promised to do all that he could.

I spent the afternoon emailing and in the process uncovered some depressing news. Three Sherpas had been killed on the south side of the mountain on the Khumbu Icefall. This was the treacherous lower part of the route where climbers had to negotiate a maze of broken ice blocks and towering seracs. I was glad we had no such obstacle on our route, despite the fact that we had a considerably longer climb on our side. It brought to four the total number of deaths on the mountain and most teams had yet to begin the actual climbing. I came across little news of Gerry Winkler, the Austrian, other than that he had arrived on the south side of the mountain and was in good health. I had to wonder if he was watching us as well.

The following morning the camp emptied still further. Sarah, together with Dickie and Ro, also departed for interim camp. Nigel and Chris, who were more familiar with the route, followed them a few hours later. Pat and I were the only ones left in camp and he decided to head off for a stroll around the other expeditions. Pat was proving quite an asset to our team. Although not a mountaineer, he had a passion for the hills and was having the time of his life. He also liked nothing more than extending our hospitality to climbers from other teams. In truth this should have been my job but I was never at ease with small talk. Pat's 'networking', as we liked to call it, was bound to pay dividends. So far we had done more favours for other teams than we had received but there was nothing wrong with getting a reputation for generosity. After all, the time might come when we needed to call in some favours.

Chris, a qualified optometrist, had taken a good look into my eye with an ophthalmoscope before heading off. The news wasn't good. There were at least half a dozen small bleeds and his advice was very definite. If I went back up the mountain in my present condition, and retriggered the bleeding, I could jeopardise my sight permanently.

I spent the afternoon drawing a timeline in the back of my diary. It was now 24 April and that left us with at least thirty days on the mountain, perhaps more if we stayed until the end of May. I knew that I could not leave base camp for another week at least. So that already took me to the end of the month. If my eye hadn't got any worse, perhaps I could head up to ABC and spend a couple of nights there? It would be only a modest gain in altitude, barely another 1,000 metres. If that trip didn't do any damage, perhaps I could go higher still? I wouldn't be back down until around 4 May and then would need a couple of days' rest before heading back up. Then maybe the North Col by 7 May? Then the long haul back to base camp again ... I stopped myself from getting carried away and threw the pencil down in despair. Some climbers had already been halfway up the mountain and I was yet to take a step out of base camp. I reckoned my chances of reaching the summit now had to be less than 10 per cent.

Patrick was great company that evening. His walk had turned into a mini-epic and he was enthusing about all the wildlife en route and the beautiful ice formations. His attitude humbled me. Here I was letting ambition take hold of me. I hadn't even noticed half of what Pat had seen. He delighted in Guillet's company especially, wanting to know everything about Tibetans and their families. We watched a film later and I went to bed determined that I should just let things take their natural course. I had to learn to slow down and appreciate my good fortune just to be here.

The following morning I rang ABC in our usual routine call. We had a satellite phone at each camp and it was useful to check that everything was fine. It also allowed us to update the plan for who was heading where and when. It was an essential safety net and I insisted that we record daily movements on a white board in the dining tent. The hike up to ABC was treacherous enough and anyone injured could soon become stranded. The news that morning was staggering. Andrew and Seb had reached the North Col the previous day. I was not the least bit surprised at Seb, but Andrew had left base camp only the day before, fully a day behind the others and on top of a couple of sleepless nights looking after his patients. Their achievement seemed to be spurring on the others and they all planned to make their way up to the Col that day. We decided to have another phone call in the evening to check on progress.

To work off some frustration, I decided it would be no bad thing to go for a walk myself and perhaps gain a bit of altitude. About a kilometre across the moraine lay a small side valley, which we had nicknamed 'the frozen river'. It soon disappeared from view, winding out of sight behind the ridge. It looked intriguing and a bit of exploration would at least take my mind off things. Pemba made me a small packed lunch of chapattis, cheese and a boiled egg, and armed with plenty of water I set off, determined to find a relaxed but steady pace. Everything at this height was further than it looked and I stopped a couple of times to admire the view over my shoulder. The mountain today looked serene against a crystal clear sky. There was a faint plume streaming away from the summit, a sure sign that high winds were still blasting the top. How incredible it was that we had come over 8,000 kilometres to this point and yet it was still so remote.

The valley was stunning. The frozen river had formed a slippery sheet, perhaps a hundred metres across in places. I picked my route carefully, gradually working my way upwards until I had ascended some 300 metres higher than base camp. Even this would be good altitude training, I decided, just pushing myself, and my eye, a little further. I had a lazy lunch, allowing my body as long as possible to adjust to the thinner air. The steep valley sides away from the river were a moonscape, barren and rock strewn. Above me lay high ridges covered in snow and numerous minor summits in every direction. To all of us hell bent on Everest it was too easy to ignore these lesser peaks, many of them comfortably over 6,000 metres in height. The famous explorer Bill

Tillman had climbed many of them. He had been a member of the Everest expeditions during the 1930s, a full decade after the disappearance of Mallory and Irvine, but they never attracted the same publicity as did the early efforts. Tillman himself had never felt at ease with extreme altitude and his experiences on the upper slopes of Everest were short-lived; instead he busied himself by climbing all around the base camp. Some thirty summits in the area have a first ascent by Tillman. In terms of exploration, it was probably a greater legacy than summitting Everest itself.

I returned to the level flood plain, but made a slight detour rather than head directly back to camp. It seemed appropriate to pay my respects at the memorial cairns that littered an outcrop in the valley. Here a British Army team had just laid a new memorial to Tony Swierzy. As a member of the 1984 SAS expedition to the mountain, he had died in an avalanche on 3 April of that year. He had been a close colleague of a team member on our expedition in 2000. I was too young to have known him, but his death had clearly affected many and his memory was very much alive. To those who have attempted SAS selection, his name is synonymous with '642', a triangulation point near Pen y Fan in the Brecon Beacons. Here his name is recorded on another brass plaque, among the hills where he trained. Our very first selection test had been to run up to the point and back with a fifty-pound pack, a one-hour return trip. Only after our descent did the instructor ask us for the name posted there. In our haste, none of us had noticed. 'Oh dear. You need to be more observant, gentlemen. Best get back up there and have another look then!' Another hour of pain ensued before the name of Swierzy was engrained on my mind for ever.

Around me were dozens of memorials, dedicated to those who had died on the slopes above. Some were formal, others simple inscriptions, carved in haste before an expedition departed. They were sombre epitaphs to many failed ambitions, and behind each was a story of tragedy. It was macabre to remember that this was no graveyard. The bodies of all those mentioned still lay high on the mountain, too remote ever to be recovered or accorded a decent burial. Below the memorial Russell Brice had his elaborate camp. Tents were laid out neatly in rows, the entire complex a village in itself. I popped in for a coffee and relaxed into a sumptuous chair, a world away from our draughty dining tent and plastic furniture. Climbers on Russell's team were paying a small fortune and this is where it went. It was a respite but I felt reassured that I would rather rough it and have over $30,000 left in my pocket.

Seb had returned that afternoon from ABC and his successful ascent of the North Col. He was typically modest about his efforts, doubly so in fact as he had descended the twenty-two kilometres in about four hours. Although they had set off together, Andrew was yet to arrive, but true to form he turned up just as dinner was being served. It was good for Pat and I to have some company again, especially as they were both on such an obvious high. There was no denying, though, that the climb had been exhausting. They both looked visibly thinner – hard to believe as it was only four days since I had last seen them. With their beards and sunburned faces, it seemed more like a month. The climb had been far tougher than they had imagined. The agony from six years earlier was still fresh in my mind and I sympathised completely.

'I was definitely unprepared for how hard it would be. At the time it was one of the hardest things I had ever done. The most I ever managed was ten steps in a row!'

Andrew agreed. 'It's utterly exhausting. The most depressing thing is that even when you reach the North Col you're nowhere near the summit. You can see it, but you're barely a quarter of the way up the mountain!'

We reminisced over dinner but as the plates were cleared away the conversation turned and I detected that something was amiss. Andrew spoke first. 'Dom, we've all been doing some thinking up at ABC. We've been looking at the whole situation with the oxygen again. In view of the fact that so many have been to the

North Col, we could have ten going for the summit. If that's the case, thirty cylinders won't be enough.'

Their unease worried me, but it was old ground as far as I was concerned. After all, I had been through all of the arrangements in Kathmandu and saw little reason to change anything. My only private concern was the danger of not being resupplied. With the oxygen needed for Pemba, things were left very tight indeed. 'The way I see it we have enough oxygen for six people to go to the summit. That's thirty bottles in total. I admit we could need more ... but if that's the case we can easily get them from Russell ... and at a good price. Nic and I have already cleared that with him.'

'But with ten going for the summit and needing five bottles each, we could need another twenty. Don't you think we should get them now? In case there aren't enough?'

'We could ... but don't forget only half the team have been to the North Col. We've just been saying it's barely a quarter of the way up the mountain. We haven't started the hard part yet! Look, I hate to sound so negative ... especially as the leader, but the chances of us sending ten people to the summit are very slim. People decide it's not for them ... or just get ill. You know that better than anyone, Andrew.'

I was referring to Tarka L'Herpiniere, the fifteenth member of our team. Tarka had accompanied the climbers on their first foray to ABC. He was relatively inexperienced and although very strong had fallen victim to HACE within just a few days. Andrew had cared for him in my absence, while I too had been ill down in Shegar. As Tarka had no option but to return home, Nic had selflessly offered to take him to the Nepalese border. It was a return trip of several days and he was yet to get back. This was a delay that would certainly affect Nic's own chances of attempting the summit.

I was doing my best to hide my frustration. Clearly a discussion of sorts had occurred in my absence and I felt my judgement was being called into question. Also, from twelve original climbers, Andrew was now assuming we were ten, twelve minus Tarka and myself. I was stung by his assumption.

Seb had been characteristically silent until now but finally spoke up. 'I think during our meeting there was a feeling that we ought to get the bottles early – just in case, really.'

'Look, Russell Brice assured us that he has plenty of oxygen on the mountain. In fact, far more than he is likely to need. However, he wanted to supply us much closer to the summit window. I trust him to do that. If I go to him now and say our team has reached the North Col and we'd like another thirty cylinders he'll fall about laughing!' At that there was a murmur of agreement, followed by silence.

My pride was dented. All I had left was a chance to run the expedition from here at base camp and I could see it wasn't going to be easy. It wasn't really about the oxygen; I had reviewed every aspect of the logistics and was still confident of the plan. It was more that my grasp was slipping. The very fact that a meeting had taken place in my absence was proof of that. I shouldn't have been surprised. After all I had been off the mountain for the best part of a week and it was naive to think that everything would be put on hold without me. Early on, Pauline and Phil had raised concerns about the oxygen we had in place but they had assured me back in Kathmandu they were happy with the plan. Now I had to wonder if that was still the case.

We tried our best to change the subject, both Seb and Andrew sensing my disappointment. To their credit they attempted to lighten the situation but conversation was awkward and after a few minutes I excused myself and headed to bed. The freezing night air had a soothing effect. I walked away from the tents until I could look back at the mountain bathed in moonlight. I so desperately wanted to climb, and staying here was like rubbing salt in the wound. I had been ill enough to head for home; only the role of leader had brought me back to the mountain. Now I could see even that was going to prove a challenge.

During the SAS expedition of 2000, nine of us had climbed to the Col, but only two had gone on to even attempt the summit. Although I couldn't say that I was counting on some not making it to the top, inwardly I had to. We were an expedition with meagre resources; those of us who had cycled were flat broke, having paid for the overland trip and taken much longer off work. I wished we could have afforded a hundred bottles of oxygen, but we simply didn't have the funds, hence the need for my 'judgement call'. I resolved that some form of compromise would be the best way forward. My eye seemed to be improving just a little and if that was the case I might head up to ABC in a few days. Maybe then we would be in a position to talk more about numbers.

I felt much better about the situation in the morning. Like it or not, people would just have to be patient and follow the plan. Of course, there was nothing to stop individuals simply going off and buying their own bottles, especially those that had the resources. But it would drive a wedge straight through the team – a team that I was desperate to keep together. I had to reinforce my position and be decisive. Naturally, that also meant standing by my decisions if I was wrong.

My newfound resolve was quickly tested during the morning phone call. Initially I spoke to Chris, who gave us details about the previous day's ascent. He and Nigel, together with Phil and Pauline, had all been to the North Col. Not only that but Chris, together with Nigel, had pushed on the next day, eventually reaching the high point of 7,500 metres, a little short of where our second camp would be. It was quite an achievement so early on. Phil and Pauline had come close, but thought the conditions too windy, so, playing safe, they had returned early to ABC. So far there was no reference to the meeting that had taken place three nights earlier. Then Chris asked about the oxygen.

'Dom, Pauline's asked when the extra twenty bottles might be coming up to ABC?'

Andrew and Seb had done their best to convince me it was just an idea. Now it seemed a decision had been taken. 'You'd better put her on the line, Chris,' I said abruptly. There was a short pause before I heard her voice, trying to sound cheery but it was more hesitant than usual.

'Hi, Dom . . . I hear there might be a problem?'

'Well, there shouldn't be, Pauline! Nothing's changed as far as I'm concerned. Russell has told me he has plenty of oxygen in place and we'll decide in a week how much we need. No sooner. You agreed to that plan in Kathmandu. I'm not sure why you're panicking? I might not be climbing any more but I can still make the decisions . . .'

Pauline was taken aback. Since our arrival at base camp, she and Phil had become inseparable. Even between the two camps they chose to trek alone. That in itself wasn't a problem but it made my job much more difficult. The last thing any of us needed was a team within a team. I longed for the Pauline of old. She put such store by teamwork and I valued her opinion enormously. I also needed Phil's support but he had already declared his hand. I knew he was here reluctantly, his sole aim to get them both to the top safely. Together they had even been given much of their own equipment. Now I suspected they saw the lack of oxygen as hampering their chances. I had to think of a way of bringing them back on board.

My mood lightened considerably when André and Jamie returned later that afternoon. They too had reached the North Col and looked shattered, their descent to base camp having taken over six hours. Despite that, they were great company and both were high on the achievement. They reported that the others intended to stay up in ABC for the time being. I was a bit disappointed to hear this, partly because I wanted a meeting to clear the air, but also for their own recovery. The North Col was a punishing ascent and afterwards it was all too tempting to collapse into ABC and just remain there. In truth, your body is constantly getting weaker at that height, irrespective of whether you are climbing or not. The best course of action is to make that extra effort and descend all the way to base camp. The improvement in Seb and Andrew's condition was already obvious. Later, we all had fun needling Pat that he was yet to escape the confines of base camp and that he ran the risk of an altitude-induced caffeine overdose.

'You guys have no idea. I'm far too busy here with important business. All this networking requires real effort you know!'

During the next couple of days, all discussion about oxygen was put aside. Welcome relief also arrived in a resupply from Mr Rai in Kathmandu. They had finally broken the blockade, but the situation in Nepal still sounded dire. I was concerned at how we would actually get back into the country if things didn't improve. For now there was little we could do and there were certainly more pressing issues. I was pleased to see that the two bottles we had used for Pemba had been replaced as promised. It was a weight off my mind and would ease the pressure on our present supply.

The last few days' meals had been getting a bit repetitive with noodle and garlic soup every evening, always followed by rice and chapattis. The soup sometimes had small pieces of floating yak gristle, but these became scarcer as the days passed. Vegetables were limited to deep-fried cauliflower and the last of the potatoes. Initially our dinner conversations had focused on politics, moun-taineering, films and books read. Now the only topics were our ultimate food desires – yearnings for buttered granary bread, bangers and mash, and even a full English breakfast. At least with the resupply things had taken a turn for the better. An aubergine curry, with a slice of yak cheese, followed a cucumber and carrot salad. We were expecting the usual dessert of tinned fruit, but with great ceremony Pemba paraded in with fresh mangoes. He was beaming from ear to ear as we applauded the upturn in our fortunes. Normally Guillet would serve the food, but tonight he had been demoted. It was a big occasion and Pemba was in charge.

It was now nearly May, and after almost three weeks on the mountain the days were not quite so cold. The layer of snow around base camp had thinned to patches since our arrival. For the first time, we took some chairs outside and read books in the sunshine. But our optimism was always short-lived; in an instant the wind could pick up or a flurry of snow or sleet would envelop us, enough to send us scurrying for the relative warmth of the tents. The daytime was bearable, but the temperature dropped rapidly when the sun dropped behind the ridge above us. We soon learned to come to dinner with duvet jackets on, and even hats and gloves ready for departure. Sometimes after eating we congregated in the dome, newer and considerably warmer than the draughty dining tent. We all fetched our sleeping bags and made ourselves as cosy as possible, packed in like sardines.

If Pat wasn't playing the guitar, the evening entertainment was usually a DVD, our limited collection bolstered by Dickie who had taken the initiative by buying the complete pirated series of James Bond movies. It reminded me of Christmas afternoons as a child. We had now seen at least a dozen and were still going strong. Of course, if the tent was full it was quite hard to see the tiny laptop screen. Often the batteries would die in the cold or a hot drink would get spilt and then chaos would ensue.

The worst part of a day in camp was leaving the warmth of the dome to return to your individual tent. By then, the temperature would have plummeted to minus fifteen. At least my bag was warm and within a few minutes I would be comfortable again. As all our water had to be boiled anyway, I had developed a practised routine. A couple of drinking bottles filled with hot water from the kitchen acted as good heaters in the sleeping bag. By the time they had cooled a couple of hours later, I would usually wake with a raging thirst. Once empty, they were then close to hand to act as the essential pee bottles. I also went to sleep wearing my head torch so that I never woke fumbling around for it in the dark. All common sense techniques perhaps, but a sign that we were adapting to the conditions and the routine.

It was now a week since I had returned to camp from the valley and my condition had improved considerably. My thoughts were increasingly turning to heading further up the mountain. If I was to have any chance of reaching the summit there was little time to lose. The others in the team were already well ahead in terms of their schedule on the mountain, although I did at least have the advantage of having climbed above the North Col before, so was familiar with the conditions and the route. Nevertheless I really needed to see how well I performed at a higher altitude and if my eye could hold up. If it didn't get any worse, I decided that I would keep pushing gently higher.

Both Andrew and Chris, who had since returned, were very anxious on my behalf and repeatedly urged me to take it easy. Andrew armed me with a long list of drugs to guard against the onset of more oedema. For my eye there was no treatment, although Chris continued to monitor it closely. It was not an unusual injury. One evening a Swedish climber came over, hearing that we had an optometrist in the camp. His prognosis was far worse than mine but he flippantly said that he would merely consider Chris's firm advice not to go any higher.

The mountain attracted no end of eccentrics and we had already met quite a few. Many had found their way on to Russell Brice's team. There was Tim, a Harley Davidson mechanic from the States, complete with tattoos. He had arrived in Kathmandu with his entire payment for the expedition, nearly $40,000, in cash. Graham Hoyland, who I had met in 2000, was also attached to the team. He was a BBC producer and great-nephew of Howard Somervell, a member of Mallory's 1924 expedition. Graham himself had summitted Everest in 1992 and had since taken a passionate interest in the history of the 1924 expedition. He remained convinced that they could have reached the top. His dream was to find the camera that Irvine supposedly had with him on the day. Perhaps the film inside could be developed and a wonderful summit shot exposed. Russell loved nothing more than winding Graham up about the camera. He joked that he had found it years previously and misplaced it in a drawer somewhere at home.

We enjoyed a great relationship with many teams, Russell's included. The Spanish and French teams camped next to us were very friendly, always popping in to say hello and share any information they had. Some teams inevitably kept themselves to themselves. We saw little of the Koreans camped across the valley, or the Indians for that matter. The most peculiar of the teams were the 'Seven Summits' expedition; they were Russian led and camped barely a hundred yards from us. I took them an official document one morning, which had been passed to us by our liaison officer. It was hard to discover who was in charge and I received a very gruff reception. Much of this was no doubt down to the language barrier, but they still seemed uninterested in mixing with other teams.

André and Jamie decided on 30 April that it was time for them to move up high again. They planned to leave the following day after an early lunch and sleep at the interim camp before reaching ABC the following day. It seemed like a good opportunity to head up myself. I had a restless night, wondering how I would react to the increased altitude. Most people with my condition would have headed for home long ago, so this was unknown territory. The good news was that my 'sats' had now increased from 60 per cent to 80 per cent in the last ten days. This was similar to others in the team so there shouldn't be too much to fear. The nagging issue remained the condition of my eye.

Most of my equipment had already gone up to ABC with the yaks when we arrived, but there was still a surprising amount to carry. Most of us had only one high-altitude bag so it needed to go with us when we travelled between camps. We also had to carry a variety of food and snacks for the two-day journey. As the camp was emptying, Seb and Andrew also decided to join us, making a party of five. That was until Seb announced that he couldn't bear the primitive conditions at interim camp and would rather leave early and walk to ABC in a single day. None of us were keen to join his ferocious pace, hence our more leisurely start. Armed with large rucksacks and a lunch packed by Pemba, it was midday before we set off.

We started by walking to our left around the snout of the Rongbuk glacier. The faint trail criss-crossed its way through the boulders and scree, worn thin by the hundreds of yaks that had passed. A few minutes later, we turned parallel to the glacier and began walking gently uphill. A vast ridge of lateral moraine marked the edge of the ice. Between this and the valley side was a narrow straight valley, perhaps fifty metres in width. It sloped gently upwards and made for easy walking. Ahead of us, framed by the head of the valley, Everest rose majestically and seemingly at arm's reach. After an hour André and I stopped for a break, resting our rucksacks on a huge boulder. Jamie was a few minutes behind but caught us up soon enough. It was a relief to be keeping up with them and for the first time in days I felt fully involved.

From here the path took an abrupt turn, striking steeply up the ridge to our left. It was a punishing climb that left you gasping if you went too quickly. I soon found the best technique was to slow my pace down to a crawl. The loose scree underfoot only made matters worse, as my feet slipped back and there was little to show for the effort. After half an hour the steepness began to ease and we entered the East Rongbuk Valley. This was the route that had for so long eluded the early Everest expeditions. In 1921 they had arrived late in the season and with no real prospect of climbing the mountain. Everest had only been seen from a distance before and knowledge of its slopes and possible routes was very thin indeed.

From the Rongbuk they had marched straight up the glacier and under the shadow of the forbidding north face. They spied the North Col, but from their side there was little hope of climbing it. It was not until mid-August that Mallory and Bullock, who had trekked many miles around the mountain, reached the Lhakpa La. This pass offered an uninterrupted view of the North-east Ridge and, most importantly, what seemed a modest ascent to the North Col. Mallory knew instantly he had seen the way to the top. Only later did they realise that the East Rongbuk, dismissed earlier as a minor glacier, curved around all the way to the foot of the col.

It was easy to forget the work of these early pioneers. The hardships they overcame just to reach the mountain were considerable. With no maps and little knowledge of high altitude, the odds were well stacked against them. I wondered what Mallory would think of the circus that we were now a small part of. Perhaps he might be just a little impressed that we had at least cycled to get here.

As we entered the valley, we came to a flat area high above a melt-water stream that gushed below. This was the likely site of the camp for the first British expeditions. Here they would have broken the long ascent up to ABC, but now yak herders used the area as a sort of impromptu grazing area for their charges. We walked adjacent to the stream for an hour or so across a gravelly flood plain. It wasn't long though before we were back on steep glacial moraine. The debris had been sculpted into narrow curved ridges, which gave way easily underfoot. In places the path was precipitous above the raging torrent of icy water below. High above and shading us from the sun were the steep valley walls, at least a couple of thousand feet high. If this valley were to be placed elsewhere in the world it would be a spectacular sight in its own right, but anyone here was en route to a greater goal, and it was all too easy not to even bother looking up.

Where the glacier began to curve gently to the south, a forest of ice towers emerged from the centre of the glacier. Like enormous white sails, the elegant sculptures crowded together, sometimes thrusting twenty metres into the air. We saw our first tents, where other expeditions had also placed their interim camps. Then, much to our surprise, Phil and Pauline appeared over the top of a steep scree slope looking drained and gaunt after their long stay at ABC. None of us had seen them for a few days, such had been the length of their stay.

We all stopped, grateful for the rest, but conversation was awkward and I let André and Jamie do most of the chatting. We conveniently ignored the thorny issue of oxygen. My stubbornness had, if anything, increased over the last few days, and I was confident that my judgement would prove correct. I was starting to feel part of the team again and was enjoying the company. It was Pauline who spoke first.

'Dom, I think we got our wires crossed the other day. The others clearly didn't get across what I had suggested. We were only swapping ideas really.'

'It's not a problem, Pauline, I understand. I just want any decisions to be taken centrally in a meeting, preferably when I'm around. I'll be back down in a couple of days so we can talk about it then, if that's OK?'

At this Pauline nodded, clearly much happier. We left it there, wishing each other luck for the remaining walk.

Our own tents were a little further on and frustratingly down a steep slope, which we would only have to reascend the following morning: two old ridge tents that looked like they had seen better days. Just a few metres away, as if taunting us, was Russell Brice's interim camp. It was about the size of our base camp. A huge modern dome for dining was surrounded by a series of smaller sleeping tents. It was in a different league to our facilities but then we were paying a fraction of what his clients were. We had a cup of tea and enjoyed the last of the weak sunshine before Andrew arrived.

Not only was I feeling fine but I could sense that Andrew was equally pleased not to have another casualty on his hands for the time being. Together we made a slippery and rather treacherous descent to the glacial stream below to collect water. The racing torrent had carved a smooth channel through the ice. Only a few metres down it disappeared beneath the surface. Falling in would have dire repercussions as it was fast flowing and incredibly cold. Back at the tents, the Tibetan cook from Russell's camp came over to offer us supper. He had no one in residence that night and we guessed, correctly, that he wanted to make an extra buck or two. This was confirmed when he whispered Russell's name and put a finger to his lips to signal we mustn't tell him. We were happy to oblige and it saved the effort of cooking for ourselves. Ensconced in the comfortable dome, we sipped on milk tea while our vegetable noodles were prepared.

Considering the altitude I slept well. Gone were the restless nights that I had experienced when we first arrived. I found that a litre of water was now enough to see me through the night, which in turn meant that I reached for the pee bottle a lot less. None of us had much appetite for breakfast, though. We shared out the left-over chapatti and jam from our packed lunch the previous day and filled up on sweet milky tea instead. The short climb back up to the main path was punishing and further than it looked. Perhaps fifty metres in total, it left us doubled over at the top and gasping for breath. I resolved to slow down and take it as gently as I could. The path eased for the next hour as we climbed a long gentle ridge of medial moraine, towers of ice soaring above on either side. I relaxed and tried to enjoy the walk, not an easy thing to do at this altitude. We were now at 6,000 metres, higher even than the summit of Kilimanjaro.

We paused to rest by a small green melt-water lake and here the glacier split again. We headed to the left, seemingly away from the mountain. Everest was now hidden from view completely behind the soaring ridges above us. The path steepened and my newfound confidence was quickly tested. Our pace slowed to a snail's crawl, as we paused, breathless, every ten steps or so. It was another long hour before the first tents of ABC came into view. André and Jamie warned me that it was still another thirty minutes as our camp was placed well back. An endless succession of small ridges and troughs delayed our arrival as long as possible. The loose scree and wet gravel slid on the ice beneath and made our progress frustratingly slow. It was with huge relief that I looked up from the last dip to see Seb at the edge of the camp, smiling down at us.

'Glad you could make it. About time!', he called out cheerfully.

'How you did that walk in a day I'll never know,' I replied breathlessly.

'I can't stand that horrendous camp, that was all that kept me going!'

Chapter 13

An Uphill Battle

It was all I could do to collapse into the dining tent. Thankfully, a smiling Nat was soon through with a flask of tea and we quickly made light of the walk. It wasn't long before discussion turned to a plan for the next few days. The others had been to the North Col already and were now looking to climb higher still; their next step to try and spend a night there before pushing up higher to Camp 2 at 7,500 metres. This was the height that Chris and Nigel had already reached, and Phil and Pauline had come close. During our meeting in Nyalam, I had suggested that this was the point everyone should reach before considering a summit attempt. It was also the model that many of the commercial teams had adopted. A night on the North Col would be good experience of sleeping at extreme altitude, while the climb to Camp 2 would be a real test of climbing stamina. On the summit attempt itself, we would begin using oxygen from that point, which would in theory make things a little easier to Camp 3.

I was tempted to join them in their bid to push higher but common sense got the better of me. Although seriously behind the others, my strength was improving all the time and I didn't want to jeopardise my recovery. The walk up to ABC had been easier than expected and my eye was no worse. The best strategy would be to descend all the way back to base camp, rest for a day or two and check that all was well. If so, I could soon reascend and push on to the North Col and perhaps sleep there. It was unlikely that I would have the time to ascend further but I simply had to take one day at a time.

Nat produced a tasty lunch of fried rice before we spent the afternoon sorting kit. The radios we would need on the mountain had to be charged from a temperamental generator outside the tent. Nigel had been persevering admirably but it was stubbornly refusing to start. It was over twenty years old and the lack of oxygen wasn't helping. For any generator to run successfully in the thin atmosphere, adjustments to the carburettor had to be made. Fortunately Karma's experience paid dividends: he walked up, kicked it a few times and it sprang into life.

The precious oxygen cylinders also had to be unpacked from their protective boxes. In common with most other expeditions on the mountain we had opted for the traditional Russian Poisk cylinders. Originally produced in huge numbers for the Russian air force, they had a reputation for being both lightweight and reliable. The genuine article was supposed to be a bottle that had been refilled in Russia. Horror stories had emerged where bottles were being filled more cheaply in India, allegedly with air rather than oxygen. Previous climbers had been unaware of this until the upper reaches of the mountain. I was assured the thirty bottles I had ordered were genuine, but they hadn't come cheap. At $12,000 it was a significant part of our overall budget on the mountain.

Most climbers used the traditional Poisk mask that came with the bottle and regulator. The regulator itself screwed on to the top of the bottle and controlled the flow of oxygen through to the mask. A small dial told you how full the bottle was, while a knob allowed you to adjust the flow rate in litres per minute. By choosing a setting of just two litres a minute we hoped to make a bottle last about ten hours, hence the need for three bottles for a full summit attempt. This would by no means make the climbing easy but it would give us an edge in an otherwise highly dangerous environment.

It is still very unusual for climbers to summit without supplementary oxygen. Of those that have made it, a significant proportion die on the way down or suffers severe frostbite. The latter is due to the oxygen-starved blood thickening and therefore not flowing properly. This in turn restricts the blood flow to the extremities and the result is rapid chilling. The chances of stroke, heart attack and collapse also increase massively; some have experienced impaired vision and even hallucinations.

Scientists are in little doubt that reaching the summit tests human physiology to the very limit. Added to this, of course, is the exertion entailed on a steep, sometimes technical climb. Reaching the top of Everest instantly, and without acclimatising, would result in unconsciousness within a couple of minutes; and death would rapidly follow. Those that have made it 'oxygen-free' have often been caught out descending due to deteriorating weather conditions. With the onset of a depression, the level of oxygen can plummet still further, suddenly equivalent to being another 200 or 300 metres higher than you actually are.

Despite the risks, perhaps even because of them, there is a 'purity' in reaching the summit without bottled oxygen that many mountaineers aspire to. Nevertheless, quite a few climbers seem to arrive on the mountain with aspirations to climb 'oxygen-free', only to compromise their ideals very quickly and submit to using the oxygen. Only the purist would stand by the maxim that 'no summit is better than a summit with oxygen'. For our team and myself especially there was no question in my mind – I would use the oxygen. To hell with principles, I was having enough trouble as it was just living at base camp. Cruelly, the physiology that determines how well you acclimatise is largely genetic and has little to do with physical condition. Success was about knowing your own limits, and I had been ill often enough to realise that I needed to be extremely careful.

We connected a cylinder through a regulator and into our new masks. I had rejected the traditional and basic Poisk mask for a new British model, the 'Topout'. Designed by Ted Atkins, an RAF flight engineer, it was adapted from a Tornado pilot's mask, making use of the oxygen that flowed into the mask while exhaling. Using a plastic cylinder to act as a reservoir in the delivery pipe, this oxygen would be stored for a few seconds, allowing more to be available when inhaling. Others had attempted to design masks, some with complex rebreathing systems that used exhaled air to retrieve oxygen. These had a very mixed reputation and we were reluctant to risk anything too technical. Ted's system was reassuringly simple, both in design and construction.

I strapped on the mask and Andrew released the regulator. At first I noticed no immediate change but the 'sats' monitor on my finger said otherwise. Where the oxygen level in my blood had hovered around the 70 per cent mark, it now climbed quickly to over 90 per cent, well in excess of even the level at base camp. It was immediately obvious that the oxygen would in effect make the mountain seem 'lower'. We took it in turns, testing each bottle and getting used to the masks and regulators. It was straightforward here in the tent but we knew adjustments would have to be made under duress. We would also have to swap bottles during summit day and for this we practised working together. One drawback of the regulator design was that it was impossible to see one's own setting as the bottle was carried out of sight in your rucksack.

The temperature plummeted that evening when the sun dropped behind the North Col. We were used to this at base camp but here conditions were colder still. We rushed for our down jackets and even big boots in an effort to stave off the cold, and by the time we huddled around the small dining table for dinner, it resembled a scene from *Scott of the Antarctic*. After dinner we played cards, but it wasn't long before the call of my sleeping bag was too strong. I retreated to my little tent and settled in as quickly as I could. Trying to read involved holding a hand out of the sleeping bag, but this only let the meagre warmth escape.

There was little rush the following morning and I waited for the sun to strike the tent and warm it up, relieved to have only a minor headache – another indication that my recovery was fairly complete, apart from the recurring problem with my eyes. We spent a leisurely morning in the tent, drinking fluids and chatting about the day ahead. The others were going to prepare for their departure to Camp 2 the following morning, while I too resolved to spend another night before descending back to base camp.

The next day, keen to get away, I headed off by nine. The sooner I was at base camp, the more rest I would get. Near the lower end of ABC, I came across Jamie McGuinness, the co-leader of the Everest Peace Project expedition. Jamie's team consisted of a loose assortment of climbers from seven different countries and five different religions, including a Palestinian and two Israeli Jews. By all accounts they were only short of a Pakistani woman to make their team complete. He was interested in our progress and had already dropped by a couple of times in base camp to chat. He looked concerned as we talked, and revealed that they were severely short of high-altitude rations. He wasn't sure if this was due to theft or some miscalculation. I promised to help him if we could but we had barely the minimum required as it was.

The descent was, of course, far easier and I made quick progress over the loose moraine. Every few minutes, though, there would be a short uphill section, which served as a sharp reminder to take it easy. I stopped on the path above our interim camp for some biscuits and a drink before pressing on. Only at the mouth of the East Rongbuk did I catch Sonam and Tshering. They had set off half an hour before me from ABC, so I was pleasantly surprised to have caught them up. They were busy sunning themselves and enjoying a well-deserved break. Sonam had been up for over two weeks now and really should have descended earlier. They beamed at me as I pulled level, hurriedly packing their rucksacks to join me.

'Ahh, sir, go very strong. Very strong,' Sonam repeated.

He had few words of English but they were always delivered with a smile. He was softly spoken and had a very warm nature.

It was hard to believe that he was a veteran of twenty-three Everest expeditions and had himself summitted five times. Tshering was his only son, and although he had a daughter she had sadly died the previous year. Now forty-three, he told me his ambition was to retire at fifty. His life was a hard one, despite representing the height of ambition for most Sherpas. Survival was always an issue for them and many died in the course of their work. On a dangerous mountain, the odds eventually catch up with the very best. Sonam had already earned enough to buy a lodge in the Khumbu valley on the south side of Everest, which his wife ran in his absence.

We arrived at base camp just as lunch was being served. In total, the descent had taken me just over four hours, about the same time that it took Seb. I was thrilled at my recovery and the air at base camp felt positively thick by comparison. The weather had also warmed considerably since our arrival and the earlier snowfalls had all but disappeared. Spring had definitely arrived and in the sunshine it was warm enough to sit out. Phil and Pauline, together with Nigel and Chris, were the only ones at base camp, with Pat still to come down. Pauline had relaxed considerably and now seemed far more at ease. It was a relief that we could get back to a level footing. To nip things in the bud, I asked Pauline later if she would mind talking to Russell about the oxygen again, just to confirm our previous arrangement. It seemed like the best way of keeping the peace and she agreed with alacrity, promising to pay him a visit in the morning. In truth, any visit to Russell's camp was a pleasure. It had the air of a Roman emperor's encampment, resplendent with carpets in the tents and fruit on the table. A shining example of how not to rough it.

I enjoyed my best night's sleep yet on the mountain. The effect of dropping to base camp was soon noticeable, not least through one's appetite. For the first time on the trip I was hungry at breakfast and wolfed down a whole pancake smeared in honey and crowned with a fried egg. My mood lifted still further when Chris examined my eyes. I thought I had detected a small improvement and he confirmed this, but he was still reluctant to advocate me going higher. Nevertheless, I was more relaxed about the chances of doing permanent damage. More than ever, I was resolved to carry on and perhaps even have a crack at the summit.

News was good the following lunchtime when we had a radio check with Nic at ABC. Seb, Andrew, Jamie and André had all pushed successfully up to Camp 2 at 7,500 metres. They had spent the previous night on the North Col and then got up early to make the five-hour climb. I was pleased with their efforts, as it now meant eight members of the team had reached this height or very close to it. That left Nic and Sarah, who had made the North Col but were yet to go higher, and me, of course, who was yet to even set foot on the climb.

Since the debate over oxygen I had been anxious to have a team meeting where we could talk things through. The following day would be unusual in that almost everyone would be at base camp. Nic and Sarah looked set to remain at ABC, but I felt I knew them both well enough to speak to them later. Events had moved forward considerably and with the summit period nearly upon us, I needed to try and cater for everyone to have a crack at the summit.

Thankfully Russell had confirmed that his supplies of oxygen were still available, but a greater restriction would be the availability of the other equipment. We had two tents in each camp, which in turn meant a limit of six in one place at one time. We also only had six masks, so there was no way that a group of more than this number could go together. This wasn't entirely accidental on my part, as I had always considered six the maximum party size. Now that everyone wanted to go, it would simply mean staggering two teams. A successful team would also need the tents on their descent, meaning that the second team could not begin until the first were off the mountain. These were the problems that I was presented with before even beginning to deal with the politics of who went first. It was the decision I most dreaded on the entire expedition. I had seen the fall-out on military trips, where some were chosen for the summit and not others. However, in the military the leader has been handed a professional authority. I had no such fallback. At least we were a group of friends and I would have to rely on the goodwill of the others to carry it through.

By the following lunchtime, Seb was the first to arrive, looking relaxed despite his descent that morning. He seemed pleased with their efforts of the previous day but was also in awe of the sheer scale of the mountain.

'It's a really punishing climb,' he explained, shaking his head. 'And the exposure to Camp 2 is incredible. I kept looking up at the rocks above but they just didn't seem to be getting any closer. It was like that for five hours without a break.'

'How do you feel about going higher still?' I ventured.

Seb was as considered and understated as ever in his reply. 'It shouldn't be too bad, I think. I'm looking forward to getting on that oxygen. It's worth a try anyway. I think we just have to be cautious, but yes . . . I'd definitely like to give it a go.'

Jamie and André arrived back into camp that afternoon, both looking shattered, and just before dinner Andrew appeared, looking cheerful but equally drained. We were learning that he was always last to arrive, usually having been delayed by a casualty en route. I put the word around that we should have a meeting after dinner in the dome and immediately there was a sense of tension in the air. I did my best to catch individuals to canvass their thoughts. If someone didn't want to go for the top, now would be the time to say. Selfishly, it would also make my calculations a lot easier.

Pat recounted the latest development in the British Army West Ridge expedition. It didn't help my unease. Their leader Dave Bunting had also announced his summit team. In an expedition of their size most would get no chance at the top and there were some very disgruntled characters. At least with us everyone should get a chance. My main concern was that there might only be one good weather window, in which case a second team would lose out. Jamie caught me before we went into dinner and in a typically selfless way said that he wasn't fussed which team he was in. He would just be glad to have a crack at the top, given the opportunity. It was a welcome gesture.

There was little room in the dome tent after twelve of us had squeezed in. With only the light from a few torches I could barely make out the individuals sitting with their backs against the wall of the tent. I was keen to stress the positive rather than repeat the whole oxygen debate.

'First, can I congratulate everyone on their efforts so far? We're in an incredibly strong position . . . as I'm sure you're aware. Few teams have as many people ready for the summit as we do. However, as you all know, this presents a problem. We can't all head for the summit together, so we're going to have to stagger different summit teams. I'm sure you can appreciate this . . . and I hope that even if the decision isn't what you were hoping for, you'll be happy to support it.'

There was a welcome murmur of content from around me before I continued. 'Clearly, if everyone elects to go for the summit, and most of you have, we are going to require more oxygen. That means more money, I'm afraid, probably $500 each. I'm proposing that we buy just an extra twelve cylinders from Russell, not the twenty that we discussed. That should give us ample and enough for every summit climber to have four full bottles. That leaves some in reserve, either for us, or for the Sherpas to use as they establish the top camp. I need to be clear that if we buy this oxygen and you change your mind, perhaps at the North Col, about going higher then you are still committed to buying the oxygen. In other words, this is the point of "no return", financially speaking. Is everyone happy with that?' Again there were nods of agreement.

'I've thought very hard about which teams should go first and I've based it on three things. Firstly, the experience of the individuals themselves. Those with more experience are more likely to succeed and should perhaps have their chance at the earliest weather window. Secondly, their performance on the mountain in the last couple of weeks. For example, Nic and Sarah are yet to go high on the mountain, as well as myself of course. Also there's the issue of how rested people are. That's down to sheer timing, I'm afraid.' I paused slightly, dreading the moment. Once this was out in the open there would be no going back.

'My suggestion then is as follows. I think Phil and Pauline, together with Chris and Nigel, should make up the first team. The second team would be Andrew, Seb, Jamie and André. Assuming they're successful, the second team can depart as soon as the first make the summit. In theory that means you will all meet on the North Col, where there'll be a bottleneck. We can get around that problem by putting an extra tent on the North Col to make three in total. That would provide sleeping space for nine people if necessary.'

I paused and was met only by silence, so I went on. 'That of course leaves Nic and Sarah and myself. The jury's still out on that one and I'm yet to speak to the other two as of course as they're not here. However, like me, they need more time, so if we go at all, it's likely to be in a very late third team. Or, if some of you drop out or choose to turn around for some reason we could take up those slots.' I took the silence that followed as a sign of general consent until Andrew spoke up.

'The thing is, Dom, I think that those of us that reached Camp 2 yesterday were a very strong team. We've also gone slightly higher than anyone else, and you did say that reaching Camp 2 was a necessary stage for anyone wanting to get to the summit. We're the only people to actually do that, apart from Chris, of course. It just seems the goalposts have moved.'

Andrew had a point, but before I could reply Phil spoke up, clearly stung at the implied criticism. His Scottish accent was soft but as always the words were very precise. 'Andrew, Pauline and I only turned round before Camp 2 because of the weather. The winds were too high to continue. That's a sound mountaineering decision. It wasn't because we couldn't have made it.'

I tried to defuse what was a potentially difficult situation. 'Look, Andrew, the four of you performed superbly yesterday, no one's denying that. You have also been higher than anyone else, but there are other factors to take into account. I would rather those with more overall experience went earlier. Their advice will be invaluable to those that follow. Remember, as a team we are still incredibly inexperienced. Also, you guys have only just got down today and you need a few days off. The other four are all rested and in theory could head off tomorrow, ready for the first weather window. I'm going to stand by my decision, Andrew; I think it's a fair one and on balance the best for everyone.'

In truth I had moved the goalposts a little, but my argument was valid. Phil and Nigel were probably the most experienced members of the team. It would be good to have their advice on the route after their descent. That aside, I felt the second team of Andrew, Seb, Jamie and André was the strongest one. What I couldn't say publicly to Andrew was that their best chance probably lay in going second. True, there might only be one weather window, but they stood to benefit enormously from the mistakes and advice of the first team. There is a huge psycho-logical advantage in being second, when others have paved the way for you. It had always intrigued me how near Tom Bourdillon and Charles Evans had come to the top of Everest in 1953. They were incredibly close to being the first on the summit but returned defeated, only for the second team of Hillary and Tenzing to grab the glory a day later. I was sure that Andrew would get his chance. Furthermore, I had a gut feeling that in practice things would unfold very differently from the plan. They always did.

All of us dispersed that evening, none of us in the mood to watch a film as we had on other nights. Holding such a formal meeting had ratcheted up the pressure, but that had been intentional. We needed to respect the severity of what we were about to embark on. Andrew, together with André and Pat, made his way to the dining tent. I sensed they might be discussing the plans and, anxious to avoid a post-mortem, I headed for bed.

The next morning, 7 May, Phil and Pauline wasted no time in beginning their preparations for the summit. With Chris and Nigel in the same team I had hoped the four of them would begin to work together but there was little evidence of that. Phil and Pauline were still very much a climbing unit, and nothing was going to disturb that. If anyone could bring a group together, Pauline could, but I detected that it was Phil who really needed to be in control of their climbing and safety. He had assumed the role of guide and partner for Pauline, anxious to get them both to the top and be done with it.

Pat pulled me aside later in the morning and gave me a much-needed confidence boost. 'Listen, mate, I just wanted to tell you that you spoke really well last night. Everyone is behind you, there's nothing to worry about.'

I wasn't so sure and said so, laughing. 'There was no dissent then last night . . . after I went to bed?'

'No, not at all. We discussed everything but that's to be expected. Look, if the weather closes in and some people don't get a chance, it's not your fault. No one's going to blame you. You're doing a great job. Everyone here knows you've got your work cut out.'

I was unconvinced, but from someone with no ambitions of his own, Pat's opinion was particularly welcome. If Andrew was at all bitter, he did nothing to show it. He had such talent and drive that he merely decided to redirect his energies elsewhere for the next few days. He announced at lunch that he would make a visit up to the West Ridge team at 'Shipton's Camp'. This was some five hours' walking away, directly up the glacier. His aim was to recruit more individuals for his eye study.[20] As the team was British, he could test them here as well as back in the UK if they all agreed. It was typical of Andrew's commitment to his research. At a time when everyone else was resting, he was actually increasing his workload.

My own agenda was very much under pressure again. I simply had to make the North Col before even considering a summit attempt. If I was going to make it at all, I would be heading for the summit in ten days or so. There was just time to climb up to ABC, then the North Col, and then back to base camp. In theory at least, things could work out, but there was no room for error. It would also give me a chance to catch Nic and Sarah, who were still at ABC. They deserved to hear from me directly what the plans were. I hoped they wouldn't be too disappointed at not being included in the main plan. I guessed not, as they were both struggling mentally with the whole prospect, Sarah especially. I still had absolute faith in their ability and was sure that our time would come as a team.

I set off after lunch for interim camp, confident that I could get there in three hours. I would be there on my own that evening so there didn't seem to be much point in arriving early. My plan was to walk up, eat a snack and go straight to bed. All being well, I would be in ABC the following morning. The walk didn't seem to come as easily as before. Perhaps I hadn't rested for long enough in base camp before reascending. In the end, I put my music on and my head down until I arrived, shattered, just after five o'clock. This time Russell's camp was occupied so there was no choice but to succumb to our tatty ridge tent. I made a half-hearted attempt to light the leaky cooker, abandoning the idea quickly after it flared up in my face. I figured the odds were already stacked against me without taking any more chances. I could see the headlines – 'Expedition leader dies in gas explosion on Everest!'

The problem is you never want a cup of tea more than when you can't have one. I could easily have asked at Russell's tent for some hot water but pride prevented me. It would be tantamount to admitting that our camp was inferior and we needed their help. I didn't need to spend $40,000 I decided, and resolved to try and get a good night's sleep. The following morning I was on my way early and soon met Nic descending in the opposite direction. We were both glad of the break and sat in the sunshine for twenty minutes while we caught up on news. He and Sarah had been to the North Col, but he didn't seem entirely at ease with himself. I sensed that he still hadn't fully acclimatised to the conditions, not just physically but mentally as well. I knew what a perfectionist he was and he was never happy in himself if things weren't just right. I explained the outcome of the meeting and he seemed resigned to the idea of going later.

'Absolutely fine. I'm simply not ready yet anyway. I think it's just taking me a while to find my feet. If the chance comes up, I'll be really grateful.'

We went our separate ways, but I couldn't help feeling that Nic seemed dejected. Perhaps he had already sensed the summit wasn't for him. He had also lost a few days escorting Tarka to the border; a big sacrifice on his part, which had placed him even further behind in terms of acclimatisation. By the time I arrived in ABC, I was also feeling a bit down. The ascent had seemed harder than a few days ago and had actually taken me a little longer. Perhaps I too was approaching my limit.

Sarah was the only one in ABC, together with two Sherpas, and she was relieved to have some company. We had a pack of playing cards, on the back of which were fifty-two different plant species. Such was her boredom that she had learned them all the previous evening, Latin names included. A quick test proved she hadn't been idle.

Sarah was disappointed by not being included in the main teams, but as always she accepted my decision with good grace.

'I just think my chances of getting to the top are pretty slim now, aren't they? The weather will have closed in before we get a chance.'

'Not at all,' I reassured her. 'Our opportunity will come and it could be sooner rather than later. Don't forget, not all of the others will make it. It's only a plan and I'm absolutely sure it will change.'

'Well, just getting to the North Col is a struggle at the moment for both Nic and I. I can't really imagine myself going higher anyway. What were your plans?'

'I was thinking of heading up there tomorrow and then hopefully spending the night. If that goes well, maybe ascend a little of the way to Camp 2. If I feel good, then I know I'm OK for a crack at the summit, although it's still a tall order, I know. If you come as well, it would give you a chance to look at the rest of the route?'

Sarah seemed happy with the plan. Her lack of confidence was more mental than physical. She had acclimatised well and I knew she was as strong as any of us. She was also very determined and could achieve anything she put her mind to. That said, she was probably the least experienced member of the team. For her to get to the North Col would, in truth, be a great achievement. But deep down she knew she had the strength, and the opportunity, to go the whole way.

After an early night and a leisurely start, Sarah and I made our way slowly out of ABC the following morning. The numerous tented camps and prayer flags en route gave it a carnival-like atmosphere. The site was strung out over half a mile along the moraine between the glacier and the steep valley wall. Unlike base camp, where there were large distances between camps, here we were barely metres apart. We said hello to familiar faces as we passed but were reluctant to stop for long. Our pace was painfully slow, and our full sacks for the night on the Col further hindered us. It was half an hour before the path came to an abrupt end at the edge of the glacier. Here, climbers had deposited barrels of equipment, walking poles and various detritus. We unshouldered our sacks and for the first time on the trip, I put my crampons on. From this point on, we would be on ice.

The glacier led us into a huge cwm,[21] above which towered the slopes of the North Col, the steep cliffs and overhanging glaciers shielding us from any wind. Like the western cwm on the far side of the mountain, it was a colossal heat-trap. The sun's rays, strong in the thin atmosphere, reflected back from the ice with a dazzling glare. The gradient was gentle, but in the fierce heat we wore only salopettes with a T-shirt beneath. Above the North Col, at an unfamiliar angle, we could make out the summit. I paused and gazed up, trying to magic it closer in some way. Never had a summit been so near but quite so far. After travelling 8,000 kilometres, it was maybe three kilometres away as the crow flies. Our journey was almost over, but the last section would prove equal to all that had gone before.

The view of the summit disappeared as we moved under the shadow of the Col. The so-called face was actually a steep but very forbidding slope at perhaps a forty-five-degree angle. It was easy to be blasé about the route up the Col. It was not technically difficult. The fixed ropes attached by Russell's team each season ensured that much at least, and with modern crampons, it was straightforward to get a good purchase on the ice. When the British first ascended the Col in 1922, it must have seemed a formidable undertaking. In true Alpine style, steps had to be cut the whole way and an array of ladders put in place to allow for porterage of loads. The expedition met with tragedy when seven porters were swept to their death by an avalanche. It was an incident that affected Mallory deeply, and for which he never fully forgave himself.

At the base of the slope we attached our jumars[22] to the fixed line and began the long ascent. The last time I had done this climb, six years previously, it had been my undoing and now I felt nervous. In the circumstances, Sarah was an ideal companion. She and I weren't the least bit in competition, and had nothing to prove, except to ourselves perhaps. We settled into a comfortable but tiring routine. Slide the jumar up, test its purchase, and then take two or three steps and repeat. It wasn't long before my lungs were straining under the effort. It was all too easy to rely on your arms to haul yourself up, but this was a bad technique. The jumar was there as a back-up and not to be hauled upon. Resting every ten steps was comfortable. Sometimes I did fifteen and occasionally twenty in a row. The latter left me breathless and doubled up over my ice axe, trying to will the oxygen into my lungs. I resolved to go as slowly as I could, eventually finding an uneasy rhythm. After a few rope-lengths and on a natural ledge I stopped and waited for Sarah. She wasn't far behind and I took some photographs of her coming over the edge. As we rested, Sonam and Tshering also appeared, making much lighter work of the slope, despite their loads. I had asked them to bring another tent to the North Col in preparation for the summit bids and they were also carrying equipment ready for the top camp. They paused briefly before pressing on and I resolved to try and keep up with them. By concentrating and counting my steps I needed fewer rest breaks and moved much more steadily. For perhaps an hour, we climbed together, before I fell behind and they sped off without me.

We continued to switchback under steep seracs and across small crevasses that had opened in the ice wall. In a couple of places we had to balance across aluminium ladders to continue on our way. After three hours we reached a steep headwall. I knew this meant we were near the top, but the final pull was exhausting. Every couple of steps I planted my feet and leaned into the slope to regain my breath. At the top was a wide shelf where an expedition had placed its tents. Ours, I knew, were higher still and another fifteen minutes away across the Col. As we made our way gingerly along the narrow ridge I counted at least fifty tents. It must have been the highest village in the world. To our left, the slope fell away to the Rongbuk glacier 1,000 metres below. Our own tents looked directly down to ABC and over the steep drop. Only when the others had ascended up to Camp 2, and looked back at the Col, did they realise how precarious our position was. Short of good sites, the Sherpas had elected to pitch them on an enormous overhanging serac. We had raised the position of the tents with Sonam, tentatively so as not to offend him, hoping he might see fit to move them.

He replied with his usual broad grin, 'No problem, sir, no problem. Very good tents, very nice place, very good view . . .'

As for the view, we couldn't have asked for better. Beyond ABC and to the south-east I could see the rise to the Lhakpa La, the pass from where Mallory had first spied the Col on which we were now camped. Beyond was the huge expanse of the Tibetan plateau, littered with virgin peaks. Immediately to our left and above the Col rose the steep and forbidding-looking Changtse, a satellite peak of Everest. To my right, of course, was the continuation of the North Ridge, the way we would have to climb. The long snow slope disappeared up into the clouds. It was impossible to gauge distance, the fixed line becoming quickly invisible. Then I detected three tiny dots high above and barely moving against the enormity of the face. The sheer scale of the mountain was breathtaking and impossible to grasp.

The tent was far from comfortable and was full of boil-in-the-bag meals strewn over the floor. I wasn't sure who had left it in this state but thought the Sherpas had slept in here last. I wasn't about to complain. Sonam and Tshering were still hollowing out a platform for our third tent further along the ridge. I helped them pathetically for a few minutes but couldn't work at their rate. The floor of our tent was desperately uneven. Pitched on snow it had melted underneath and it looked as though a good night's sleep would be unlikely. Eventually, with a lot of rearranging of kit, we made ourselves as comfortable as we could and got the stove on.

Sarah and I talked for hours, reminiscing about the cycle journey, but the highlight of the evening was the food, which I had been looking forward to for weeks. The army 'boil-in-the-bag' rations were a godsend. Although heavy to carry, they were easy to heat in a pan, and the hot water could then be used for yet another cup of tea. I knew Phil and Pauline had brought their own dehydrated meals with the aim of saving weight but in my opinion ours were far easier and, though heavier, probably more nutritious as well. Our appetites sated, we settled in for a long night's sleep, water at the ready. That night would be a big test, I knew. If I could sleep comfortably at this altitude and, importantly, not damage my eye further, then I knew I would be good for a summit attempt.

With the wind whipping away at the fabric of the tent all night, it was always going to be a restless sleep. I checked the thermometer on my watch in the small hours: eighteen below zero, and that was inside the tent. We were glad when the first rays of light struck us early in the morning. In our exposed position, it was much earlier than at base camp, barely six o'clock. I was too warm and comfortable to move, but Sarah was already getting her climbing kit on. I knew for her own peace of mind she was anxious to investigate the route up to Camp 2. I reluctantly offered to join her but she didn't seem too fussed.

'I just need to try it a bit,' she said, 'see what the exposure is like. Peace of mind really.'

I watched her head off across the last bit of the Col. The snow was blown across the fixed line and sparkled in the early sunshine. She disappeared from view for a few minutes where the ridge dipped, before appearing again perhaps a hundred metres away. I watched her begin the climb, looking minute against the breadth of the ridge.

Sarah returned a couple of hours later, by which time at least I had the tea on. I was feeling lazy but also very relaxed about the prospects for the next fortnight. The weather would now be the main variable, but that was completely beyond my control. We packed our kit before returning down the fixed ropes to the glacier and ABC. Descending was far easier and we were down the line in a little over half an hour, but the march across the glacier seemed interminable. After removing our crampons, we began the hot exposed trail back into ABC. We stopped only once and that was to talk to Caroline Letrange, a member of a tiny French team consisting of her husband and another friend. Caroline spoke good English, and already knew Sarah, who had been helping her with a computer problem. It was good to talk to someone who shared our ideals, an amateur expedition like our own, in contrast to the huge teams around us.

Back at ABC, Phil and Pauline had already arrived. I was concerned that there was no Chris and Nigel; they were apparently a day behind and would be here for lunch tomorrow. It worried me again that a supposedly close-knit group of four were not working together. There was little I could do at this stage; matters would have to take their course. It was obvious, though, that they wouldn't be climbing together as the team I had envisaged. While we chatted, Sarah packed her things to descend straight to base camp that afternoon. She had been in ABC for the best part of a week and was anxious to get down. Her confidence seemed renewed and I too was feeling buoyed by my recovery. The summit was now a real possibility. I was less fussed about heading down that day, too tired to do the walk as quickly as last time. I resolved to spend another night and then descend the following morning.

Chapter 14

Summit Fever

Twenty-four hours later and we were in the pub. Pat had suggested a trip from base camp down to the Tibetan village of tents that surrounded the road-head. Together with Seb and André, we stepped out across the gravel flood plain and picked the first half-decent establishment. Parting a thick woollen blanket, we stumbled into the smoke-filled interior and found a rug seat against the tent wall. We refused their offer of homemade chang and played safe with the bottled Everest beer. It was an exorbitant $3 each but one could hardly begrudge their enterprise. The owner tried to entertain us with some kind of simple guitar. Barely visible beneath his yak coat and worn balaclava, he plucked away painfully, while his wife scurried back and forth doing all the chores. Inevitably, Pat took over and provided amusement for us all, our host included, even borrowing his jacket for effect. Then he stopped mid-strum, his eyes wide with excitement.

'This is the place! It's just perfect. Guys, how many people do you think we could get in here?'

'Dozens. Why? What are you planning?' André said suspiciously.

'Well, in a couple of days I have a friend coming to base camp, a sort of guest celebrity. I thought it might be the chance for a party. You know, invite all the other teams and have a knees-up. What do you reckon?'

'Who is it? We might not even be here ...' we all pleaded in unison, but Pat was not giving anything away. 'Ahh, you'll just have to wait and see ... Let's just say he's very, very famous!' He returned to his rendition of Tibetan folk songs.

While Pat's attempt to lift our spirits was very welcome, we were all feeling apprehensive. Whether a success or failure, the outcome of the next few days was sure to be dramatic. The conversation turned to summit teams and I sensed the restlessness of Seb and André. They were both desperate to get home and for very similar reasons. Seb was father to three children and had missed his daughter's first birthday while on the trip. His middle son Jago, also my godson, had been very ill for the last couple of weeks, although he was now on the mend. It had been a stressful time for Seb and he needed to get back as soon as he could. André was in a similar position. He had two boys, and the youngest, Will, had been born only a month before André left to join the expedition. He too was missing home. I had purposely not factored in these considerations when planning the summit teams. It seemed heartless on the one hand, but I knew it was fair to consider only the present situation on the mountain.

That said, there was no reason why Seb and André could not join the other four in their summit bid. I would have hesitated if they had already gelled as a team but that plainly wasn't going to happen. Maybe the addition of another two team members would make a strong party of six? It was likely that at least a couple would turn around but that would still leave a foursome in place. I knew Phil and Pauline were determined to stay together but there was every chance that one of them might not make it. What would the other do in that case? We talked openly about the permutations and I had to concede that there was little reason why they shouldn't go ahead. It would leave five of us, who in theory could make a strong second party. This also had the advantage that we would need only two periods of stable weather, rather than the three my original plan had called for.

There was little time to waste, and the following morning Seb was off to ABC like a shot. If for any reason his climb was delayed, I had no doubt he would be off home soon anyway. André was more reticent, I could tell. He wanted the two days to climb to ABC and ideally a day's rest afterwards. It was now 12 May so that meant the others could set off for the summit on the 15th, weather permitting. That would place them on top on the 18th, which would actually be ideal. The second team would then be able to follow three or four days behind.

André was nervous and, to make matters worse, he had an upset stomach. Both served to delay his departure until after lunchtime. During the six o'clock phone call, I let Pauline know that Seb and André would be joining them. Allowing for André's day of rest in ABC, which seemed perfectly fair, I told her that they would be free to head up on the 15th, three days from now. There was some hesitation and I could tell there were other plans afoot.

'The thing is, Dom, we're really keen to make the most of the weather here. The conditions look brilliant and we're happy to wait for Seb if he's coming up today, but by the time André's ready it may be too late. I'm not sure we can wait that long.'

'I hear what you're saying, Pauline, but André deserves a chance to be in that team. If you've already gone, then he'll be left high and dry. He's not well and he deserves a day in ABC after he's arrived, to prepare. Then you can all head up as a strong team of six together.'

'Let me put you on to Phil . . .'

Phil was calm and measured as he explained their situation, but the argument remained unresolved. By asking them as leader to follow my wishes, I was also throwing down the gauntlet. They had clearly determined their own agenda and whatever I said I knew they weren't going to wait. I felt their urgency was unfounded. Although they were anxious to get going, there was huge security in climbing as a group and I thought they would welcome the addition of André. We had identified early on that our strength as a team was our greatest asset and now we were abandoning that very premise. André also deserved better and I couldn't help feeling I had let him down.

Phil and Pauline made it quite clear that their preferred date would be the 14th. That would at least allow André to join them if he was feeling up to it, but he would get no time to prepare. I had no way of communicating this to André as he was now at interim camp, but it seemed like an uneasy compromise. He would now have to fight his own battles when he arrived at ABC. It was another low for me. I felt let down that we were no longer working for the good of the team.

Despite the strong temptation to declare a 'free for all', I resisted. There would have to be some semblance of control, but every time leadership is undermined it makes it much harder to continue. I didn't sleep easy that night but I told myself that now was not the time to lose focus. I had my own summit chances to consider and knew that the best-laid plans often went astray. The whole of the first team might be defeated by bad weather and then we would have the better chance. Who was to know?

It was a restless couple of days in base camp. Those of us down below no longer felt part of the action and I was yearning to be back at ABC. André rang on the night of 13 May to say he had arrived safely but was unlikely to go up the following morning. The others were itching to get going and he was reluctant to hold them up. He was being more than generous and I apologised that he did not have longer. He seemed reassured when I told him that he could always join our team, as with five of us there would be a spare slot. Finally I determined to leave base camp two days later, on 15 May. While I would miss the departure of the first team, I would arrive on the night of the 16th, the day before they went for the summit. This meant I would at least be there to wish everyone luck on the radio and monitor their progress.

The night before departure we trooped down to the village for Pat's mystery party. By now he had become social coordinator for the entire base camp, and the humble tent was packed with climbers of all nationalities, buzzing with expectation. Our Tibetan host had never seen anything like it, and he gratefully served beer by the crateload, stuffing the wads of dollars into his hat. Then, to rousing cheers, a familiar figure emerged from the darkness at the back of the tent. Yes, it was Elvis himself. 'Good evening, Tibet!' Complete with guitar and jumpsuit he soon had the crowd singing along to a string of hits. It was just as amusing to watch the Sherpas, staring open-mouthed at the spectacle of Pat doing his party piece.

This time I had Andrew and Sarah for company on the long walk up. The novelty of the spectacular scenery had worn off and I consoled myself that whatever the outcome this would probably be my last time. Once again we had the use of Russell's tents at the interim camp and we didn't even bother to haggle. For the princely sum of $5 each, we ate as much as we could, but my appetite was pitifully small and I was wasting away. While the cycling had made me lose the weight I needed to, my body simply hadn't stopped shedding the pounds. According to the weekly weigh-ins, I had lost another ten kilos while on the mountain. Much of this was now muscle. My arms had shrunk away and my shoulders felt hopelessly weak. Dreaming of the food we might eat back in Kathmandu had now become a daily ritual.

We arrived in ABC for lunch to find both André and, surprisingly, Nigel. He had made it to the North Col but had suffered a restless night with a hacking cough. It wasn't an uncommon ailment at altitude, and had defeated many in the past. Reluctantly he had decided to retreat, but was already doing a sterling job of organising ABC and manning the radios. News from up high was mixed. Seb and Chris were going well and as we spoke were heading up to Camp 3. Hopefully they would go for the summit the following day, 17 May. I was confused about the whereabouts of Phil and Pauline, as they had all spent the night on the Col together. My hopes that the four would climb together were quickly dashed when Nigel explained the new plan.

'Phil and Pauline had to turn back. She was struggling with the weight of her sack and couldn't make Camp 2. Now they're back on the North Col.'

I was disappointed for her but it wasn't all bad news. Nigel continued. 'Apparently she's found a Sherpa up there who's willing to carry her sack all the way to Camp 2 tomorrow. They're going to have another go.'

'You must be joking! It can't be one of our Sherpas; they're all down here. She must be paying someone from another expedition?'

'I guess so,' said Nigel. 'Either way, they've now had two nights on the North Col which is hardly ideal.'

The first success came later that afternoon when Dickie and Ro staggered back into camp after reaching the North Col. With all the politics and palaver of organising the summit teams I had been neglecting their steady progress. It had always been their stated ambition to try and reach the North Col, an increasingly common target for less ambitious climbers, or those on a budget. At a height of 7,000 metres, it was no mean feat, but for these two, who had no previous climbing experience, it was an exceptional achievement. Dickie, in particular, was shattered and was staggering with exhaustion by the time he reached the tents. I was delighted for him. He had arrived on the trip overweight and very unfit. His determination and Nic's guidance as his fitness guru had got him to this point. Ro looked remarkably fresh and could probably have gone further, but she too was thrilled to have made it.

With all of us ensconced in the dining tent, we waited next to the radio for any news. Eventually, Seb's voice came through so clearly that we thought he was next door.

'Hello, ABC, this is Seb and Chris, over.'

'Hello, Seb, this is Dom. How are you getting on up there, over?'

'Good.' There was a pause while he took a breath from the masks they would now be using. 'It was easier than yesterday . . .

The oxygen makes a big difference. There's a bit of a problem with the camp though, over.'

'Go ahead, Seb, we're listening, over.'

'We're at the tents ... but they're only at a height of 8,000 metres. We understood from the Sherpas ... that they would be at 8,300 metres. It's going to affect our chances.'

'OK, Seb. Stay close to the radio. I'll talk to Sonam, wait, out.'

This was bad news. Almost every other team had placed their camp some way above 8,000 metres. With Camp 2 at 7,500 metres and the summit at 8,850 metres, it meant they had just completed a modest climb, and left themselves with a daunting summit day ahead. Better-resourced expeditions, such as Russell Brice's, even had three camps between the North Col and the summit. We, of course, had no such luxury but had been relying on our Sherpas to pick a good spot at the correct height. We called in Sonam from the kitchen tent next door.

'Sonam, do you know where our Camp 3 is? What height?' I was keen to get his version of events.

'Yes, sir. 8,300 metres. I am very sure. Dorjee tell me 8,300 metres.'

'Did he have an altimeter, do you know? Is it before the other camps?'

'Don't know, maybe a little below other camps. Little tent space, I think.'

It was a fruitless discussion and I was far from impressed. True, space for tents was always at a premium. Tent shelves had to be levelled out from the snow and gravel on the forbidding north face. If our camp was lower than the others, though, I failed to see how they knew there was lack of space above. I feared they had pitched the camp as low as they dared and I could hardly blame them. Carrying loads at that height was an enormous effort. A more assertive and experienced leader than me would have given the Sherpas very strict instructions. I had probably lapsed on this point and they had taken advantage. For now there was nothing that could be done. I relayed this back to Seb and apologised.

'Not to worry . . . I guess we'll just have to leave a little earlier. Probably . . . nine this evening.'

'OK. Do you want to call us just before you head off, over?'

We agreed to have a radio check later that evening. I walked out of the dining tent and stared up at the high ridge. The wind had dropped now and despite the gathering darkness the mountain above shone in a glaring white. I looked hard at where their tents must be but the enormity of the mountain was overwhelming. It was strange to be relatively comfortable here, while a mere two or three kilometres away our friends were on the very edge of existence: now in the 'death zone', the hours that their bodies could survive were strictly numbered. They had a very long day ahead, but I had absolute faith. I knew both of them were strong and was convinced they could make it.

We made a call down to base camp that evening to report that all was well and that Seb and Chris were both poised for success. The news from Patrick was not so good. A life had been lost high on the North Ridge above us. The story had been breaking on 15 May as I left base camp but it had now been confirmed that the climber was British and had probably been descending from the summit. At the time, we knew little about him, other than that his name was David Sharp and he had died below the second step. This was also the final resting place of an Indian climber,[23] who had sought shelter in a small cave beneath the rock and even today his legs protruded from it. He had been nicknamed 'Green Boots' by the scores of climbers who had since passed.

At our radio check that night Seb and Chris both sounded breathless but excited. It wasn't the greatest confidence boost, but I had to tell them of the death above. David's body still lay right on the route and it was better that they were prepared. They seemed as confident as ever and I wished them luck on behalf of us all. We agreed that they would radio us when they reached the 'second step', the trickiest part of the climb. Hopefully that would be at about 5 a.m. and we would then monitor their progress for the last couple of hours to the summit.

I took the radio to bed and crawled into my sleeping bag. Conditions were perfect but it was a bitterly cold night. I thought of David Sharp lying alone on the ridge and how we were all still prepared to step over him in our own bid to reach the summit. I slept fitfully, listening for any static or murmur from the radio. The alarm was set for 5 but I resisted the temptation to call them. We had agreed they would call us, after all, and I was anxious not to hassle them.

By breakfast, we had still heard nothing and I grew increasingly concerned. We sat silently, each of us lost in our own thoughts, just praying for news. Another hour passed before my feelings of dread made me feel physically sick. There were numerous explanations, I told myself. The batteries on the radio for a start were notoriously fickle, especially at low temperatures. I tried calling them but to no avail. It was gone eight o'clock before the radio crackled into life. I heard Seb's familiar voice, deadpan, and strained with exhaustion.

'Hello BC . . . this is Seb, over.'

'Go ahead, Seb, how are you getting on, over?'

'Not great, actually . . . we reached the summit,' he said matter of factly. 'But we're having a few problems . . . Chris seems very weak and is struggling. He's collapsed on me a couple of times . . . I'm not sure he can get down, over.' I was stunned into silence, as was Andrew, who was standing beside me. I tried to gather my thoughts.

'Where are you, Seb . . . do you know what height you're at? And is Chris still with you?'

'He's ahead of me at the moment . . . since I stopped to call you. The second step is going to be very tricky for us.'

'Seb, listen, you simply have to get him down the second step. Can you abseil alongside him, over?'

I was annoyed at my own naivety. In truth, it was pointless dispensing advice from down here. Their lives were simply in their own hands. I handed over to Andrew, who I thought might talk more sense.

'Hi Seb, Andrew here. Look, if you can get level with him, you can give him a shot of Dex.[24] That will make a big difference and see him down the trickiest bit. Can you do that, over?'

'Sure I can try, but I'll have to catch him first . . . he's ahead of me now. I'll call you when we get to the second step.'

We came off the radio and a silence descended. I guessed we were all thinking the same terrible thoughts. What if? What now? Nigel, calm as always, suggested that he and Sarah wander up to some of the other camps to ask for advice. Other teams might have climbers also descending. I agreed it would do no harm and they headed off. There was little to do otherwise but wait things out. A strange calm ensued while we sat tense and quiet, the dining tent feeling like a hospital waiting room. Dickie had acquired a two-week-old copy of the *Daily Mail* and we silently swapped pages, my eyes skimming over the pictures, absorbing nothing. My head spun with a thousand thoughts. What were we thinking that we could do this without risking our lives? Other more experienced climbers had already lost theirs. Why couldn't we take the hint? What would I say if I had to ring Alicia, Chris's wife? I had spoken to her only two days previously when I arrived at ABC. Chris had been unable to get through to her before he left for the summit, so had asked me to call.

Sarah and Nigel returned to say that they had had a muted response from most teams. In fact a few seemed to be mired in crises of their own. The only positive response was from Russell. His camp was higher than anyone else's and would be the first Seb and Chris reached on their descent. We were welcome to use their tents and oxygen, if need be, in an emergency. It was generous and at least gave me something to relay to Seb. Another half-hour passed.

'Dom, this is Seb . . . We're just approaching the second step . . . I think Chris is still ahead of me, though . . . over.' I was slightly reassured. If Chris was staying ahead of Seb, he must be moving well and at least down the mountain. Every step lower was closer to safety or even help. The worst scenario was a fallen climber or one who refused to move.

'That's good, Seb. Russell Brice has said you're welcome to use his HIMEX tents at the first camp you come to. There are cookers there and oxygen if you need it, over.'

'Thanks ... That's good to know ... Hopefully we'll be able to push on down ... I just don't know at this stage.'

Seb was starting to sound exhausted himself and I detected a slight edge of desperation. But I felt just a little encouraged. That first call was enough to make me think it was all over, but now we knew Chris was still moving and I tried to will him along. 'Just get lower,' I thought, 'just get lower ...' There followed a delay of another hour before the radio burst into life again. Then I heard the best possible sound, in a clear and strong voice.

'Hi Dom, Chris here. Just to let you know all is well. Rather lost it for a bit up there. But feeling fine now, over. Thanks.'

In an instant, all of us were beaming with delight and relief simply washed through me.

'Hi Chris, Dom here, great to hear your voice. I knew you were just testing us! We knew you'd be fine, over.'

'Well, all good now, though ... and getting lower ... Well, we're still above 8,000 metres ... but feeling good.'

'Great, Chris, we'll let you get on. Give us a call when you're back at the top camp. Out.'

Sarah went back up to Russell's camp to report that all was well. I suddenly felt embarrassed that we had asked for help, but it had been the right thing to do. We simply had to be grateful that the panic was over, though they had a long descent remaining. The good news was that Phil and Pauline were already on their way to Camp 3. Pauline had made it to Camp 2 the day before, with the help of a Sherpa. Now on oxygen, they were going well and should make the top camp at about the same time as Chris and Seb would be descending. While it was possible for all of them to stay at the top camp, Seb and Chris really needed to push on down to Camp 2. The lower they were, the quicker would be their recovery.

As we were celebrating our good fortune, more bad news began to circulate around the camp. Tomas Olsson, a Swedish extreme skier had also died on the north face. Together with his Norwegian colleague, Tormod Granheim, he had summitted the day before Chris and Seb – 16 May – but only after a very demanding climb. They had then attempted to ski down the Norton Couloir, the steep gulley that marks the left-hand edge of the summit pyramid. At around 8,500 metres, a steep drop-off marked the gully. With their progress checked, they had no choice but to abseil down the fifty-metre cliff. It was then that the anchor holding Tomas gave way and he plunged to his death down the north face.

Andrew and I were keeping a macabre tally of the deaths so far on the mountain. With four on the south side and the death of Russell's Sherpa early on, the total had been five. But the recent deaths of David Sharp and Tomas Olsson brought that tally up to seven. Sadly, we knew that probably wouldn't be the end of it. The summit period was still only just beginning and more drama was sure to unfold. The worst season on record had been the spring of 1996, when twelve lost their lives. We only hoped that no records would be broken in that department.

It was mid-afternoon before Phil and Pauline reached Camp 3. They briefly swapped information with Seb and Chris, who to my relief then pushed on down to the safety of Camp 2. It had been a long twelve hours for everyone. In base camp we were exhausted, if only emotionally. We just hoped that Phil and Pauline weren't going to be faced with a repeat of the whole scenario. My very reason for wanting us to climb in fours had been demonstrated all too clearly. But now there was little we could do.

One of Chris's problems, we later learned, had been with his mask. It appeared that one of the valves had become clogged with ice and he hadn't realised in time. This in turn had reduced his oxygen intake and led to the problems. However, such information was invaluable for Phil and Pauline as they prepared to set off later that night.

Again, I went to bed with the radio and this time everything went smoothly. Pauline called from above the second step, sounding breathless but confident and fully in control. They were only an hour from the top and it was about six in the morning. I climbed out of the tent wrapped in my down suit. The sun was yet to rise in ABC and it was intensely cold. Looking up, I could see the upper reaches of the summit pyramid already bathed in a yellow glow. The sky above was cloudless, a crisp shade of even blue, and the moon was just appearing over the ridge. It was still waxing and would be full in a couple of days as we began our own ascent.

I enjoyed a quiet moment before waking the others. The aim of the expedition was all but completed. With Pauline's ascent, the first cyclist from the team would make the summit and the 'longest climb' would be over. It was more with relief than pride that we had got to this stage. We had been lucky, Chris's close call had told us that much. Was there any point in risking my own ascent? My health had already suffered enough. The objective had been reached and we could walk away perfectly content. Just pull the plug and head back to Kathmandu and home. I knew this wasn't going to happen, though – it simply wasn't an option. Despite the drama, even the recent deaths, I still had a hunger for the summit. I tried to put it down more to curiosity than ambition, but I needed to be up there; high at the edge of the atmosphere, feeling what few others had ever felt. Everything I had read about Everest, the stories of Mallory and Irvine, and so many others, had taken place high on that stage. Ironically, the recent deaths made the summit even more alluring. We knew it was dangerous anyway, but here was a chance to risk your life in a simple duel: pitting yourself against a mountain and ultimately against your own self. It was a potentially deadly game but one we all needed to know we could win.

The others gradually emerged from the tents, looking sleepy and cold. We huddled around in a group outside the dining tent. The reception was better here and we didn't want to risk missing anything. By the time the radio sprang to life we were freezing cold and desperate for the warmth of the tent. That was quickly forgotten with the familiar sound of Pauline's voice. We all broke into broad smiles.

'Hello, ABC. We have completed the longest climb on earth!' Pauline sounded breathless but ecstatic. 'Are you all there, over? Dom, Sarah, Nic, Jamie . . .'

'We're here, Pauline. Congratulations, we're all very proud of you here . . .' It was indeed a great achievement. Pauline had battled hard and the success was well deserved.

The others beckoned for the radio so we passed it around in turn to offer our congratulations. With the summit looking so beautifully clear and the great reception, they could have been stood next to us. In truth we found out later that conditions were exceptionally cold that morning and Phil in particular was anxious for them to get off the top and keep moving. The events of the previous day with Chris would also have made them doubly nervous.

Pauline talked for far longer than she should have, and eventually we thought it best to sign off and let them descend. We retired to the mess tent where Pemba bought us tea and an early breakfast of porridge. Then reality hit. After two stressful days monitoring the others, it was now our turn.

Andrew was thinking the same and was the first to speak, chuckling as he did so. 'Well, that's fabulous. But now it's our turn and we've barely slept for two nights! Hardly ideal preparation . . .'

He wasn't wrong. But the weather still looked good and we didn't want to delay. Anyone going for the summit would have to head off today and be on the North Col that evening. The spotlight had switched to us very suddenly and caught us a little unawares. Andrew and I decided that we would leave fairly late, probably three o'clock. We saw little point in going earlier as we would just sit on the North Col. The others were more cautious and resolved to leave after an early lunch at about midday. Either way we would all be together that evening at 7,000 metres.

There was plenty of apprehension. André was unusually quiet and he spoke to me mid-morning to say he had decided not to go up. I felt incredibly sorry for him. He was bitterly disappointed, I knew, but it was a wise and well-thought-out decision. Chris's experience had hit him quite hard. André also had a new baby boy to think of. In short, he had too much to lose and I could see he wasn't in the right of frame of mind. I had spent long enough around base camp to see that those who succeeded were often in bullish and confident mood. Those that saw sense often lacked the tunnel vision necessary for success. They, of course, were the sensible ones.

André wasn't the only apprehensive member of our team. Sarah had been in tears several times over the last couple of days, and was torn over what to do next. She desperately wanted advice, I could tell. Somebody to say, 'look, just go for it', or perhaps 'stay put, you don't have the experience'. Cruelly, I refrained from saying anything to her. She simply had to decide for herself. I wasn't about to persuade someone to climb this mountain, especially someone less experienced. Chris's close call had scared me enough, and I knew just how strong he was – in fact, probably the strongest person on our whole team. It had to be a personal decision, just as André had made his.

If Sarah was nervous, Jamie and Andrew were as relaxed and confident as ever. I had an uncanny feeling they were going all the way to the top. Nic I wasn't too sure about: he had been painfully quiet over the last few days and was struggling with some inner demon. His determination had been immense during the cycling ride and for him not reaching the summit would perhaps hurt the most. If I failed, I at least had the satisfaction of having organised the expedition. Sarah and Jamie were both young and recently graduated; they could easily return another day. But Nic had staked a huge amount of effort and financial resources on the trip. This was his big chance, perhaps his only one, and no one deserved success more.

Without André, there were five of us packing our kit that morning. I glanced up at the mountain often, knowing I was as ready as I could be. Despite my earlier ill health, my recovery had been miraculous. I was weakened from weight-loss but there was only time for one attempt anyway. All we needed was some good weather and a dose of luck.

Chapter 15

Space Walking

Nic was away first from ABC, closely followed by Jamie and Sarah. Andrew and I enjoyed a leisurely lunch. But my heart sank when I came out of the dining tent an hour later, and saw Nic making his way back to camp. He looked devastated and told me he was going to call it a day. There was little I could say – anything would have sounded flippant. He sounded so matter of fact, as if he had just changed his mind about not going to the shops, but I knew he was trying to be positive. The expedition he had signed up for two years earlier, and played a key role in for six months, was now over. He had proved the most loyal to our cause, the most committed from the very start. He was just a couple of thousand metres short of the longest climb, but it must have felt like a million miles.

Andrew and I set off an hour later. We picked our way slowly through the tents of ABC, talking to few people. The other expeditions were either busy with their own summit bids or picking up the pieces from some recent tragedy. Lost in our own thoughts, we said nothing, steadying our breathing and preserving all our effort for the climb ahead. Reaching the base of the Col, we could see Sarah half an hour ahead of us, making good headway. Andrew quickly clipped on to the fixed ropes, and so began the laborious haul upwards.

I paused for a few minutes, happy to be at the back of the line. The cooler conditions made the ascent easier than the previous week, but we would have to be cautious. When the sun went down, the temperature would plummet and we would need to be under cover by then. I was keeping Andrew within sight, a couple of rope-lengths ahead, and saw him draw level with a descending climber. They stopped to talk. As I came closer, I could see that the stranger was in floods of tears. He turned to me briefly before descending. 'Bon chance. Please be careful. Be very careful . . .'

Andrew and I paused on the narrow shelf. 'That was Philippe,' said Andrew. 'He made the summit with his team but another French climber has died just below the summit.'

We were both stunned. That another life had been lost was bad enough, but this was a team closer in size to ours. This was the first time I had witnessed the result of a death on the mountain. Philippe did nothing to dissuade us from carrying on, but his distress said it all. Andrew and I sat for a few minutes, trying to make sense of it all. We both felt and said much the same. Philippe's distress should have discouraged us, perhaps made us rethink our plans, but the die was cast and we were not about to turn around.

Nearing the top of the fixed ropes, we could see a short line of climbers on a steep section below the Col itself. It took a while for them to clear and for the climbers to disappear over the crest. As I drew nearer, I could see Sarah at the back of the line, talking to someone slumped on the ground. Other climbers had stepped over the prone climber and by the time I reached the spot there was no one around. He was lying face down, grasping the rope and seemingly lifeless. I couldn't easily climb past him – he had rather inconveniently paused just below the crest, where it wasn't easy to stop. Perhaps this explained why so many others had walked past. I hoped he was alive, but if so why would he have stopped here of all places?

'Hello, can you hear me?' There was little response. I would have to unclip from the rope in order to move alongside him, but first I hacked away at the slope with my axe to make a small shelf so I could crouch safely. The effort left me exhausted, and I struggled to regain my breath before I had another go.

'Can you hear me?' I shouted this time and shook his shoulder roughly with my hand, determined to gain some response. This time the figure raised his head a fraction but I could hear nothing.

'Why aren't you climbing up ... why have you stopped?' I asked, leaning only inches from his face.

This time I could hear his response. 'I'm going down. I'm going down to ABC!' he mumbled, sounding annoyed. Numerous others, including Sarah, must have asked him the same thing, but I was amazed. It was a long way down to ABC and the temperature was dropping steadily. Aside from that, he was blatantly making no effort to move.

'Why don't you go back up to the tents, just for tonight? It's too late for you to go down now.'

'I have to go down ... be fine.'

I paused for a response as he raised himself slightly, revealing his face. I thought I recognised him.

'It's Vince, isn't it? What happened? Did you make the summit?' We had met Vince, a Canadian, a couple of weeks earlier at base camp when he had dropped in to introduce himself. He had no climbing partners, and had joined a loose commercial team, but with the very bold objective of trying to reach the summit without oxygen. We had all been sceptical of his chances, particularly with so little support.

'I've been to Camp 2 ... had some bad headaches ... came back down today.'

Over my shoulder, I could see Andrew ascending the last rope behind me. He joined us and we agreed that we had to get him back up to the Col and the safety of the tents. The nearest ones were barely fifty metres away and belonged to our friends from the Irish team, so we called down to Nic in ABC, asking him to check that it was fine to use them. Andrew was concerned that Vince's condition could deteriorate further and offered to stay with him while I went up to our camp to get some oxygen. Any other assistance I could get would be an added bonus.

I couldn't deny my frustration. What had been a straightforward climb to the North Col was now being thwarted. We should have already been in the tents drinking tea and relaxing rather than being out in the cold. There was little option, though. The temperature was plummeting and it was clear that if we didn't help Vince no one else was going to. We were almost certainly the last on the ropes that day. Left alone, Vince would die. The climbers ahead of us must have eased their conscience, seeing that there were others behind them.

I passed the empty Irish tents and climbed the last ladder up to the Col. The first big camp belonged to the massive Russian-led team. To my relief, there seemed to be plenty of activity and I entered the open door of their central tent. Such was the size of their operation that they had erected a full dining tent on the Col, more typical of most teams at base camp. There were perhaps a dozen climbers inside, of all nationalities, and some Sherpas. Most had not long arrived and were in the process of taking off kit or sipping mugs of tea. I guessed they were the ones who had passed Vince ahead of me.

'Can anyone help me? There is an injured climber on the rope. We need to get him back to a tent. It will only take a few minutes if I have some help.'

A stony silence descended and not one of those around the table even looked up. A Sherpa to my side beckoned me over and told me to speak to the leader outside. I ducked outside to see a tall blond Russian coming out of his tent. He acknowledged me but said nothing at first. I repeated my plea for assistance.

'Why is this man there?' he grunted. 'He is your team . . . yes?'

'No. No, he's not,' I said, annoyed that that should be an issue. 'We just found him. He's a solo climber from Canada. Look, I am just asking for help from a couple of your Sherpas for a few minutes. Is that really a problem?'

'My team are very tired and now they have removed their equipment. It is not possible, I think.'

I held his gaze, looking for a glimmer of compassion. I was left speechless – surely he would relent. But he gave me an icy stare in return before turning away and heading back into the tent.

Humiliated, I went up to our tents, still another ten minutes' climb away. Jamie and Sarah already had the water boiling and offered to help but there was little point in us all getting cold. I grabbed the oxygen and headed back along the ridge still seething. Why on earth would I want to climb this mountain if it's come to this? Is this what I came here for? Darkness was looming now and the wind was rising. I balanced myself with the axe in one hand and two oxygen bottles under the other arm, pausing outside the Russian camp again. A lamp was now on inside and I could hear voices and even laughter. I couldn't resist the urge to make a point and opened the flap of the tent. I held it there, hoping that the cold wind might blow straight through and disturb their dinner. I was met with some disapproving glances before they lowered their heads.

'There is still an injured climber on the ropes below us.' I paused. 'I'm taking him some oxygen from our team. Some help would be useful. It will only take a few minutes.'

There was no reply and I expected none. I paused for a few seconds, both to let the warmth seep out of their tent – and my words sink in.

'OK. Good night. Enjoy your dinner and have a safe climb.' I turned and headed away, relieved not to have lost my cool, but also regretting a little that I hadn't. As I reached the ladder, I heard the familiar squeak behind me of crampons on the snow. Turning around, I saw a Sherpa had followed me from the Russian camp. 'I come to help,' he said simply and took an oxygen bottle from me. I smiled and thanked him before we descended the ladder gingerly.

Incredibly, Andrew had coaxed Vince to the top of the rope and Nic had radioed back to say we were welcome to use the Irish tents. It had seemed the worst was over, but Vince's so-called 'team' down in ABC were reluctant to send any Sherpas. Perhaps this was because Vince had refused their advice and help during the ascent. He was clearly a stubborn character and perhaps not the most cooperative member of a dysfunctional group, but even now that his life was at stake there was little response from his team.

I thanked the Sherpa who helped us, later regretting that I didn't get his name. Andrew was reluctant to leave Vince and decided that he would stay and monitor his condition for a couple of hours. He said there was no real point in me staying as well and so I headed back slowly to our tents, leaving him with a radio. As a doctor, he had been called upon frequently throughout the expedition. Now it was happening again, perhaps rather unfairly on his own summit bid. For Andrew, though, there was no compromise. Caring for others came well ahead of his personal ambition. I climbed back to the tent, thankful that he was coming to the summit with me.

It was dark by the time Andrew made it to our camp. Vince's condition thankfully stabilised, he reported. Some Spanish climbers on the same permit had offered to come up to the North Col the following morning and guide Vince back down. I lay awake that night, feeling that perhaps we should just take the hint and turn back. The death toll was mounting steadily and tonight there had nearly been another. Our oxygen supply had also diminished, with the loss of the two bottles given to Vince. Furthermore, the weather didn't look promising. We had forgone the luxury of satellite forecasting and instead relied on the goodwill of other teams, and of course our own judgement. That was now called into question with the wind battering the side of the tent in powerful gusts.

It had abated only slightly the following morning so we resolved to sit things out for a while. The three of us sat up warm and comfortable in our bags, brewing tea, while Andrew left to check on Vince and wait for the Spanish rescue party to arrive. With a six-hour climb ahead, we could delay things for a few hours perhaps, but not too long. We waited patiently for the radio check at eight o'clock with ABC. Nic had already done a sterling job recruiting help for Vince, and now he was doing his best to give us information on the weather. But before signing off he said that Chris needed to speak to me and passed me over. Nothing could have prepared me for what I was about to hear.

'Dom, it's Chris. You may have heard about Jacques, Caroline's husband. He died a couple of days ago, probably a few hours after Seb and I summitted.'

It dawned on me that this was the death that had so upset Philippe. Sarah and I had talked to Caroline Letrange, his wife, only a few days previously.

'He died a little below the summit, perhaps only a hundred metres below. The Sherpas haven't been very specific, I'm afraid. Caroline has asked that if we have anyone reaching the summit, would they be able to retrieve some of his effects?'

I paused before answering, my head reeling with the implications. Death on this mountain seemed more real than ever. Someone's life was over. Someone I had met a few days earlier had lost her husband and now she was in ABC asking us to do something desperately personal. Her courage in just asking was immense. There was only one response – 'Yes, of course.'

'OK, Dom, there's a camera, a prayer string around his neck, on which is tied his wedding ring. Also perhaps some snow samples that he was taking. Caroline has said she doesn't want you to risk yourselves. That's important – I think she knows it's a long shot.'

I came off the radio stunned at the task we had just been handed. The mountain felt more like a war zone. We were surrounded by a spiralling death toll and constant bad news, through which we had to battle. Or did we? We had no cause to uphold, or anything to fight for. We were here to have fun, but events were unfolding at such a pace it was hard to make sound judgements. Jamie and I said nothing to each other but sat in silence for a few minutes. Again doubts about proceeding up the mountain quickly vanished. What we had been asked to do actually gave us the purpose we needed.

Andrew returned half an hour later, satisfied that Vince was in good hands. The Spanish had come to the rescue, despite some of them having summitted only a few days previously. They must have been exhausted, but their efforts were in the true spirit of climbing and it made up for the selfishness I had witnessed the previous afternoon. As we discussed our options, Phil and Pauline arrived at the tents, from Camp 2, looking shattered. Their advice to us was very measured and Pauline freely admitted that she had been terrified on the ascent. At one stage, the line to her mask had become entangled and she had panicked as her oxygen supply was suddenly cut off. The route was also much more technically demanding than they had expected. We passed on the news of Jacques and they were devastated. Pauline had known Jacques and now realised they had passed his body just below the summit. At the time, they had no idea who it was, let alone that he had died only a day earlier.

We were ready to set out. The wind had eased a little and there seemed no reason not to continue. Getting ready in the cramped tent was exhausting. It took half an hour just to pull on our massive insulated boots and do up a harness. We had already ripped the fabric of the tent with our crampons and the door was in tatters. Outside the wind was biting but it was good to be in the fresh air and away from the confines of the tent. Jamie and I readied ourselves while Andrew and Sarah finished their preparations. Sarah was deep in conversation with Pauline inside the tent, still weighing up her decision about going for the summit. Pauline's advice was perhaps what Sarah needed. She was climbing well but I had severe doubts that she was mentally prepared for it. Jacques's death had also hit her hard. By the time she emerged her mind was made up. She would come with us to Camp 3 but no further.

It was ten o'clock by the time we said farewell to Phil and Pauline and began our slow crawl along the fixed rope. The Col itself was relatively flat but within a few minutes we reached the long slope that led to Camp 2. Our pace slowed immediately and we settled back into the routine of pausing every ten steps. The wind blasted across the ridge from the west, covering the rope with snow. In the icy cold, my jaw and throat soon turned numb. I pulled my scarf over my mouth and nose but that made it harder to breathe. I constantly reminded myself to slow down. We had all day and I had to find a rhythm. It's not a race, I told myself – the snail always wins – it's not a race.

My resolution to enjoy the climb was short-lived. Every time we stopped I would be bent double over my axe, face just inches from the slope in front, struggling for breath. Raising my head to look around required a conscious effort. There was no discussion between us. We were a comfortable distance apart, perhaps ten metres, to allow for more slack on the fixed rope. Each of us had raised the hood on our jacket to gain some protection from the elements. The result was tunnel vision; the only view was the fixed rope and the jumar in front. I resisted the urge to look up. I knew the rocks above which marked the camp were still 2,000 feet higher, though they appeared much closer. Instead I relied on my altimeter to tick off the distance and played with numbers in my head. Five hundred metres to climb ... only ten lots of fifty metres. The first fifty metres of ascent took half an hour ... that's five hours, I thought to myself. Not so bad, we could be there for three o'clock. Keep going ... keep going.

At 7,400 metres the slope eased a bit and Jamie and I paused to take photos of Sarah and Andrew climbing up from below. We were now level with the summit of Changtse, its huge bulk looming out of the cloud to the north. The sky was an ominous leaden grey. I knew from the others that we were close to the tents, but they were still out of sight. Above I could see only snow and rocks. We were nearly as high as we would go without oxygen and though the cylinders would give us a boost, I was under no illusions about what lay ahead.

It was with sheer relief that we drew level with the tents. The two yellow domes were pitched only a few metres from the fixed rope on a narrow shelf. It was a secure spot at least; two or three metres wide with just enough space to remove kit and sort ourselves out. I just slumped into a heap and admired the staggering view. I couldn't bring myself to look up; the summit was still another 5,000 feet above us.

With no time to waste, we made ourselves comfortable and started melting snow. The next couple of days would be a major battle with hydration and we had to do all we could to drink fluids. It was a slow process, shovelling the snow into the pan and trying to melt it, let alone bring it to the boil. We had drunk nothing during the ascent and we also needed plenty for the night to come. Then, in the morning, we would have to begin melting again ready for the climb to Camp 3. Working in pairs made the process much easier and Jamie and I took it in turns to watch the stove. Every manoeuvre in the tent had to be carefully measured. Nothing was easier – and more infuriating – than knocking over a pan and having to start over again. To make more room, we stacked the oxygen out of the way in the tent porch. We had budgeted for a bottle each for the coming night. Putting it on a low flow, it should last as long as twelve hours, but we both refrained from using it just yet. We felt fine, and we had at least another sixteen hours in the tent, possibly more.

Sarah and Andrew were in the tent next door, just within shouting distance. I admired the decision she had made earlier, knowing it was a wise one. No one doubted she had the stamina to make it, but in her words, 'the risk far outweighs the gain'. Sarah seemed much more at ease now and determined to enjoy the rest of the climb. Her plan was to stay at Camp 3 while we struck out for the summit. It would help us enormously to have the support. Just to be able to descend to the top camp and have water ready would be a huge bonus. That evening we also heard on the radio from ABC that two of the Sherpas might join us. A few days earlier they had been reluctant, too tired after lifting oxygen to the high camps. Now Karma and Tshering were at the North Col and preparing to catch us up.

Jamie leant precariously out of the tent porch, scanning the valley below.

'How's the weather looking?' I had to shout to be heard over the wind.

'Not bad, there's thick cloud below us now in the valleys … hardly any peaks showing through … it's like being in a plane.'

Indeed, we were so high up it was exactly like looking through an aircraft window. We joked that all we needed was a hostess trolley and a crap film to watch. The valley was so far below that any detail would have been obscured, even without the cloud.

My appetite was still intact and we set about trying to consume as much food as we could. We both knew things would get progressively harder from now, so we might as well eat while we had the chance. Downing two 'boil-in-the-bag' meals wasn't easy but we rose to the challenge. Then, after dinner, it was straight on with the oxygen. Without it, our bodies would be unable to digest the food properly.

The long night passed slowly and I woke frequently. Whether through restlessness or nervous energy I couldn't tell, but the unfamiliar mask made me feel panicked and constricted. It was difficult to register any immediate benefit from the oxygen but it had to be doing us some good. It would ensure my lungs were clear and help us be stronger for the following morning. In the safe cocoon of the darkened tent, I struggled to believe we were at 25,000 feet. The mask and the low hiss of the oxygen in the darkness made my surroundings feel like a small spaceship. I spent much of the night in a dream-like trance. Here we were, isolated and lonely at the edge of the world.

We could afford a late start, which was just as well as the whole brewing process had to be repeated. We made several cups of luke-warm tea and then used the rest to fill bags of water, which would slip inside our down suits. With any luck, they wouldn't freeze during the day. Andrew stuck his head through the door, ominously wearing a stethoscope.

'What the hell are you doing with that?' I mumbled through my mask.

'Just thought I would give you a bit of a check-up!' There was no stopping Andrew, who found it impossible to forget about his day job. But his concern was well founded. It was only three weeks since my bout of HAPE, and climbing Everest so soon was not recommended. Andrew had said as much to me down at base camp and even emailed consultants back home to canvass as many opinions as possible. I reassured him that I had never felt better but was happy to submit to his judgement – any signs of fluid in my lungs would mean an end to my summit bid. There were a tense few seconds, while I took the obligatory deep breaths. Having had to take my shirt off I could feel the warmth ebbing out of me.

'All good,' said Andrew, relieved. 'You'd better get your shirt on before you get exposure, though!'

Getting ready seemed to take twice as long as the previous day. We manoeuvred ourselves out of the tent and into our boots and crampons, now further hampered by the oxygen apparatus. While I waited for the others, I took the chance to gaze up at the route ahead. The angle of slope was similar, but this time craggy outcrops littered the icy face above. There would be a lot of scrambling and we would have to pick our way more carefully. At least it would be more varied than the previous day's long slow plod.

It took an age to find a rhythm. The oxygen took the edge off the gulps for breath that we had grown used to, but our overall pace was no quicker than the day before. The summit seemed tantalisingly close. I knew Mallory had died not far above us, in 1924. Just eight years ago, his body had been found at a height of 8,155 metres. The exact circumstances of his death are still unknown, but what is certain is that he had broken his leg and fallen some distance. Whether it was on the way to or from the summit no one knows.

The steepness of the face was intimidating – this was no place for the faint-hearted. Over my shoulder, I could see tents on the North Col, now 3,000 feet below us. I was glad of the fixed rope, which offered us modest security. The early climbers had had no such safety net. I wanted to know if I could climb without it and tried unclipping for a couple of minutes at a time. The going was straightforward enough but a slip would quickly prove fatal. Stopping yourself on an icy slope requires real determination and in our oxygen-starved state would be very difficult to do. Mallory perhaps returned from the upper reaches of the mountain late in the day. Exhausted and, most likely, separated from Irvine, one slip was all that it took.

It was several hours before we reached an altitude of 8,000 metres and formally entered the 'death zone'. We paused on a rocky shelf for our only rest of the ascent and looked back at the route. For the first time we could see beyond the Rongbuk Monastery and the faint line of the road we had cycled along. The sheer enormity of the distance we had come was overwhelming, and for a moment the summit seemed unimportant. Just reaching this height offered a true taste of the mountain. For years I had longed to be at this altitude. For the first time on the journey I felt that if we couldn't make the summit, I would still be more than content.

It was three o'clock when we arrived at Camp 3. It was perched on a dangerously thin ledge, which made even crossing the two-metre gap between the tents an adventure. I was no longer sure if I could have continued without the fixed rope. Once you were unclipped, every move had to be considered carefully. Despite this, the nervousness of the last few days had evaporated and at long last the odds were on our side. All of us were healthy and climbing well, and I wondered briefly if Sarah might reconsider her decision. Her mind was made up, though, and she resolved to stay the full night here and wait for our return. She herself was thrilled to have made it this far, as we all were.

We radioed back to ABC that all was well. I purposely didn't ask for the forecast – there was little point. From now we'd have to rely on our judgement, and, of course, sheer luck. None of us were that hell-bent on reaching the top that we couldn't retreat if conditions worsened. Our plan was simple. To move quickly and strongly and get down as soon as possible. Every half-hour or so we stuck our heads through the door and monitored the conditions. It was windy and although the summit looked calm the reality was probably very different. The valleys below were still blanketed by a layer of cloud and only the very highest summits pierced through, like sentinels around our own mountain.

We decided to leave at eleven o'clock that night. Andrew was anxious and keen to set off earlier but I was trying to put the brakes on things. Seb and Chris had left too early, arriving at the second step in the dark. With a seven-hour climb to the step, I wanted to make it for first light at six o'clock and then hopefully to the summit a couple of hours later. That would allow ample time for the descent.

On Everest there is an understandable paranoia about cut-off times, that is to say, the point at which, on summit day, a team has to admit it is too slow to enable a safe descent and therefore to retreat. The formula is well rehearsed by modern commercial teams such as Russell Brice's. He positions himself on the North Col during summit day and monitors his climbers through a telescope and by radio. If they are too slow at his key points he orders them to descend. His decision is final and although sometimes unpopular, it has accounted for a superb safety record.

In the well-publicised Everest disaster of 1996, twelve climbers lost their lives. Most of them were inexperienced climbers arriving at the summit late in the day, and were caught out by tiredness and weather during the descent. Andrew was keen to have a cut-off time for our ascent, perhaps at the second step. It was sensible but I was reluctant to be too specific, preferring to rely on our judgement as the climb unfolded. Either way we would have to arrive early at the higher reaches of the mountain to allow plenty of daylight for the descent. Summitting late in the day had without a doubt led to the demise of David Sharp a few days earlier, and for all we knew, possibly Jacques Letrange as well.

A little after nine o'clock we heard sounds approaching and soon the faces of Karma and Tshering appeared in the door. They were happy to wait but we ushered them inside and made them tea. They were blanketed in a thick layer of frost on their clothes and even their faces – and they were already shivering despite their down suits. The temperature was dropping rapidly. With four of us, the tent was impossibly cramped and getting ready was harder than ever. Earlier that day I had put my boots on safely in the porch at Camp 2. Here, if we dropped a boot, it would disappear down the face. The consequences were too drastic to even consider.

Outside, the cold felt like a thousand needles on my face. The small thermometer on my jacket recorded minus thirty and that took no account of the wind. When Andrew and Sarah were ready, we clipped on to the fixed line and headed into the night. It was impossible to grasp the magnitude of our surroundings. My only view was the yellow pool of light from my head torch upon the snow in front. My crampons squeaked and crunched into the ice under my feet, and there was the constant but reassuring hiss of oxygen streaming into my mask. Not for the first time I felt like a lone astronaut stepping into the unknown, into a place where we had no right to be and from where there might be no return. The inky blackness was like outer space – all-enveloping, cold and harsh.

The rope followed a meandering line through and over outcrops of rock. There was always good purchase, but the face was steeper than I had imagined, and I began to appreciate the darkness. It offered some comfort, protecting us from the huge exposure. The hours ticked by and we paused occasionally to catch our breath. I knew we were making good time when I saw that the rock below us had turned to dull ochre yellow in the torchlight. This was the famous 'yellow band', a stratum of fossil-rich shale preserved from the mud of the Tethys Sea over sixty million years ago. Now these rocks had been pushed up more than five miles into the atmosphere. It was amusing to think it was just geology that had brought us all this way.

I had constant problems with my gloves. Every time we had to unclip the jumar or adjust a mask, we had to slip off our huge down mitts to allow for some movement. Underneath we all wore thinner gloves to avoid frostbite. My inner gloves were still too thick, and on several occasions I had to remove them completely. Andrew saw me struggling and generously waited to lend me his spares. They were considerably thinner but fitted perfectly. The problem solved, we pressed on.

We had now pushed past 8,300 metres and were drawing close to the North-east Ridge itself. Soon we would leave the relative shelter of the face. Then we would turn right on to the ridge and a succession of three steps that would lead to the summit. There was no sign of other climbers until I turned to look to across at the enormity of the West Ridge a few kilometres away. There I saw two head torches, pinpricks of light, impossibly small but strangely close. It had to be the army team, battling with their own route, but ultimately in a bid for the same goal. Half an hour later, we passed through a gap in the rocks and emerged on to the North-east Ridge. I had read it was like stepping on to the wing of an airliner in full flight. But even that failed to prepare me for the impact of the experience.

The ridge was narrower than I had anticipated, perhaps only five metres wide. The far side dropped away instantly to the Kangshung glacier, 10,000 feet below. The exposure was incredible and the view the most staggering that I had ever seen. It was as though we had stepped from a darkened room into daylight. At first I thought dawn must have rushed up on us, but it was still too early and the light too grey. The full moon had risen in the east, and until now had been hidden from us in the shadow of the face. A few miles away rose the imposing sight of Makalu, and beyond were hundreds of other peaks, all bathed in the eerie moonlight. I felt as if I had reached up to the edge of world and was looking out into another. I could have stared at the sight for hours but this was a cold and dangerous place. The wind was light but bitingly cold as we sat and huddled together to check our oxygen. We had now been on the go for six hours but there should be plenty left. We planned to swap the bottles nearer the summit and the second one should see us through our descent.

'Dom – yours is nearly empty!'

I hoped I had misheard, but there was no mistaking Jamie. We wound each other up continually but this was no joke. Surely not even Jamie would do that now? I unshouldered my bottle to inspect it properly, my mind racing and my heart sinking. I knew that my ascent was effectively over. It was far too early to swap bottles and press on. There just wouldn't be enough to get down again. I looked at the dial – there was only 10 per cent left. I must have had the flow on at too high a rate, a simple but very costly error. Perhaps I'd knocked the dial during the ascent? The Sherpas might have a spare but they were yet to catch us up and I didn't feel like waiting here in the extreme cold with limited oxygen. Andrew and Jamie were equally silent, the consequences no doubt playing through their minds. I shook the bottle and tapped the regulator furiously. The dial sprang back to life and I gulped a welcome sigh of relief. There was still over a third left, plenty to see me through another couple of hours.

The drama over, we prepared to move off. Andrew went first, followed by myself, then Jamie. The gradient was easier now since the ridge was nearly horizontal. We took a precarious route just to the north in the lee of the wind and made quick progress. It was just ten minutes before Andrew checked his pace. The dawn was rising behind us, and in its weak light, I saw the reason why. Ahead of us was a body lying face down. It had to be that of David Sharp who had died three days earlier. He was lying with his arms drawn under him, outside the shelter of the overhanging rock. We had to step over his feet as he lay directly under the line itself. Tucked under the shelter of the rock behind him I could see the emerging legs and fluorescent colour of 'Green Boots', the Indian climber who had died there in 1996. His face was hidden and his upper body contorted from having pulled himself into the shelter. It was a macabre sight and only served to make our surroundings even more unearthly.

The first of our climbing obstacles was the 'first step'. From below in base camp it was barely discernible – a blip high on the ridgeline. Now it seemed daunting, but in practice presented little technical difficulty. We heaved our way over small shelves that reminded me of scrambling on the beach as a child. We even descended a little, down to the second step. This was a far more serious challenge, split into two stages, and totalling some thirty metres in height. Back home it would have made an interesting Sunday afternoon rock climb. Here at 8,500 metres it was far more intimidating and the crux of the whole route. The slope fell away steeply to our right now, all the way to the Rongbuk glacier two miles below. It was exposed and dangerous and had defeated others before us. In all probability, Mallory could not have climbed it, and almost certainly not on his own. There were ways around the step, but they presented their own, perhaps greater, dangers.

It's believed that the first to overcome the step were the Chinese in 1960. After the invasion of Tibet ten years earlier, they were anxious to make their mark on the summit that now lay in their possession. The enormous expedition allowed no room for error, and they even constructed the dirt road that now led all the way to base camp. Failure was not an option for a team numbering some 214 members and with national pride at stake. The four-man summit team ascended the second step using pitons,[25] even standing on one another's shoulders at one point. The latter resulted in the loss of toes for one climber after he removed his boots. Their successful ascent was long doubted by Western climbers, and the claim that they had left a bust of Chairman Mao on the summit even more so. What was not in dispute was that in 1975 the Chinese returned, and this time a lightweight aluminium ladder was placed on the upper step as a permanent fixture to overcome the steep headwall. They also erected a small summit tripod for surveying purposes. British climbers Doug Scott and Dougal Haston later discovered this, after their climb of the south-west face later the same year.

At the foot of the step we came across another climber and a Sherpa. They were busy using a rope to make some kind of seated harness, as if to haul each other up the face. It was an almost comical sight, but we were starting to get frustrated. We had moved quickly until this point and were now being held up through no fault of our own. I assumed they were from the Russian team, whom I'd approached for help at the North Col two days earlier. Their Camp 3 had been much higher than ours so they would have set off with a head start. We were closing on them, but crucially at just the wrong point. At the foot of the second step it was hard to find any shelter. The wind and the cold quickly combined to drain us of warmth and energy, to devastating effect. I felt for the first time the fear of being immobile at this altitude – life ebbing steadily away with the inactivity.

Jamie tapped me on the shoulder and mumbled through his mask. 'Dom, I might have to call it a day, mate . . . I'm getting too cold . . . What do you think?' I too was wavering. We had been waiting for half an hour and our momentum had gone. I wondered how the sight of dead bodies had affected Jamie. It was perhaps less of a shock to Andrew and I, but Jamie was still only twenty-three, and for him it was another first.

'Look, why don't we try and get over the step? If we're still cold . . . and it's too late . . . then we'll turn around.' He nodded his agreement. None of us wanted to admit defeat before the crux of the climb. I had read and heard so much about the step that I wanted to experience it for myself. If after that we had to head down, then so be it.

Eventually our fellow climbers pulled themselves over the first section, clearing the way for us. Andrew quickly got going. The first ledge was at chest height and covered in verglas[26] and a dusting of powdery snow. He tried to heave himself on to it, but slid back to where he started, crampons screeching on the rock. At the second attempt he was over, and I waited a couple of minutes to give us some space. There were at least a dozen old ropes in front of me. Somewhere amongst them was this season's fixed rope but it was hard to see which one. Any thoughts I had of free-climbing vanished. I hooked my axe over a lip of rock and in my other hand grabbed a bunch of ropes, hoping that their combined strength would hold me. I heaved myself on to the next boulder. A succession of desperate lunges left me breathless. I doubled over, trying to breathe through my mask. The oxygen couldn't come quickly enough and I frantically pulled the mask to one side to get fresh air. There was nothing to breathe and I was left sucking on emptiness. I cursed myself for being such an idiot and hurriedly replaced the mask. It was a good two minutes before my breathing returned to normal. I saw Jamie below had surmounted the ledge and was beginning to close on me. I pressed on and moved to the upper section of the step.

Although this section was steeper than the earlier part, the ladder was there and tied loosely against the cliff. Andrew was nearing the top of it and I waited until he was well clear. It wasn't as difficult as I had feared. The rungs fitted neatly into my crampons and I tried to climb deliberately slowly to keep my breath, focusing only on my hands and feet. To my right was the deep abyss. I had no intention of going that way if I could help it. The top was a tangle of frayed ropes so I stepped gingerly over them and on to a broad snow slope. We were clear of the second step – above lay the final hurdle, the summit pyramid. We crouched down and helped each other change oxygen bottles as Jamie joined us. The wind was still strong but a weak sun was shining now, the feeble warmth an added boost to morale.

Ahead we could see a couple of figures picking their way over the jumble of rocks that marked the third step, and though most of the summit pyramid was clear, the very top was hidden from view. While Andrew helped Jamie with his oxygen, I led the way, looking around, determined to absorb the view. To my right, the slope dropped away steeply, and to my left was the Kangshung face and another sheer drop. I was shocked to notice a figure some ten metres away from the fixed rope, leaning sideways on his rucksack. I thought he was staring at me, then realised it must be another body. That was until he beckoned at me furiously.

I was reluctant to unclip from the security of the line. The wind was strong and the climber was close to the edge of the

Kangshung face. I knew it was dangerously corniced and he could easily be on a fragile snow shelf. There was enough slack in the line to allow me to move within two or three metres of him. I knelt close by while he continued his frantic hand signals. With one hand he clutched his rucksack, and with the other he motioned as though to slice it open. All the while, he looked intently at me.

'What do you need? What do you want?' I yelled across the noise of the wind, having taken off my mask. I was determined to resolve the situation quickly and press on. He replied in what sounded like Russian. It made little difference – we simply couldn't communicate. I shook my head and patted my chest to signal that I had no knife.

'You must go down!' I yelled and pointed. He nodded and then gestured at two figures now descending through the third step. They looked strong and I guessed they were his friends from the same team. If they had been to the summit already, they would be able to lead him down or at least help him. I turned around to see Andrew and Jamie catching up, so I made my way back to the natural line of the fixed rope and together we continued our ascent. I soon lost sight of the figure I had tried to help.

As we met the two climbers on their way down, I pointed to their friend, making sure they would stop and help their team mate. The lead figure nodded before pointing back at the summit with the shaft of his axe. 'Cold . . . very, very cold,' he repeated in a thick accent. 'Good luck.' In no time they were gone and we were left alone. We scrambled through the jumble of rocks that was the third step, drawing closer, but I still feared the weather would get the better of us and the wind prove too strong. I glanced behind to see that Karma and Tshering were closing on us. They had done well to catch up, but in truth were only a little quicker. With renewed vigour and momentum, our enlarged team pressed ahead.

This time we let the Sherpas take the lead. The line veered to the right of the pyramid and seemingly away from the summit.

Soon we were back on the north face of the mountain, traversing along a narrow snow shelf. It was exhilarating, but we were horribly exposed. The drop to our right was over two miles, all the way down to base camp. For a few minutes we were in the shade and, mercifully, in the lee of the wind. The sudden quiet was unnerving and the gloom left me longing to be back in the sun. We picked our way cautiously, anxious to avoid any mistakes at this late stage. Andrew was a few metres ahead of me when we saw what we had been expecting.

Jacques was lying on his back a few metres beneath us. There was another piece of frayed rope off the line leading down to him. I wasn't sure of the purpose of this. Had he lowered himself off the route? Or had Roland perhaps put him there to keep him away from the line? He was a big man, but thankfully for us his face was covered. There was no mistaking his clothing and boots, just as Caroline had described. Andrew and I looked at each other, but there was little to say. We had already decided that we would go to the summit first and, time permitting, we would retrieve the effects from Jacques's body on our descent.

Just a few metres away the line turned abruptly to the left and almost back on itself. Ahead rose a narrow but protected gully. I glanced at my altimeter and my heart sank. Still another hundred metres' ascent to go – that meant over an hour yet. Andrew was pulling ahead and moving as strongly as ever and I did my best to keep up. Only when we emerged from the narrow gully into the sun and wind did my mistake become clear.

There was the summit, barely two minutes away. Karma and Tshering were almost there. As I drew closer, I could see the top was actually an enormous snow cornice arching far over the Kangshung face. It looked perilous and no bigger than the roof of a small house. Half buried in the snow and whipping in the wind were the colourful remains of prayer flags. Those last minutes were painless, the least tiring of the whole ascent. My altimeter had deceived me and the exhilaration of knowing we had made it outweighed any exhaustion.

I paused just five metres below the top to catch my breath. Buried in the snow at my feet was a Union Jack. Smiling at my good fortune, I prised it loose and held it aloft just as Andrew raised his camera to get a shot. It was a fortuitous moment and I could see Andrew had removed his mask and was beaming. I climbed the last steps and we hugged each other. I sat on the snow and choked back some tears, not of happiness, just sheer unadulterated relief. True, the descent was still to come, but for me the 'longest climb' was over. I looked again at my watch to see it was 8.35 a.m. and the date 21 May. Five months, almost to the very hour, since we had left the Dead Sea.

Chapter 16

Downhill All the Way

No sooner had I stopped moving than I began to feel the biting cold, the wind robbing me of what little warmth remained. Jamie was just three minutes behind and I could sense his relief as he made the final steps. Both choked up, we hugged each other but said little more than a muffled 'well done'. Somewhere behind me, I was aware of Andrew talking on the radio before he passed it over. I turned my back to the blasting wind, before speaking briefly to ABC. Neglecting to remove my mask meant they didn't understand a word, but it was probably for the best. Words could never express how deliriously happy I felt. We snapped away taking pictures, recording as much as we could and relishing the moment, but now with all five of us on top there was hardly room to manoeuvre. Tshering turned around too sharply, only to dislodge an old oxygen bottle. We watched helplessly as it shot off in the direction of the south-west face, turning within seconds into a lethal high-speed missile.

After just eight minutes, I beckoned at the others, anxious that we should get moving. At the back of my mind was the task ahead with Jacques's body as well as the long descent. I turned around for one last look into Nepal. Far below I could see the summit of Lobuje, a peak I had climbed years earlier. At the time it had seemed enormous; now 2,000 metres below it looked improbably tiny. Past it ran the Khumbu glacier, up which I had carried my bicycle as a teenager so many years before. I put my head back and stared up into space where the sky turned to a deep blue. Again, I felt like an astronaut about to float into the unknown, or a diver staring into the depths.

We gathered ourselves together and I led us off the summit, desperate to outrace the worsening weather. It was only a couple of minutes before we were back in the cold of the gulley, but at least sheltered from the wind. Andrew and I led, with the Sherpas behind, as we drew level with Jacques.

'I'm happy to get the stuff if you could belay me?' said Andrew.

I was relieved by his suggestion. Although at this point I was so keen to get down, I really didn't mind who did it. Just as long as we didn't dwell too long.

'I'll use this to lower you,' I said as I slipped off my outer mitts. I pulled in the slack rope and made a figure of eight in it before passing it to Andrew to clip in. I wrapped the slack around my body and tried to make a firm stance for myself. Andrew was unlikely to fall anywhere but the slope was dangerously steep and none of us were particularly secure. Gingerly he made his way down towards Jacques, who lay perhaps five metres below. I paid out the rope for the few seconds it took for Andrew to draw level with him on the small shelf. He methodically removed his gloves before crouching next to him. He seemed to pause for a few seconds, lost in thought, before unzipping Jacques's jacket. The three days since his death had already caused everything to freeze and nothing would move easily. He reached gently inside his clothing to grasp the string around his neck. On this we knew was his wedding ring.

'Can you get it, Andrew?' I called.

'Yeah, but I can't untie it.'

'Just snap it, it doesn't matter'.

Andrew yanked at the string and it gave way easily. I saw him gingerly hold the ring before safely stowing it in a zipped pocket.

He managed the cool detachment of a doctor at work but he too had his wedding ring tied around his neck. We all thought the same; it could so easily have been us, lying here in this lonely place. I could see Karma and Tshering were getting restless. They were as keen to get down as we were, perhaps even more so. It suddenly occurred to me that they had no idea what we were doing with Jacques's body. For all they knew, we might have been stealing his effects. I turned to Karma to explain.

'He is a friend. We must get his wedding ring. For his wife.'

Karma acknowledged this with a nod but seemed unmoved. Andrew joined us back on the line and unclipped from the belay. There was insufficient time to look for his other possessions and it didn't really seem right. His camera was supposed to be on his waist belt but of that there was no sign. At least we had the thing that was most precious to Caroline.

I led off down the fixed line, making very quick headway. At the third step we got caught again behind two of the Russian team. They had failed to reach the top, presumably playing safe in the high winds. Now they were descending impossibly slowly. It was a frustrating few minutes and they made no attempt to let us pass although we were blatantly quicker. Instead I unclipped and without the security of the line scrambled through the rocks before rejoining the route. There was no sign of the man I had seen earlier who had appeared to be in trouble. I just hoped he had been picked up by his colleagues and led down to safety. Thankfully I was now ahead of those descending and the route was clear to the second step. I knew this was a bottleneck, just like the one we had been caught in on the ascent, and I was anxious not to be delayed. I looked behind me just once, urging the others to follow my lead and overtake.

Descending the step was tricky, and for this reason I had planned all along to abseil rather than climb down. For the purpose I had on my harness a lightweight abseil device through which I could feed the rope. The reality was a little more daunting. I arrived at the top of the cliff to be met by the jumble of tatty decaying rope I had seen on my ascent. In the daylight, I could more easily identify the new fixed line but there was no natural abseil. If I clipped in here the natural line below would take me directly over the north face and not into the corner I needed to reach. I simply had to use the ladder as a guide to get back to the right place. I settled on a compromise, passing the rope through to make an abseil and using it as a guide to reach the ladder. The icy ledge sloped away over the drop and I chose my steps carefully, desperate not to slip at this stage. 'Just be careful, just be careful . . .' I muttered to myself. How stupid would it be to fall off this thing now?

Exactly a week earlier, it was rumoured that a member of the Indo-Tibetan Border Police expedition had fallen to his death on the second step after a successful summit. I reached the top of the ladder, anxious to grab hold of something attached to the cliff. If I could descend the ladder using my abseil for security it should be straightforward. I kicked away at the bundle of rope surrounding the first step and placed my crampon on the rung. The first step was the hardest but I soon had my hands on the top rung. Mistakenly I thought I was safe.

My right foot seemed to be caught up and I glanced down. With horror, I noticed the strap had come undone and the back of the crampon was hanging free in the tangle of rope. I gingerly tried to raise my foot so I could at least grab it. That way I could hang on to it and reattach it at the bottom. It was looser than I thought and instantly it fell away from my foot. 'Please please, just land at the bottom!' But it smacked on to a rock under the ladder twenty feet below, and bounced away out of sight.

A wave of panic washed through me. I simply had to have the crampon to descend. I felt scared, annoyed, and extremely vulnerable. 'What a bloody idiot,' I cursed myself. 'Now I'm going to die up here like the others. Just when it was in the bag I had to blow it.' I recalled the first time I had been shown how to use crampons up in Scotland as a teenager. 'Check them regularly, check them regularly.' Here it was, a schoolboy error and I could see it now. No glamorous high-altitude death ... 'He just died because his crampon fell off!' Feeling dreadfully exposed, I descended the rest of the ladder and clipped into the jumar, too scared to move further.

My right foot felt naked and utterly useless on the ice-covered rocks. Calming myself, I tried to assess the situation. I scanned around for the crampon and to my initial relief saw it just five metres away. Then, to my dismay, I realised it was perched on a small snow cornice above the abyss of the north face. To reach it I would have to unclip from the fixed line and edge myself over a 10,000-foot drop on unstable snow – and all with one crampon. I looked disdainfully at it, trying to will it towards me. It sat there, of course, siren-like, luring me closer, but I wasn't tempted. It was far too dangerous.

In my selfish haste to descend, I had all but forgotten the others. Karma now appeared above me and I pointed out the crampon on its precarious perch. He had both crampons on and probably more courage. I hoped I might get a 'No problem. I can reach it. Wait here.' He looked for some time before turning to me and shaking his head. Even through his mask I could hear his response.

'Big problem. Very dangerous.' He pointed at my right boot. Thanks, Karma, I thought. Like I needed telling.

The next few minutes were a nightmare. I was reluctant to leave the crampon there, convinced that I couldn't descend without it. Was it worth risking my life to retrieve it? I couldn't make up my mind but eventually admitted defeat. We still had much of the step to descend and so I clung to the fixed rope like the lifeline it now represented. In a delicate manoeuvre, I let the Sherpas go around me on the tight shelf, Karma first and Tshering following very nervously. The bottom section was extremely steep and he hesitated repeatedly, uncertain how to descend. The Sherpas, unlike us, had no abseil devices and their weak rope skills sometimes left them floundering. We all carried prussics, thin nylon ropes that could be wrapped around the main line to generate friction. This would have been a perfect time to use them, but it only occurred to me then that they might not know how. Eventually Tshering, using brute force, took a giant leap, landing neatly in the snow at the base of the step. I abseiled down and forced a huge sigh of relief.

My problems were only just beginning, but I relaxed a little, took some deep breaths, and steeled myself for the day ahead. It's only half past nine in the morning, I reassured myself. I can do this if I just take it easy and keep going. A grim determination came over me. I knew I was still feeling strong and there was no way I was staying up here, like David, like Jacques and even 'Green Boots'. Karma offered to wait for Andrew and Jamie, who we presumed were starting to descend behind us. Reluctant to slow the others down and make them wait, I told Karma I would make a head start. I moved very slowly along the ridge, retracing the steps of a few hours previously. It wasn't as bad as I feared, although dreadfully slow. In the morning sun, the crisp surface had turned into softer snow. This meant that my right foot gained a little purchase. The face sloped away to my left now, and thankfully this was the cramponed side. I moved the crampon forward first and made sure I planted it firmly. Only then did I ease the more vulnerable right foot up to join it. In this shuffling style, I proceeded painfully along the ridge, at least making progress.

I thought little about the others, focusing entirely and selfishly on rescuing myself. My single aim now was to get off this mountain safely. It was almost an hour before I approached the body of David again. In the sunlight the scene was not as ghostly as the night before. I paused next to where he lay and sank to one knee. I tried to spare a thought for him and how desperately sad it was that he hadn't made it. My day would be long, but I was becoming increasingly confident that I would get down safely. The panic and isolation I had experienced had lasted only a few minutes. David's would have been ever-increasing to the point where he must have known he was going to die. I looked carefully at his kit to see if he was well equipped. Unbelievably his crampons were of exactly the same type as mine. My head started to spin. In the oxygen-starved atmosphere I couldn't string together a logical chain of thoughts. Just a few feet away was a spare crampon . . .

'All I need to get to safety is sitting right there . . . simple. Don't be ridiculous, you can't steal kit from a dead man's body! What would his family think? What would he think, more to the point?' I wished suddenly I had known him. With the macabre sense of humour many climbers possess, he might even have laughed. 'Don't be a fool, go for it . . . just take it. I don't need it, do I?'

I sat there for several minutes, wrestling with my moral dilemma. Half-heartedly I tugged at the frozen strap but it was immovable. In the end the easier solution was not to bother and push on regardless. I had been making fair progress anyway, albeit very slowly. I left David where he lay, exposed to the elements and just a few metres from Green Boots. At least now he was at peace.

The others were still to catch me up, so I couldn't have been doing too badly. I had to change style abruptly when I reached the spot where the route took us back on to the face. This was the point I dreaded. Now I would be descending steeply and there was no way I could get the purchase necessary. The best technique was to walk facing straight downhill, using the fixed rope as a flimsy handrail. The crampons were crucial for this, and without one of them it was simply impossible. Instead, I decided to play safe and resort to my abseil device. In this way, I began walking backwards down the fixed line, feeding the rope through as I went. The thin line, only three or four millimetres across, wasn't designed for this. It slipped repeatedly but I was at least relatively safe.

At every anchor point, I had to remove my outer gloves, and then undo and reattach the 'descendeur' on to the next stretch of line. Here I was most at danger. With poor purchase on my feet, I had to be doubly sure that I had a good stance before unclipping myself. It was a tiresome process but I continued to make progress through the late morning. All the while, I could hear the radio crackling away inside my jacket. Nic at ABC was talking to Sarah at the top camp. They had heard nothing from us since the summit and were obviously concerned. I should have rescued the radio from my pocket and called them back, but I resisted. Everything required such enormous effort and I wanted to preserve every ounce of energy for getting back down.

I couldn't believe how far we had climbed the night before, the darkness concealing the true scale of our ascent. Only after six hours of descent did I spot some tents and begin to feel safe. Ours were much lower still, but at least I would be there within the hour. I sat down and called up Sarah. I hoped she would get some water on as I was incredibly dehydrated. I hadn't touched the two litres inside my jacket and had eaten nothing for fifteen hours. Glancing over my shoulder, I could see figures high above and closing on me. I was sure Andrew's distinctive yellow suit was amongst them. Encouraged, I got to my feet, with fresh motivation to press on.

Sarah was not only relieved to see us but also glad to have some company. It was now three o'clock and she had been on her own since our departure – a total of some sixteen hours. It was a lonely vigil up here in the death zone but her efforts were much appreciated. There were already full water bottles and another two pots on the boil. Karma and Tshering were keen to press on and get to the lower camp, but for us there was no question. We squeezed into Sarah's tent and gulped tepid tea and soup. We mocked her that we couldn't tell which was which as she had muddled so many bottles. Not that it mattered; none of us had drunk anything during the entire climb so we were desperate. We knew that we too should aim to get lower, as was the practice, but I wasn't too concerned. Our top camp was the lowest of all the expeditions, which at least now was proving an advantage. We also had quite a bit of oxygen left. This meant that another night here would not be too uncomfortable or unsafe. The others readily agreed, although Sarah understandably was probably desperate to get down. She did a fantastic job of looking after us as we settled into an exhausted stupor. Jamie was already in a deep sleep, muttering to himself and replaying the events of the day. I too was shattered but didn't feel like sleeping. I just felt lucky to be alive and wanted to relish every minute of our newfound safety.

That evening passed in a blur of chilled sleep, interspersed by warm drinks. Most of the descent was still ahead, but I knew we could make it safely, even with my one crampon. Jamie and I had brought only one sleeping bag between us in an effort to save weight. As darkness fell the temperature fell steeply again. Inhibitions disappeared and we huddled together in an effort to preserve all the warmth we could. There was enough oxygen for the night so we set a low flow and tried our best to sleep. My mind raced with thoughts of Jacques and David, the summit, and the entire journey that was now behind us. No one could have guessed that events would reach such a dramatic conclusion. Luck had been on our side. All being well, we would be one of the few teams on the mountain to emerge unscathed from all the tragedy.

Stiff with cold and tiredness, we made a painfully slow start the following morning. We packed as much equipment and rubbish as we could to take down the mountain, leaving just the empty tents. Dorjee was already climbing up for these and would take them down later that day, saving us a huge amount of effort. When we set off, the others quickly moved ahead of me. I was jealous as they disappeared off down the ropes and I was left fiddling with my laborious abseil technique. It took three hours to reach the safety of Camp 2; still only half what it had taken me to ascend. The stoves were already roaring away for yet more fluid and we basked in the warmth of the tent. The noon sun at this height was powerful and for once there was little wind. Inside the tent it was too hot but we didn't care. We let the heat roast us and make up for the last forty-eight hours. We looked back wistfully at the summit through the open door. Today was actually a far better day for weather.

The descent to the North Col became incredibly tiresome. I soon resolved to spend the night there rather than descend further and urged the others to continue. I was going so slowly it would take me for ever to reach ABC and it was best done on my own. Nic had asked Dorjee to bring some spare crampons up for me, but I was yet to see any sign of him. It was worth waiting, as it would make the final leg considerably safer.

I sat for a while in the tent, sipping tea, and listening to the familiar rustle of the snow blowing gently over the flysheet. I felt totally relaxed and happier than I had been in months. My job was almost done, we were off the mountain safely and our success had exceeded our wildest hopes. The tragedy of the last week had, if anything, reinforced our success. It helped us to realise what odds we had overcome. I wasn't short of food that night and ate my way through three hot meals and several teas. Then I settled into a deep twelve-hour sleep, unhindered by the constraints of the oxygen mask.

I packed up the remainder of the food in the morning and struggled across the ridge with an enormous load. Aside from Dorjee, I would be last off the mountain and I knew I would feel guilty if we left rubbish. He had brought me an extra crampon but annoyingly it didn't fit. Now, what should have been straightforward quickly became an exhausting struggle. I trudged painfully across the glacier before I reached the moraine and saw people for the first time. Nic and Patrick were walking up and waved as I drew closer. We all embraced as they offered their congratulations. Despite Nic missing out on the summit he had earned his team credentials faultlessly, manning the radio for hours on end, along with Nigel. I was pleased for Pat, who had taken two months to get this far but now at least was seeing the mountain close up. Following behind them was Guillet, our Tibetan helper, smiling from ear to ear. He bowed his head when he saw me and grasped my hands in his. He looked so pleased to see me and was incredibly gracious. He insisted on taking my rucksack and I resisted rather pathetically. Unhindered, I followed the others gently back to base camp. I tried to savour every step on the solid moraine, knowing that in all likelihood I would never come this way again. When I reached the tent, a smiling Nigel thrust a can of beer into my hand. It didn't even touch the sides.

The others were equally shattered after their long descent but that afternoon they set off towards base camp. I stayed in ABC with Nic, Pat and Nigel and together we helped the Sherpas begin to dismantle the camp and pack equipment. When I did descend to base camp the following day, the descent that I had previously reduced to four hours now took six. I was running on empty and had lost a dangerous amount of weight. Devoid of energy, I fuelled myself on boiled sweets and dried fruit to keep me going. My appetite was certainly stronger than it had been earlier on the mountain, but in truth there seemed little point in eating. Every meal in base camp had proved a struggle, but I had forced it down to maintain my strength. Now I no longer had to, I was content to sip tea and just pick at the food in front of me. The rations on the mountain had been a lifesaver. I dreaded going back to Nat's stodgy pancakes and slurry porridge.

I wasn't in as bad a way as some of the team, though. Dickie was in a dreadful state after his ascent to the Col a week earlier. He sat in the dining tent hacking up phlegm from deep in his lungs. His face looked so pained I thought he would explode. Phil had drifted into some kind of high-altitude trance and emerged reluctantly from his tent only at the behest of Pauline. The spark that had existed at mealtimes seemed to have gone. The objective that had been the constant topic of conversation was now achieved. We were just tired and dreaming of home. Even conversation required a conscious effort.

I missed the company of Seb, Chris and André. Anxious to get home, they had descended to base camp a week earlier and left on the same morning we had summitted. I had had a very idealised view that the whole team would stick together, perhaps all the way home, but in practice things were bound to be different. Most teams on the mountain become fractured in the end, with team members cutting away once they have summitted. Seb and André were needed at home and could not wait to see their young families. Chris's mother was also dangerously ill and I knew he needed to get back as soon as possible. He had come close to leaving the trip earlier for that very reason.

There was little opportunity for the rest us to depart ahead of schedule, unless we wanted to pay a vast amount in dollars. We had booked the yaks weeks earlier to bring down our stuff from ABC on 27 May. Our actual departure from base camp in the jeeps was booked for three days later. Any attempt to bring this forward was quickly dismissed by the Chinese officials and so we had to sit tight. It was a frustrating five days, but we busied ourselves by tidying up and packing equipment.

On our penultimate evening we decided to host a dinner party for some of our neighbours. Nat went the extra mile with the meagre supplies he had left. First on the invitation list were two of the nearby Catalan team. It was a masterstroke by Pat, who knew they had an enormous supply of cured hams hanging in their tent. They didn't disappoint and duly arrived with the delicious starter.

We also invited Russell Brice over, who amazingly arrived with a couple of bottles of wine. The mood lifted and we all swapped stories of the ascent and some of the characters at base camp. My conversation with Russell turned inevitably to David Sharp. News was already circulating in the press and on the web that David had been left to die by Russell's team. Climbers ascending on the morning of the 15th, one of the main summit days, had apparently found him still alive; Mark Inglis, a double amputee and part of Russell's team, rather unfairly had borne the brunt of the criticism despite the many other climbers who had played their part.

Russell was stung by the criticism. The implication that he was a ruthless commercial leader made him very uncomfortable and he defended his position in a quiet but determined manner, maintaining he was the one who repeatedly had to deal with the aftermath of deaths on the mountain. When David had died, Russell had visited the team's base camp to find a complete apathy about his disappearance. He went to David's tent personally, unsure at the time that David was definitely missing. There he found a few possessions, a little money, a bible and, of course, his passport. He used the passport details to contact David's parents and break the news.

David Sharp had been just thirty-four years old and, by all accounts, it had been his third time on Everest. It was suggested he had succumbed to 'summit fever' and that, with a combination of other factors, probably led to his death. Initial information was scanty because he had apparently been climbing on his own. He had reached the summit late, probably in the afternoon or evening of 14 May. He then started his descent, and we know that he made it only as far as the Green Boots cave, 1,000 feet below the summit. He had stopped to seek refuge, maybe even with thoughts of spending the night there, but his body would already have been in decline. Stopping to rest was a false economy – and he never got up again.

I felt for Russell. He had an air of stubbornness about him but he was also a compassionate man. Some saw him as a ruthless operator who suffered no fools, but the death of David Sharp was certainly not his fault. For starters he wasn't even there at the scene. Those who passed David would have to make their own judgements as mountaineers as to whether they should have helped. The classic defence, of course, is that in the 'death zone' it is all you can do to look after yourself. Rescues have been carried out very high on the mountain but sometimes at enormous risk and cost. In truth, David probably could have been rescued. He was below the second step, conditions were good, and there was a small army of people to help. That forty people passed him by will shock some, but it doesn't leave me at all surprised. The more people there are, the easier it is to leave decisions to someone behind you. We had experienced the same when finding Vince, the Canadian, slumped at the North Col. Above 8,000 metres, hidden behind your mask and goggles, it is easy to remain oblivious.

Russell was at best frustrated at the 'cowboy operators' who allowed climbers on a limited budget to go up the mountain, his point being that in a well-run expedition such as his own, a climber would never be left alone or without adequate Sherpa support. He was in favour of some method of licensing that would regulate those operating on the mountain. He clearly had an agenda here and I wondered where that left teams such as us. After all, we were a budget outfit, not unlike David Sharp's team. Under a licensing system, we would probably never have got on the mountain at all. However, we had emerged as probably the strongest team: seven of us had made the summit with limited support and had emerged unscathed.[27] Even Russell's team had descended with some dreadful frostbite injuries. To my mind, our team had got closer to the romantic ideals of the early Everest expeditions. We were amateur adventurers, non-commercial, and had attempted a genuine first. But those days are drawing to a close: Everest has already become an expensive and dangerous high-altitude playground.

The following morning brought yet more tragic news. Igor Plyushkin, a Russian Snow Leopard,[28] had been a member of the infamous Seven Summits team. By all accounts he had been just one of twenty climbers heading to the summit on the same day as us, although I had no recollection of seeing that number. Four of them, including Igor, had apparently turned around at 8,600 metres. With sadness I realised that Igor was probably the man that had asked for my help just below the third step. He had at least made it down to the safety of their Camp 2 at 7,800 metres. However, the following morning he had walked only fifteen metres from the tent before collapsing. Despite attempts to revive him, he was pronounced dead an hour later.

The death toll was now into double figures but more drama was still unfolding. We were shocked to learn reports of the death of Lincoln Hall, one of Australia's most experienced high-altitude mountaineers. It was the first I knew that he was even on the mountain. Lincoln was the author of *White Limbo*, the inspirational account of a small Australian team climbing the north face in the 1980s. Now fifty years old, he had reached the summit on 25 May, again with the Seven Summits team. Somehow on the descent he had become lost and disorientated and been left for dead by one of his Sherpas. Like David Sharp he had spent a night in the open, but contrary to the early reports he had actually survived. In the meantime, his expedition had already reported to his family that he had died on the mountain.

At 7.30 the following morning, a team led by American climber Dan Mazur found Lincoln stranded on a ridge between the first and second steps. He was delirious and had removed his gloves and was even attempting to remove his shirt. He later reported that he felt as though he were afloat on a boat and wanted to dive over the side. He was successfully led to safety and survived, albeit with some severe frostbite. His survival was not only a credit to his own stamina but to those who took the time and effort to rescue him. They had remained with him for several hours, restoring him with hot drinks and oxygen before a Sherpa team arrived to lead him down. Dan Mazur and his team had in the best possible way restored a little of the mountain's reputation by rescuing a climber from extreme altitude, especially as he had been in a very similar position to David Sharp.

Lincoln's survival did little to alter the fact that it was a disastrous year. Thomas Weber, a German climber also attached to Seven Summits, died, as did Vitor Negrete, a Brazilian who had shared a tent with David Sharp. In total, some eleven climbers had lost their lives. All this muted our success as we descended from base camp in the jeeps on 30 May. I couldn't help but feel blessed that we had been so fortunate to return uninjured. That people as experienced as Lincoln Hall had come unstuck showed that our survival was as much down to luck as skill.

We stopped briefly at the Rongbuk Monastery to donate to them our medical kit and the solar panel we had used. The remainder of the journey was blissful in comparison to the ascent two months earlier. Within ten hours, we were on the border again in Zhangmu, drinking beer and sitting on proper chairs. Zhangmu looked much less miserable now, the air was thick and heady and drawing breath was just sheer delight.

The last leg over the border and to Kathmandu was frustratingly slow, but late the following evening we found ourselves ensconced in Fire and Ice, drooling over the menu. My enormous pizza, of which I had been dreaming, defeated me after just two slices. The final three days passed in a blur of packing, long boozy lunches and even some interviews. Only on our last night's celebration did the expedition throw up one final and timely surprise.

The character who tapped me on the shoulder in the bar was small, wiry and bearded. He smiled inanely as if he didn't have a care in the world. At first I thought he was drunk or simply crazy, perhaps both. Only when he persisted in his broad Germanic accent did the penny finally drop.

'EVEREST*MAX* yes? You are Dom? My name is Gerry. Gerry Winkler!'

In the drama of the preceding weeks, Gerry and his quest to complete the longest climb had almost been forgotten. He had after all been on the south side of the mountain, so news had been very scarce. To his credit he had also summitted on 20 May, the day before Jamie and I, but after Pauline. The dates seemed a little academic and it was of no consequence to him that he hadn't been the first. We met for lunch the next day and talked about the incredible journey he had experienced. He was modest, describing himself as neither a great cyclist, nor a great mountaineer. Instead, what you needed to be, he told me defiantly, was 'a great traveller'.

Gerry's achievement had to be admired far more than our own, though. He had planned his trip some years previously but had developed cancer. Only in remission from this had he decided to seize the opportunity to make the journey. He was also a diabetic so had surmounted enormous odds to make the summit. I was genuinely pleased for him, as was Jamie, who had dismissed his previous doubts. I watched them laughing and joking across the table, knowing that after everything we now shared a special bond. The privilege of surviving the 'longest climb'.

Epilogue

London 2007

I stepped out across Hyde Park following much the same route from Paddington as I had almost twenty years earlier. Then, I had been about to begin life as a reluctant student at Imperial College. My life had been in a muddle. With only a rucksack full of clothes and a few books, I had a gut feeling I wouldn't be staying long. I had no better ideas of course, but instinctively I knew London wasn't for me. I stuck it out, but my love/hate relationship with the city continues to this day.

A few days after my arrival I had watched as the great storm, frightening in its intensity, had raged all around. It seemed a fitting backdrop to my life at the time: chaotic and destructive. Now the scene couldn't have been more different. Replanted trees were rich in autumn colour, and above was simply cloudless blue, marred only by criss-crossed vapour trails from planes. A sharp east wind made it chilly, but still there were families enjoying themselves and children running into the huge piles of crisp leaves, shouting with delight. I rarely visit London now, but I have learned to draw comfort from the city and be objective about the melancholy it once represented. Perhaps, because that had been a low point of my life, it reassured me that I was so much happier now.

Behind the Albert Hall I dropped down the steps, and passed the Royal Geographical Society, where a few months earlier we had celebrated the expedition with a sell-out gala for 800 guests. On the surface at least the event brought everything to a fitting close, but there was still something missing, something that I was today hoping to put right, if only for my own peace of mind. I was to meet Jacques's wife, Caroline, who was trying to make a new life here in London. We had met only once since the events on the mountain, when she had come to the gala evening. The event was so hectic that we had shared barely a few words in passing, promising to meet in the future. We both knew it was something that had to be done.

Now, six months later, I stood in the Great Hall of the Natural History Museum, a place that has always been a comfort to me: the cathedral-like expanse, the vast galleries and its anonymity all oddly reassuring. I searched earnestly for Caroline and spotted her smiling back at me. She looked serene, elegant in a long black coat, and strangely fragile against the backdrop of that huge space. We embraced silently before strolling around looking at photographs, and eventually retiring to a nearby café for lunch. We talked for hours, reliving the expedition and friends and events of the past, laughing at memories of the different characters and their foibles.

At first I felt awkward quizzing Caroline, but I had so many unanswered questions. She was quick to reassure me that she was now coming to terms with Jacques's death, and of course she was happy to talk. By her own admission, Caroline's life had been torn apart by the events of that May. When the Sherpa on her team had relayed the bad news, it had been 'like the world opening up and swallowing me'. All of the practicalities had to be dealt with. She waited for Roland, their close friend and the third member of the party, to descend – exhausted and traumatised by what had happened. She had to telephone her parents, and, of course, Jacques's family. Three days later they had packed up the camp, leaving Jacques where he lay, and descended back to Kathmandu and the tattered remains of her life. His parents flew out to Kathmandu, unable to quite comprehend the death of their son. Only after our own descent, when Andrew gave them the wedding ring, could they fully accept that their son was lost.

Caroline had sensed on the mountain that something was wrong. It had been a brief farewell at Camp 3 after she had decided not to climb further. She had reminded Jacques to take his spare gloves, but in the morning she had found them outside the tent. We will never know, but perhaps he was already developing the early symptoms of HACE. No one doubted his strength and stamina, but they had not summitted until midday and exhaustion or illness were to get the better of him. Roland had stayed with him for hours, risking his own life and pleading with his friend to move. All to no avail.

Caroline was anxious to talk more of the future than of the past. She was establishing her own company to take clients back to Everest. Her resilience and strength were astounding, but then they had to be. She hadn't lost just her husband, but everything they had hoped and lived for. She and Jacques had planned to have children on their return from Everest and to build on the success of their climb. She had remained close to Roland, who had struggled to come to terms with the events of that day. He had returned to his job in America and had also found it difficult to pick up his life. They had been a great support for each other.

Later I retraced my steps and found the courage to turn off Exhibition Road and into Prince's Gardens. It was here I had first lived as a student and I couldn't help but smile at the building site that now existed. The old halls of residence had been demolished and no trace remained. It was a cleansing moment which made it easy to believe that that episode of my life had never even existed. Perhaps Caroline was right – the only way to look is ever forward, without dwelling on the past, not even for a moment. It was sound advice and I too tried to reassure her that from a bad event can come something good. I have never believed in fate. Life can take very cruel turns, but from those setbacks good fortune can be just a moment away.

Would I go back? Yes, probably, given the chance. Those few minutes at the top of the world were all too brief. I was overwhelmed and I would risk it all again just to look into that inky blackness, straining for every breath. Call it obsession perhaps, but they say those who ask will never understand why. In this day and age, in our closeted existence, there are few opportunities to return to a base level, ultimately one of life and death. It's a dangerous game, of course, but then it wouldn't be worth playing if it weren't. The intensity of the experience is not easily described; I know that from trying to recount it. Every day since, in the months that have passed, I have treasured the memories of those brief moments as something very precious, something to grasp in a quiet moment, and no one can ever take that away from me. Was it worth it? Yes, for me, but then I didn't lose anyone close. I have thought of Jacques almost every day since, but not knowing him made the task of retrieving the ring so much easier.

And what about David Sharp and so many others? Some maintain that at extreme altitude the normal rules of compassion do not apply. Even your brain works differently. Should he have been helped? Yes, I would say so. Would he have survived? Yes, quite possibly. And would I have helped him? No, probably not. The sheer focus required just to climb at that height is such that little will distract you. I experienced that when I spoke to Igor, but knew I was in little position to assist him. That said, I can't deny that I am ashamed of my selfishness. If I was dying on Everest I would like to think that someone would help me, not climb on. Even comfort me if all else was lost. What could be worse than others blindly heading past, as you lie stranded? At least Jacques had the comfort of knowing that his closest friend did not abandon him. It bears more than a passing resemblance to the Good Samaritan parable and all of us would hate to be the victim.

There lies the gulf between obligation and compassion. The former is an all too common defence of those who pass a stranded climber. Of course they are not obligated. The victim made a choice to be there, perhaps on a limited budget, or perhaps they were even reckless. A passer-by can easily protect their moral stance on that basis. But a true Samaritan has to show compassion – kindness that stems from no obligation. It is a rare quality in a modern world. What leaves me so ashamed is that we met many Samaritans on our journey. Often the very poorest of people who shared the little they had. They were under no obligation; they would not even see us again. What did they have to gain? That question bothers me a lot, because I think that in their position I would have felt justified in putting myself first. Climbers on Everest often have money, some are positively wealthy, and at the end of the day it is but a hobby. If we cannot be compassionate then – when will we ever be? Somewhere we have lost sight of what is truly important. No summit is ever greater than a life.

Our success on Everest was part good planning and teamwork. But all you can ever do is reduce the risk. At those altitudes, the difference between success and failure is so very slim. The weather can worsen and a toss of a coin might as well decide your fate. Jacques's misfortune and my good luck have left me very cynical. We emerged unscathed from the whole experience and for that alone I am grateful. I hope I can honour Jacques's memory, and that of the others who died by being forever humble, not triumphant, and passing on the lessons learned from our experience. It is for that reason that this book was written. Our journey was a great one, not for being the first, nor for breaking any records, but because the memories of it grow richer every day. The best journeys mature over time, mellowing in your own mind as you sometimes recall a previously forgotten conversation or a wonderful view. For a few months, I enjoyed the privilege of living and working with an amazing group of people. That alone was worth a thousand summits.

Notes

1. Our team was stranded in the mountain town of Skardu after hundreds of Shias died there in riots, ruthlessly suppressed by President Zia and a then-unknown Osama Bin Laden. Together with his Sunni tribesmen, Bin Laden had been given free rein to suppress the uprising. Just as the protests subsided the president was assassinated in a revenge attack, killed by an exploding fruit basket, and the country descended into yet more turmoil. They were heady times.

2. Lydia Bradley fell out with her team mates but later that season became the first woman to summit without oxygen on 10 October 1988. Her claim is disputed by some.

3. The first two soldiers to the top of Everest in 1976, Brummie Stokes and Bronco Lane, were from 22 SAS regiment. The SAS mounted another independent expedition in 1984 to the north side but it ended in tragedy when Tony Swierzy was killed and several members were injured in an avalanche. The Army returned unsuccessfully, on several occasions, before 21 SAS mounted their attempt in 2000.

4. A torr is a unit of pressure equivalent to 1/760 of an atmosphere. Its origin lies in the fact that the atmosphere will support a column of 760 millimetres of mercury.

5. Jean-Marc died two years later while BASE-jumping from Angel Falls in Venezuela. BASE is an acronym for Bridge, Antenna, Span and Earth. Only by jumping off each of the four categories, with a parachute, can someone call themselves a fully-fledged BASE-jumper.

6. After Hadrian visited Palmyra in AD 130 he declared it a free city, but a hundred years later Palmyra was formally annexed and the citizens became Romans. Fifty years on, the rebel Queen Zenobia seized power. Within five years she had conquered Egypt, declaring herself Queen in the process, and extended her influence far into modern-day Turkey. She was defeated by Emperor Aurelian and eventually paraded through the streets of Rome in gold chains. She was well-treated by all accounts, and even settled and married into Roman society.

7. The landscape was beautifully empty but I knew this was a sad legacy of the conflict a hundred years earlier. The land had once been home to the Armenians, victims of a genocide that took place at the height of the First World War. Driven from their villages by Turkey's Ottoman rulers, many were force-marched south towards Syria and the empty desert, the very direction from which we had cycled. It is estimated that at least a million died en route. Some say past events can leave a shadow on a landscape. It was certainly an eerie atmosphere that morning, the bold jade green of the lake against the threatening winter sky and a chill wind. It was a comfort to think the countryside had in some way been touched by past events – a haunting tribute to all those lost souls.

8. MERLIN (Medical Emergency Relief International) was one of three charities for which the EVERESTMAX team raised funds – some £50,000 in total. MERLIN was one of the first charities 'on the ground' in Bam and provided crucial medical relief in the aftermath. They then established clinics to provide ongoing healthcare during the city's recovery. Other

charities supported were ITDG (the International Technology Development Group) for the construction of bicycle ambulances in Nepal, and SOS Children's Villages. While in Pokhara the team visited one of the supported villages and attached schools for the children of Tibetan refugees. Money raised later went to providing computer facilities for the children.

9. The Durand Line was established in 1893 by Sir Mortimer Durand, the foreign secretary of the British Indian government, when the British forced Afghanistan to come to an agreement and establish a firm border between British India and Afghanistan. Recent international pressure to build a fence along the border has met with fierce political opposition, and its construction seems unlikely. Pakistan, meanwhile, continues to blame both India and Iran for fanning insurgency in Baluchistan.

10. The problems with water are ongoing as supplies are traditionally brought by the twice-weekly train between Zahedan and Quetta. The RAF put Dalbandin's nearby airfield into service during the Second World War but later fell into disrepair. It has since formed a key launching point for operations in nearby Afghanistan, conducted by the United States Marine Corps. It was also near this location that Pakistan detonated their first nuclear device in 1998.

11. Although Rudyard Kipling used the phrase the 'Great Game' in his novel *Kim*, it is thought to have been coined by Sir Arthur Conolly, to describe the clandestine war between Russia and Britain in a bid for supremacy in central Asia.

12. Only on our return from the expedition did I find out that Dera Ghazi Khan was indeed officially off-limits to foreigners. Home to many of Pakistan's nuclear facilities, it is a highly sensitive area. That also explained the large numbers of tetchy police, soldiers and security officials. It made it all the more incredible that we had managed to return there the following day.

13. In the years building up to Indian independence in 1947, separate homelands for Muslims and Hindus had become inevitable, hence the need for Partition and the formation of two distinct nations. Widespread bloodshed was anticipated if the two religions were compelled to live alongside each other. When the border was finally established, the so-called Radcliffe Line was to prove highly divisive, and many Muslims and Hindus now found themselves on the wrong side of the tracks. What followed was one of the largest and bloodiest migrations in history. Well over ten million people were uprooted and some 500,000 lost their lives in the widespread violence.

14. Holi, or the Hindu festival of colours, is a spring festival during which the participants throw coloured water at each other. It has medicinal origins, as the coming rains are expected to bring fever and illness. It is hugely popular with children who delight in throwing coloured paints at each other.

15. The 'collision zone' is a term used by geologists to describe the uplift and area of deformation that ensued when India collided with Asia. After the collision, the forward rate of India's advance halved, and so began the resulting rapid uplift and formation of the Himalayan chain.

16. The sirdar – or sardar – is the leader of the porters and Sherpa staff. He helps to organise the logistics on the mountain and acts as the link between the Sherpas and the climbing party.

17. The quality of the oxygen is best assessed by weighing, as a cylinder half-full weighs considerably less than a full one. The overall weight when full is some 2.7kg. Measuring the pressure when full is unreliable as the value is subject to fluctuation with temperature.

18. It was this route that led to the deaths of Peter Boardman and Joe Tasker in 1982. It was first successfully climbed in 1988 by Russell Brice from New Zealand and Harry Taylor, a British climber and member of the SAS, although they had to descend via the conventional North Ridge route.

19. High-altitude pulmonary oedema (HAPE) occurs when extra-vascular fluid collects in the lungs. It tends to happen when ascent to high altitudes has been too rapid, especially when accompanied by intense exercise. It is now widely recognised that some people have a genetic susceptibility to HAPE. If untreated it can effectively drown the patient as the lungs receive less oxygen. The most effective means of treatment is always descent.

20. Andrew had brought with him an ultrasound scanner design-ed to take an image of the eye and optic nerve. The aim was to record the diameter of the so-called optic sheath – the membrane around the optic nerve – which is continuous with the membrane around the brain. Doctors have long suspected that the brain swells with altitude, hence the onset of cerebral oedema in extreme cases. Measuring of intra-cranial pressure swelling is very difficult, particularly in a climbing environ-ment, and Andrew hoped instead that by measuring the optic nerve diameter at different altitudes he would find a correla-tion between height and brain swelling. It was an ambitious study but was ultimately very successful.

21. Of Welsh origin, 'cwm' describes the head of a glaciated valley. In France the equivalent term is 'cirque' and in Scotland a 'corrie'. The western cwm on the south side of Everest is the main approach route to the summit.

22. A jumar, or ascender, is a lightweight device that will slide in only one direction along the rope. It offers a degree of safety should the climber slip and is an essential tool for high-altitude mountaineers. It is attached to the harness via a short sling or piece of rope.

23. Most probably the body is that of Head Constable Tsewang Paljor, who was one of eight climbers who died on 11 May, in the infamous season of 1996. He was a member of the Indo-Tibetan Border Police expedition and died along with two other members of his team. In a similar controversy to the unfolding David Sharp story, a Japanese expedition had

been accused of passing the Indians on their way to the summit – an accusation they later denied.

24. Dexamethasone is a drug carried by many climbers venturing to extreme altitude. A climber suffering from HACE (high-altitude cerebral oedema), effectively a swelling of the brain, can experience a variety of severe symptoms. The drug can counter those effects by relieving hypertension or high blood pressure. This may restore the climber's faculties sufficiently to allow him to descend safely to a lower altitude.

25. Metal spikes or wedges that can be hammered into the cliff face for security.

26. A layer of slippery and sometimes invisible hard ice that coats rock surfaces.

27. Seb Bullock and Chris Owen made the summit on 17 May. Pauline and Phil Sanderson followed on 18 May. On 21 May Dominic Faulkner, Jamie Rouan and Andrew Sutherland summitted accompanied by Sherpas Karma and Tshering.

28. The title 'Snow Leopard' is accorded to those elite mountaineers who have ascended all five 7,000-metre peaks that lie within the confines of the old Soviet Union.

Acknowledgements

As with any large expedition, the list of those who made it possible extends well beyond those lucky enough to take part. The EVEREST*MAX* team were sustained by the efforts of hundreds of friends and official supporters en route, and as a team we will be for ever in their debt. Before our journey even began, almost two years of logistical planning and fundraising had taken place. During the latter part of this preparation the work of the entire team was crucial – but especially that of Sarah Lyle and André Zlattinger. Their persistence and eternal optimism were an unqualified support, and André's return to the mountain in May 2008 meant that he finally reached the summit he so richly deserved.

Such was the length of the expedition that our families were placed under a considerable burden, and the strain of watching things from home was quite possibly as arduous as being on the trip itself. We are all extremely grateful for their understanding and for their toleration of our selfish endeavours.

Countless people on our journey showed us generosity that knew no bounds and which we had little opportunity to return. Most will never get to read this account, but I hope I can at least acknowledge the large part they played in our eventual success.

Numerous companies and individuals offered their support and blindly put their faith in our efforts. Among them were Morans of Cheltenham, Sotheby's, Cotswold Camping, Bloc Eyewear, Western Computers, Khyam tents, Sign Studio, Polaris Apparel, NSSL Satcom Solutions, Whatmore plastics, Commercial Group Cheltenham, Wombat Clothing UK, Blackbrick Building, Select Solar, Badger Rugby, Honda, Buff Headwear and Whyte Bikes (suppliers of Marin). John and Vicki Parfitt were a constant support throughout the expedition and did a great job of holding the fort while we were away. Cheltenham College and Nigel Archdale supported us admirably with the use of facilities for much of our fundraising.

It was never my intention to write a book about the 'longest climb', and it proved to be a daunting process. My sincere thanks must go to Charlie Campbell, my agent, for his support and patience, and to Louisa Joyner for her invaluable advice throughout the editing process, along with the whole team at Virgin Books. My mother and stepfather were there as always, not only throughout the expedition but even making suggestions after the first draft.

My last and biggest thank you is reserved for Becka. Not just for waiting for me while I was away, but also for then putting up with me during the long evenings of writing. You are more than I deserve.